Symmetry/Asymmetry of Differential Equations in Biomathematics

Symmetry/Asymmetry of Differential Equations in Biomathematics

Guest Editors

Liang Zhang
Junli Liu
Tailei Zhang

MDPI

Basel • Beijing • Wuhan • Barcelona • Belgrade • Novi Sad • Cluj • Manchester

Guest Editors

Liang Zhang
College of Science
Northwest A&F University
Yangling
China

Junli Liu
School of Science
Xi'an Polytechnic University
Xi'an
China

Tailei Zhang
School of Science
Chang'an University
Xi'an
China

Editorial Office
MDPI AG
Grosspeteranlage 5
4052 Basel, Switzerland

This is a reprint of the Special Issue, published open access by the journal *Symmetry* (ISSN 2073-8994), freely accessible at: https://www.mdpi.com/journal/symmetry/special_issues/3ZAY11LK9A.

For citation purposes, cite each article independently as indicated on the article page online and as indicated below:

Lastname, A.A.; Lastname, B.B. Article Title. *Journal Name* **Year**, *Volume Number*, Page Range.

ISBN 978-3-7258-6568-0 (Hbk)
ISBN 978-3-7258-6569-7 (PDF)
https://doi.org/10.3390/books978-3-7258-6569-7

Contents

symmetry

MDPI

Editorial

Symmetry/Asymmetry of Differential Equations in Biomathematics

Liang Zhang [1,*], Junli Liu [2,*] and Tailei Zhang [3,*]

1 College of Science, Northwest A&F University, Yangling 712100, China
2 School of Science, Xi'an Polytechnic University, Xi'an 710048, China
3 School of Science, Chang'an University, Xi'an 710064, China
* Correspondence: zhanglsd@126.com (L.Z.); jlliu2008@126.com (J.L.); tlzhang@chd.edu.cn (T.Z.)

Differential equations serve as powerful mathematical tools for studying biomathematics, where symmetry and asymmetry are fundamental phenomena in biological systems. Investigating these properties in differential equations is crucial for uncovering the underlying mechanisms of organismal interactions and dynamic behaviors.

This Special Issue highlights recent advances in the application of differential equations to biomathematics, with a particular focus on the roles of symmetry and asymmetry in biological modeling. Key topics include the following:

- Mathematical modeling in biology—Development and analysis of differential equation-based models.
- Computational methods—Novel techniques for solving biologically relevant differential equations.
- Complex biological systems—Exploration of symmetry and asymmetry in ecological, physiological, and evolutionary dynamics.

By bridging mathematics, biology, and computational science, this Special Issue seeks to foster interdisciplinary collaboration, stimulate innovative research, and advance the field of biomathematics.

The Special Issue contains eight papers contributed by researchers from China, Lithuania, and the USA, encompassing a broad range of critical issues and cutting-edge research topics. These topics include Positive Periodic Solution of Phytoplankton–Zooplankton Model on Time Scales [1]; Stability Analysis of Biological Systems Under Threshold Conditions [2]; Modeling the Digestion Process by a Distributed Delay Differential System [3]; Diffusion Mechanisms for Both Living and Dying Trees Across 37 Years in a Forest Stand in Lithuania's Kazlų Rūda Region [4]; Optimal Harvesting Strategies for Timber and Non-Timber Forest Products with Nonlinear Harvesting Terms [5]; Bogdanov–Takens Bifurcation of Kermack–McKendrick Model with Nonlinear Contact Rates Caused by Multiple Exposures [6]; Stability and Hopf Bifurcation of a Delayed Predator–Prey Model with a Stage Structure for Generalist Predators and a Holling Type-II Functional Response [7]; and Dynamics of a Stochastic SVEIR Epidemic Model with Nonlinear Incidence Rate [8].

We anticipate that this Special Issue will serve as a valuable resource for mathematicians, biologists, and computational scientists seeking to engage with contemporary advancements in differential equations and their applications in biomathematics.

Author Contributions: L.Z.: conceptualization, investigation, writing—original draft. J.L. and T.Z.: discussing, writing—review and editing. All authors have read and agreed to the published version of the manuscript.

Funding: This research received no external funding.

Data Availability Statement: No new data were created.

Conflicts of Interest: The authors declare no conflict of interest.

References

1. Li, Y.; Zheng, F. Positive Periodic Solution of Phytoplankton–Zooplankton Model on Time Scales. *Symmetry* **2026**, *18*, 45. [CrossRef]
2. Mahbuba, J.E.; Wang, X.-S. Stability Analysis of Biological Systems Under Threshold Conditions. *Symmetry* **2025**, *17*, 1193. [CrossRef]
3. Liu, J.; Guo, Z.; Guo, H. Modeling the Digestion Process by a Distributed Delay Differential System. *Symmetry* **2025**, *17*, 604. [CrossRef]
4. Petrauskas, E.; Rupšys, P. Diffusion Mechanisms for Both Living and Dying Trees Across 37 Years in a Forest Stand in Lithuania's Kazlų Rūda Region. *Symmetry* **2025**, *17*, 213. [CrossRef]
5. Zhang, Y.; Hao, L.; Zhang, S. Optimal Harvesting Strategies for Timber and Non-Timber Forest Products with Nonlinear Harvesting Terms. *Symmetry* **2024**, *16*, 806. [CrossRef]
6. Li, J.; Ma, M. Bogdanov–Takens Bifurcation of Kermack–McKendrick Model with Nonlinear Contact Rates Caused by Multiple Exposures. *Symmetry* **2024**, *16*, 688. [CrossRef]
7. Liang, Z.-W.; Meng, X.-Y. Stability and Hopf Bifurcation of a Delayed Predator–Prey Model with a Stage Structure for Generalist Predators and a Holling Type-II Functional Response. *Symmetry* **2024**, *16*, 597. [CrossRef]
8. Wang, X.; Zhang, L.; Zhang, X.-B. Dynamics of a Stochastic SVEIR Epidemic Model with Nonlinear Incidence Rate. *Symmetry* **2024**, *16*, 467. [CrossRef]

https://doi.org/10.3390/sym18010067

symmetry

MDPI

Article

Positive Periodic Solution of Phytoplankton–Zooplankton Model on Time Scales

Yan Li and Famei Zheng *

School of Mathematics and Statistics, Huaiyin Normal University, Huaian 223300, China; liyan@hytc.edu.cn
* Correspondence: hystzfm@163.com

Abstract

This paper addresses a phytoplankton–zooplankton model on time scales. Based on a fixed point theorem of strict-set-contraction, some sufficient conditions are established for global existence of positive periodic solution to the considered system. Finally, two examples are presented to illustrate effectiveness of the results. The main purpose of this paper is to study a more general class of biological system and to investigate the existence of positive solutions for the aforementioned system using strict-set-contraction theory. It is interesting that the results of this paper are applicable to both discrete and continuous systems. Periodic behavior is widely present in biological systems and also reflects symmetry in nature. Therefore, studying the periodic solutions of biological systems can help us better understand the dynamic behavior of biological systems.

Keywords: positive periodic solution; existence of periodic solution; phytoplankton–zooplankton model

1. Introduction

In 2002, Chattopadhyay et al. [1] introduced a toxic phytoplankton–zooplankton model, as follows:

$$\begin{aligned} x'(t) &= r_1 x(t)\left(1 - \frac{x(t)}{k}\right) - \frac{ax(t)y(t)}{c+x}, \\ y'(t) &= -r_2 y(t) + \frac{bx(t)y(t)}{c+x}, \end{aligned} \tag{1}$$

where x and y denote toxic phytoplankton and zooplankton populations, respectively, r_1 is the intrinsic growth rate of x, k is the environmental carrying capacity of x, c is the rate of predation, a is the conversion rate of x, r_2 denotes the natural death rate of y, and b is the conversion rate of y. All coefficients of system (1) are positive constants. Plankton are the most abundant form of life floating freely near the surfaces of all aquatic environments, including rivers, lakes, oceans, and estuaries [2,3]. Almost all aquatic life depends on plankton. Pphytoplankton are the plant forms of plankton community. Zooplankton are the animals in the plankton community. In the past few decades, studying the release of toxic substances by phytoplankton has been one of the hot topics. In [1], the authors studied toxic substances released by plankton, which play an important role. Sarkar and Chattopadhyay [4] investigated a toxic phytoplankton–non-toxic phytoplankton–zooplankton systemwith environmental noises and obtained the dynamic properties of the system. In [5], a delay differential equation model on harmful algal blooms in the presence of toxic substances was proposed and analyzed, and the authors described a suitable mechanism to explain the cyclic nature of the above system. In [6], the effects of the Texas (USA) brown tide alga on planktonic grazers were studied. Saha and Bandyopadhyay [7] studied a toxin-producing phytoplankton–zooplankton system and proved the existence of local Hopf bifurcation and the existence of stability switching phenomena. Sarkar et al. [8] studied two producing plankton and their effect on a phytoplankton–zooplankton system. We list more results for phytoplankton and zooplankton models as follows: stationary distribution and ergodicity [9], stochastic periodic solution [10], effects of toxin delay on the dynamics [11], dynamical behaviours [12], and so on.

To the best of the authors' knowledge, there are few results for system (1) on time scales. Hence, we study the following non-autonomous phytoplankton–zooplankton model on time scales:

$$\begin{aligned} x^{\Delta}(t) &= r_1(t)x(\sigma(t)) - \frac{r_1(t)x^2(t)}{k(t)} - \frac{a(t)x(t)y(t)}{c(t)+x(t)}, \\ y^{\Delta}(t) &= -r_2(t)y(\sigma(t)) + \frac{b(t)x(t)y(t)}{c(t)+x(t)}, \end{aligned} \tag{2}$$

where $t \in \mathbb{T}$ is a periodic time sale (see [13]), Δ is the delta (or Hilger) derivative, and σ is the forward jump operator. All coefficients of system (2) are positive periodic functions with the period ω. For the background material concerning notations and calculus on time scales, see [14].

We found that research on phytoplankton–zooplankton models is mostly focused on continuous and stochastic systems, with little attention paid to discrete systems and systems on time scales. Since the system on the time scale unifies both discrete and continuous cases, the results of this paper generalize existing related results. In addition, periodic phenomena are widely present in biological systems, and studying them can help understand the operational mechanisms of biological systems. Therefore, this article has high research value in studying positive periodic solutions. We list the following innovations of this paper:

(1) We first study the existence of a positive periodic solution for a phytoplankton–zooplankton model on time scales and expand the scope of research for phytoplankton–zooplankton models.
(2) We develop a fixed-point theorem of strict-set-contraction for studying periodic solution problems on time scales.
(3) The results of this article are applicable to both discrete and continuous systems.

The remainder of this paper is organized as follows. Section 2 gives the preliminaries. Section 3 explores the existence of positive periodic solutions of system (2) by using a fixed-point theorem of strict-set-contraction. In Section 4, we give two examples for illustrating the main results. Finally, we summarize the entire article and provide possible research directions for the future.

2. Preliminaries

A time scale $\mathbb{T}$ is a nonempty closed subset of real numbers. The forward jump operator σ, backward jump operator ρ, regressive *rd*-continuous functions $\mathcal{R}$, and positive regressive *rd*-continuous functions $\mathcal{R}^+$ can be found in the book [14]. The interval $[u,v]_{\mathbb{T}}$ means $[u,v] \cap \mathbb{T}$. The intervals $(u,v]_{\mathbb{T}}$, $(u,v)_{\mathbb{T}}$, and $[u,v)_{\mathbb{T}}$ are defined similarly. For $s,t \in \mathbb{T}$, the exponential function $e_{\delta}(t,s)$ is defined by $e_{\alpha}(t,s) = \exp\left(\int_s^t \xi_{\mu(v)}(\alpha(v))\Delta v\right)$, where

$$\xi_{\mu(v)}(\alpha(v)) = \begin{cases} \frac{1}{\mu(v)} Log(1+\alpha(v)\mu(v)), \ \mu(v) > 0, \\ \alpha(v), \ \ \mu(v) = 0, \end{cases}$$

where $\mu = \sigma(t) - t$ is the graininess function.

https://doi.org/10.3390/sym18010045

Lemma 1 ([14]). *Let $\zeta, \eta \in \mathcal{R}$. Then*

[1] $e_0(t,s) \equiv 1$ *and* $e_\zeta(t,t) \equiv 1$;
[2] $e_\zeta(\rho(t),s) = (1-\mu(t)\zeta(t))e_\zeta(t,s)$;
[3] $e_\zeta(t,s)e_\eta(t,s) = e_{\zeta\oplus\eta}(t,s)$;
[4] $e_\zeta(t,s) = \frac{1}{e_\zeta(s,t)} = e_{\ominus\zeta}(s,t)$;
[5] $e_\zeta(t,s)e_\zeta(s,r) = e_\zeta(t,r)$.

Definition 1 ([13]). *A time scale $\mathbb{T}$ is periodic if there is $T > 0$ for each $u \in \mathbb{T}$, such that $u \pm T \in \mathbb{T}$. For $\mathbb{T} \neq \mathbb{R}$, the smallest positive T is the period of time scale.*

Definition 2 ([13]). *Let $\mathbb{T} \neq \mathbb{R}$ be a periodic time scale with the period T. The function $f : \mathbb{T} \to \mathbb{R}$ is periodic with period γ if there exists a natural number n such that $\gamma = nT$, $f(\gamma \pm u) = f(\gamma)$ for each $u \in \mathbb{T}$. When $\mathbb{T} = \mathbb{R}$, f is a periodic function if κ is the smallest positive number, such that $f(x \pm \kappa) = f(x)$ for each $x \in \mathbb{T}$.*

Lemma 2. *(Schauder's fixed-point theorem [15]). Let Θ be a closed, convex and nonempty subset of a Banach space B. Let $G : \Theta \to \Theta$ be a continuous mapping such that $G\Theta$ is a relatively compact subset of B. Then, G has at least one fixed point in Θ.*

For obtaining the existence of a periodic solution of system (2), we use a fixed-point theorem of strict-set-contraction. Let B be a Banach space and P be a cone in B. The semi-order induced by the cone P is denoted by "$\leq$", that is, $u \leq v$ if, and only if, $v - u \in P$. For a bounded subset $\Omega \subset B$, let $\alpha_B(\Omega)$ be the (Kuratowski) measure of non-compactness, as follows:

$$\alpha_B(\Omega) = \inf\left\{\gamma > 0 : \text{there exists a finite number of subsets } \Omega_i \subset \Omega \text{ such that } \Omega = \cup_i \Omega_i,\ diam(\Omega_i) < \gamma\right\},$$

where $diam(\Omega_i)$ denotes the diameter of Ω_i. Let B and C be two Banach spaces and $D \subset B$. A continuous and bounded map $\Gamma : \overline{\Xi} \to C$ is called $k-$set contractive if for any bounded set $E \subset D$ we have $\alpha_C(\Gamma(E)) \leq k\alpha_B(E)$, where $0 \leq k < 1$, then Γ is strict-set-contractive.

Lemma 3 ([16]). *Let P be a cone of the Banach space B and $P_{r,R} = \{x \in P : r \leq x \leq R,\ R > r > 0\}$. Assume that $\Gamma : P_{r,R} \to P$ is strict-set-contractive such that one of the following two conditions holds:*

(i) $\Gamma x \not\geq x, \forall x \in P, ||x|| = r$ *and* $\Gamma x \not\leq x, \forall x \in P, ||x|| = R$;
(ii) $\Gamma x \not\leq x, \forall x \in P, ||x|| = r$ *and* $\Gamma x \not\geq x, \forall x \in P, ||x|| = R$. *Then Γ has at least one fixed point in $P_{r,R}$.*

3. Existence of Positive Periodic Solution

Let

$$\Gamma = \{u = (u_1, u_2)^T : u_i(t) \in C(\mathbb{T}, \mathbb{R}),\ u_i(t+\omega) = u_i(t),\ i = 1,2\}$$

with the norm $||u|| = \max |u_i|_0$, $|u_i|_0 = \sup_{t\in\mathbb{T}} |u_i(t)|$, $i = 1,2$. Obviously, Γ is a Banach space. Let

$$P = \{u = (u_1, u_2)^T \in \Gamma : u_i(t) \geq \lambda |u_i|_0,\ t \in \mathbb{T},\ i = 1,2\},$$

where $\lambda = \min\{\frac{\rho_1}{\rho_2}, \frac{\rho_3}{\rho_4}\}$, ρ_i is defined by (5) and (6), $i = 1, \cdots, 4$. From $\lambda = \min\{\frac{\rho_1}{\rho_2}, \frac{\rho_3}{\rho_4}\}$, (5) and (6), we have $0 < \lambda < 1$.

https://doi.org/10.3390/sym18010045

Lemma 4. *Assume that $-r_i \in \mathcal{R}^+$, where $i = 1, 2$, $\mathcal{R}^+$ is positive regressive rd−continuous function space. Then system (2) exists a periodic solution $u = (x, y)^T$ if, only if,*

$$x(t) = \frac{1}{e_{\ominus(-r_1)}(t, t-\omega) - 1} \int_{t-\omega}^{t} \left[\frac{r_1(s)x^2(s)}{k(s)} + \frac{a(s)x(s)y(s)}{c(s) + x(s)} \right] e_{\ominus(-r_1)}(t, s)\Delta s,$$

$$y(t) = \frac{1}{e_{\ominus(-r_2)}(t, t-\omega) - 1} \int_{t-\omega}^{t} \left[2r_2(s)y(\sigma(s)) - \frac{b(s)x(s)y(s)}{c(s) + x(s)} \right] e_{\ominus(-r_2)}(t, s)\Delta s.$$

Proof. Let $u = (x, y)^T$ be a periodic solution of system (2). We change the first equation of system (2) into the following equation:

$$x^{\Delta}(t) - r_1(t)x(\sigma(t)) = -\frac{r_1(t)x^2(t)}{k(t)} - \frac{a(t)x(t)y(t)}{c(t) + x(t)}. \tag{3}$$

Multiplying both sides of (3) by $e_{-r_1}(t, 0)$ and integrating them from $t - \omega$ to t, we obtain

$$\int_{t-\omega}^{t} [e_{-a_1}(s, 0)u(s)]^{\Delta}\Delta s = \int_{t-\omega}^{t} \left[\frac{r_1(s)x^2(s)}{k(t)} - \frac{a(t)x(s)y(s)}{c(s) + x(s)} \right] e_{-r_1}(s, 0)\Delta s. \tag{4}$$

Dividing both sides of (4) by $e_{-r_1}(t, 0)$, we have

$$x(t) = \frac{1}{e_{\ominus(-r_1)}(t, t-\omega) - 1} \int_{t-\omega}^{t} \left[\frac{r_1(s)x^2(s)}{k(s)} + \frac{a(s)x(s)y(s)}{c(s) + x(s)} \right] e_{\ominus(-r_1)}(t, s)\Delta s.$$

Similar to the above proof, we also have

$$y(t) = \frac{1}{e_{\ominus(-r_2)}(t, t-\omega) - 1} \int_{t-\omega}^{t} \left[2r_2(s)y(\sigma(s)) - \frac{b(s)x(s)y(s)}{c(s) + x(s)} \right] e_{\ominus(-r_2)}(t, s)\Delta s.$$

Since the above proof is reversible, the proof is completed. □

For $s, t \in [0, \omega]_{\mathbb{T}} = [0, \omega] \cap \mathbb{T}$, by $-r_1 \in \mathcal{R}^+$ we have

$$\begin{aligned} e_{\ominus(-r_1)}(t, s) &= \exp\left(\int_s^t \frac{log(1 + \ominus(-r_1(u))\mu(u))}{\mu(u)} \Delta u \right) \\ &= \exp\left(\int_s^t \frac{log\frac{1}{1 - r_1(u)\mu(u)}}{\mu(u)} \Delta u \right). \end{aligned}$$

Thus,

$$\rho_1 := \exp\left(-\int_0^{\omega} \left| \frac{log\frac{1}{1 - r_1(u)\mu(u)}}{\mu(u)} \right| \Delta u \right) \leq e_{\ominus(-r_1)}(t, s) \leq \exp\left(\int_0^{\omega} \left| \frac{log\frac{1}{1 - r_1(u)\mu(u)}}{\mu(u)} \right| \Delta u \right) := \rho_2. \tag{5}$$

From the proof of (5), there exist positive constants ρ_3, ρ_4 such that

$$\rho_3 \leq e_{\ominus(-r_2)}(t, s) \leq \rho_4,\ s, t \in [0, \omega]_{\mathbb{T}},\ -r_2 \in \mathcal{R}^+. \tag{6}$$

Define the mapping $F : P \to P$ by

$$(Fu)(t) = ((Fx)(t), (Fy)(t))^T,\ t \in \mathbb{T},\ u = (x, y)^T \in P,$$

https://doi.org/10.3390/sym18010045

where

$$
\begin{aligned}
(Fx)(t) &= \frac{1}{e_{\ominus(-r_1)}(t,t-\omega)-1}\int_{t-\omega}^{t}\left[\frac{r_1(s)x^2(s)}{k(s)}+\frac{a(s)x(s)y(s)}{c(s)+x(s)}\right]e_{\ominus(-r_1)}(t,s)\Delta s,\\
(Fy)(t) &= \frac{1}{e_{\ominus(-r_2)}(t,t-\omega)-1}\int_{t-\omega}^{t}\left[2r_2(s)y(\sigma(s))-\frac{b(s)x(s)y(s)}{c(s)+x(s)}\right]e_{\ominus(-r_2)}(t,s)\Delta s.
\end{aligned}
\tag{7}
$$

Let $f(t)\in C(\mathbb{T},\mathbb{R})$ be a bounded function, denote

$$f^+=\sup_{t\in\mathbb{T}}|f(t)|,\ \ f^-=\inf_{t\in\mathbb{T}}|f(t)|.$$

Throughout the entire paper, we need the following assumption:

Hypothesis 1. *The following inequality holds:*

$$2r_2(t)-b(t)\geq 0 \text{ for } t\in\mathbb{T}.$$

Since $e_{\ominus(-r_i)}(t,t-\omega)$ does not depend on t, let

$$\mu_i=\frac{1}{e_{\ominus(-r_i)}(t,t-\omega)-1},\ \ i=1,2, \tag{8}$$

where $\mu_i>0$ is constant.

Lemma 5. *Assume that Hypothesis 1 holds, then $F:P\to P$ is well defined.*

Proof. For $u=(x,y)^T\in P$, we have

$$
\begin{aligned}
(Fx)(t+\omega) &= \frac{1}{e_{\ominus(-r_1)}(t+\omega,t)-1}\int_{t}^{t+\omega}\left[\frac{r_1(s)x^2(s)}{k(s)}+\frac{a(s)x(s)y(s)}{c(s)+x(s)}\right]e_{\ominus(-r_1)}(t+\omega,s)\Delta s\\
&= \frac{1}{e_{\ominus(-r_1)}(t,t-\omega)-1}\int_{t}^{t-\omega}\left[\frac{r_1(u)x^2(u)}{k(u)}+\frac{a(u)x(u)y(u)}{c(u)+x(u)}\right]e_{\ominus(-r_1)}(t+\omega,u+\omega)\Delta u\\
&= \frac{1}{e_{\ominus(-r_1)}(t,t-\omega)-1}\int_{t}^{t-\omega}\left[\frac{r_1(u)x^2(u)}{k(u)}+\frac{a(u)x(u)y(u)}{c(u)+x(u)}\right]e_{\ominus(-r_1)}(t,u)\Delta u\\
&= (Fx)(t).
\end{aligned}
\tag{9}
$$

Similar to the proof of (9), we also have $(Fy)(t+\omega)=(Fy)(t)$. Hence, $(Fu)(t+\omega)=(Fu)(t)$. From the first equation of system (7), for $u=(x,y)^T\in P$ and $t\in[0,\omega]_{\mathbb{T}}$ we have

$$|Fx|_0\leq\mu_1\rho_2\int_0^{\omega}\left[\frac{r_1(s)x^2(s)}{k(s)}+\frac{a(s)x(s)y(s)}{c(s)+x(s)}\right]\Delta s.$$

Thus,

$$
\begin{aligned}
(Fx)(t) &\geq \mu_1\rho_1\int_0^{\omega}\left[\frac{r_1(s)x^2(s)}{k(s)}+\frac{a(s)x(s)y(s)}{c(s)+x(s)}\right]\Delta s\\
&\geq \frac{\rho_1}{\rho_2}|Fx|_0\geq\lambda|Fx|_0.
\end{aligned}
\tag{10}
$$

In view of Hypothesis 1, for $u\in P$ and $t\in[0,\omega]_{\mathbb{T}}$, we have

$$
\begin{aligned}
&2r_2(t)y(\sigma(t))-\frac{b(t)x(t)y(t)}{c(t)+x(t)}\\
&\geq\Big(2r_2(t)-b(t)\Big)\lambda|y|_0\geq 0
\end{aligned}
\tag{11}
$$

https://doi.org/10.3390/sym18010045

and $(Fy)(t) \geq 0$. Similar to the proof of (10), by (11) we have

$$(Fy)(t) \geq \frac{\rho_3}{\rho_4}|Fy|_0 \geq \lambda|Fy|_0. \tag{12}$$

From (9), (10) and (12), the proof is completed. □

Let $\Xi_R = \{u = (u_1, u_2)^T \in \Gamma : |u_i|_0 < R,\ i = 1,2\}$ and

$$k = \max\left\{\mu_1\rho_2\frac{r_1^+\omega}{k^-}2R + \frac{\mu_1\rho_2 a^+\omega}{(c^-)^2}(2c^+R + R^2),\ 2\mu_2\rho_4 r_2^+\omega + \frac{\mu_2\rho_4 b^+\omega}{(c^-)^2}(2c^+R + R^2)\right\},$$

where ρ_2 and ρ_4 are defined by (5) and (6), μ_1 and μ_2 are defined by (8).

Lemma 6. *Assume that Hypothesis 1 holds and $k < 1$, then $F : P \cap \overline{\Xi}_R \to P$ is strict-set-contractive.*

Proof. Obviously, F is continuous and bounded on $P \cap \overline{\Xi}_R$. Now, we show $\alpha_\Gamma(F(E)) \leq k\alpha_\Gamma(E)$, where $E \subset \overline{\Xi}_R$. Let $\xi = \alpha_\Gamma(E)$. For any positive constant $\varepsilon < k\xi$, there is a finite family of subsets E_i with $E = \cup_i E_i$ and $diam(E_i) < \xi + \varepsilon$. For $u_1 = (x_1, y_1)^T$, $u_2 = (x_2, y_2)^T \in E_i$, we have

$$|x_1 - x_2|_0 \leq \xi + \varepsilon \text{ and } |y_1 - y_2|_0 \leq \xi + \varepsilon. \tag{13}$$

For $u_1 = (x_1, y_1)^T$, $u_2 = (x_2, y_2)^T \in E_i$, $t \in [0, \omega]_{\mathbb{T}}$, by (13), we have

$$\begin{aligned}
|(Fx_1)(t) - (Fx_2)(t)| &\leq \mu_1\rho_2\int_0^\omega \frac{r_1(s)|x_1^2(s) - x_2^2(s)|}{k(s)}\Delta s \\
&\quad + \mu_1\rho_2\int_0^\omega \left|\frac{a(s)x_1(s)y_1(s)}{c(s) + x_1(s)} - \frac{a(s)x_2(s)y_2(s)}{c(s) + x_2(s)}\right|\Delta s \\
&\leq \mu_1\rho_2\frac{r_1^+\omega}{k^-}2R(\xi + \varepsilon) + \mu_1\rho_2 a^+\int_0^\omega \left|\frac{x_1(s)y_1(s)}{c(s) + x_1(s)} - \frac{x_2(s)y_2(s)}{c(s) + x_2(s)}\right|\Delta s.
\end{aligned} \tag{14}$$

Considering the term $\left|\frac{x_1(s)y_1(s)}{c(s)+x_1(s)} - \frac{x_2(s)y_2(s)}{c(s)+x_2(s)}\right|$ in (14), we have

$$\begin{aligned}
\left|\frac{x_1(s)y_1(s)}{c(s) + x_1(s)} - \frac{x_2(s)y_2(s)}{c(s) + x_2(s)}\right| &= \left|\frac{c(s)[x_1(s)y_1(s) - x_2(s)y_2(s)] + x_1(s)x_2(s)[y_1(s) - y_2(s)]}{(c(s) + x_1(s))(c(s) + x_2(s))}\right| \\
&\leq \frac{1}{(c^-)^2}\Big(c^+R(|x_1(s) - x_2(s)| + |y_1(s) - y_2(s)|) + R^2|y_1(s) - y_2(s)|\Big) \\
&\leq \frac{1}{(c^-)^2}(2c^+R + R^2)(\xi + \varepsilon).
\end{aligned} \tag{15}$$

From (14) and (15), we have

$$|(Fx_1)(t) - (Fx_2)(t)| \leq \left(\mu_1\rho_2\frac{r_1^+\omega}{c^-}2R + \frac{\mu_1\rho_2 a^+\omega}{(c^-)^2}(2c^+R + R^2)\right)(\xi + \varepsilon). \tag{16}$$

By (15), we also have

$$|(Fy_1)(t) - (Fy_2)(t)| \leq \left(2\mu_2\rho_4 r_2^+\omega + \frac{\mu_2\rho_4 b^+\omega}{(c^-)^2}(2c^+R + R^2)\right)(\xi + \varepsilon). \tag{17}$$

From (16) and (17), we have

$$||Fu|| \leq k(\xi + \varepsilon).$$

https://doi.org/10.3390/sym18010045

As ε is arbitrarily small, it follows that $\alpha_\Gamma(F(E)) \leq k\alpha_\Gamma(E)$. Therefore, F is strict-set-contractive. □

Theorem 1. *Assume that Hypothesis 1 holds and $k < 1$. Then, system (2) has at least one positive ω−periodic solution, provided that*

$$\mu_2\rho_4\omega\left(2r_2^+ - \frac{b^-\lambda^2 r}{c^+ + 1}\right) < \lambda \text{ and } \mu_2\rho_3\omega(2r_2^+ - b^+)\lambda > 1. \quad (18)$$

Proof. Let $R > \frac{k^+}{\mu_1\rho_1\omega\lambda^2 r_1^{-1}}$, $r < \min\{\frac{\lambda}{\mu_1\rho_2\omega}\left(\frac{r_1^+}{k^-} + \frac{a^+}{c^-}\right)^{-1}, \frac{2r_2^+(c^+ + 1)}{b^-\lambda^2}, 1\}$, where $0 < r < R$. Based on Lemma 6, F is strict-set-contractive on $P_{r,R}$. Considering Lemma 5, if there is a point $u^* = (x^*, y^*)^T \in P$ such that $Fu^* = u^*$, then u^* is one positive periodic solution of system (2). We first show that $Fu \not\geq u, \forall u = (x,y)^T \in P, ||u|| = r$. Otherwise, there exists $u = (x,y)^T \in P$ with $||u|| = r$ such that $Fu \geq u$.

Case 1: $||u|| = |x|_0 = r$. Since $Fu \geq u$, then $(Fu - u) \in P$. Thus,

$$(Fx)(t) - x(t) \geq \lambda|Fx - x|_0. \quad (19)$$

We also have

$$\begin{aligned} |Fx|_0 &\leq \mu_1\rho_2 \int_0^\omega \left[\frac{r_1(s)x^2(s)}{k(s)} + \frac{a(s)x(s)y(s)}{c(s) + x(s)}\right]\Delta s \\ &\leq \mu_1\rho_2\omega r\left(\frac{r_1^+}{k^-} + \frac{a^+}{c^-}\right)|x|_0 \\ &< \lambda|x|_0. \end{aligned} \quad (20)$$

From (19) and (20), we have

$$|x|_0 \leq |Fx|_0 < |x_0|$$

which is a contradiction.

Case 2: $||u|| = |y|_0 = r$. Since $Fu \geq u$, then $(Fu - u) \in P$. Thus,

$$(Fy)(t) - y(t) \geq \lambda|Fy - y|_0. \quad (21)$$

By (18), we have

$$\begin{aligned} |Fy|_0 &\leq \mu_2\rho_4 \int_0^\omega \left[2r_2(s)y(\sigma(s)) - \frac{b(s)x(s)y(s)}{c(s) + x(s)}\right]\Delta s \\ &\leq \mu_2\rho_4\omega\left(2r_2^+ - \frac{b^-\lambda^2 r}{c^+ + 1}\right)|y|_0 \\ &< \lambda|y|_0. \end{aligned} \quad (22)$$

From (21) and (22), we have

$$|y|_0 \leq |Fy|_0 < |y_0|$$

which is a contradiction. Next, we show that $Fu \not\leq u, \forall u \in P, ||u|| = R$. Otherwise, there exists $u = (x,y)^T \in P$ with $||u|| = R$ such that $Fu \leq u$.

Case 1: $||u|| = |x|_0 = R$. Since $Fu \leq u$, then $(u - Fu) \in P$. Thus,

$$x(t) - (Fx)(t) \geq \lambda|x - Fx|_0. \quad (23)$$

https://doi.org/10.3390/sym18010045

Furthermore, for $t \in [0,\omega]_{\mathbb{T}}$, we have

$$\begin{aligned} |Fx|_0 &\geq \mu_1\rho_1 \int_0^{\omega} \left[\frac{r_1(s)x^2(s)}{k(s)} + \frac{a(s)x(s)y(s)}{c(s)+x(s)}\right]\Delta s \\ &\geq \mu_1\rho_1\omega\lambda^2 R^2 \frac{r_1^-}{k^+} \\ &> R. \end{aligned} \tag{24}$$

From (23) and (24), we have

$$R < |Fx|_0 \leq R$$

which is a contradiction.

Case 2: $||u|| = |y|_0 = R$. Since $Fu \leq u$, then $(u - Fu) \in P$. Thus,

$$y(t) - (Fy)(t) \geq \lambda |Fy - y|_0. \tag{25}$$

Furthermore, for $t \in [0,\omega]_{\mathbb{T}}$, by (18), we have

$$\begin{aligned} |Fy|_0 &\geq \mu_2\rho_3 \int_0^{\omega} \left[2r_2(s)y(\sigma(s)) - \frac{b(s)x(s)y(s)}{c(s)+x(s)}\right]\Delta s \\ &\geq \mu_2\rho_3\omega(2r_2^+ - b^+)\lambda R \\ &> R. \end{aligned} \tag{26}$$

From (25) and (26), we have

$$R < |Fy|_0 \leq R$$

which is a contradiction. By Lemma 3, F has at least one nonzero fixed point in P. Therefore, system (2) has at least one positive periodic solutions. □

Remark 1. *In general, Mawhin's continuation theorem of coincidence degree theory can be used for studying the existence of periodic solutions to differential equation, see [17–21]. However, Mawhin's continuity theorem struggles to estimate the prior bounds of solutions when studying the existence of positive periodic solutions. Therefore, this article uses a fixed-point theorem of strict-set-contraction to study the existence of positive solutions for system (2), which can overcome the above difficulties. In fact, in recent years, with the continuous development of strict-set-contraction theory, a large number of achievements have been published. In [22], the authors used fixed-point theorems for studying fractional and differential equations. Proinov [23] obtained a new fixed point theorems assuming that the operator T satisfies a contractive-type condition, the results extended and unified many earlier results. Mehmood and Ahmad [24] applied strict-set-contraction theory for studying fractional order boundary value problem with nonlocal non-separated-type multi-point integral boundary conditions In [25], fixed points and continuity of contractive maps were systematically investigated.*

4. Examples

Example 1. *For the case $t \in \mathbb{R}$, consider the following system:*

$$\begin{aligned} x'(t) &= r_1(t)x(t) - \frac{r_1(t)x^2(t)}{k(t)} - \frac{a(t)x(t)y(t)}{c(t)+x(t)}, \\ y'(t) &= -r_2(t)y(t) + \frac{b(t)x(t)y(t)}{c(t)+x(t)}, \end{aligned} \tag{27}$$

where

$$r_1(t) = 9 + 2\cos 200\pi t,\ r_2(t) = 6 + 4\sin 200\pi t,\ a(t) = 0.03 + 0.02\cos 200\pi t,$$

$$b(t) = 4 + \cos 200\pi t,\ c(t) = 0.1 \times 10^{-5} + 0.05 \times 10^{-5}\sin 200\pi t,\ k(t) = 2 \times 10^{-5} + 10^{-5}\cos 200\pi t.$$

By simple calculation, we have

$$r_1^+ = 11,\ r_1^- = 7,\ r_2^+ = 10,\ r_2^- = 2,\ a^+ = 0.05,\ a^- = 0.01,\ b^+ = 5,$$

$$b^- = 3,\ c^+ = 0.15 \times 10^{-5},\ c^- = 0.05 \times 10^{-5},\ k^+ = 3 \times 10^{-5},\ k^- = 10^{-5}.$$

$$\omega = 0.01,\ \mu_1 \approx 11,\ \mu_2 \approx 16,\ \rho_1 \approx 0.91,\ \rho_2 \approx 1.09,\ \rho_3 \approx 0.94,\ \rho_4 \approx 1.06,\ \lambda \approx 0.89.$$

Choosing $r = 7$, $R = 8.5$, we obtain

$$\mu_2\rho_4\omega\left(2r_2^+ - \frac{b^-\lambda^2 r}{c^+ + 1}\right) \approx 0.54 < \lambda \text{ and } \mu_2\rho_3\omega(2r_2^+ - b^+)\lambda \approx 1.56 > 1.$$

Then, all conditions of Theorem 1 hold, so system (27) has a positive periodic solution. The simulation of the positive periodic solution to system (27) is given as Figure 1. It follows from Figure 1 that the solution of system (27) is positive periodic.

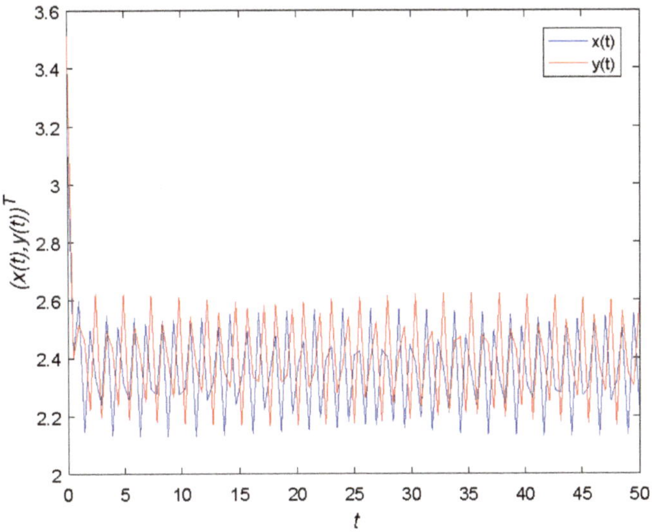

Figure 1. Positive periodic solution to system (27).

Example 2. *For the case $k \in \mathbb{Z}$, consider the following system:*

$$\begin{aligned} \Delta x(k) &= r_1(k)x(\sigma(k)) - \frac{r_1(k)x^2(k)}{k(k)} - \frac{a(k)x(k)y(k)}{c(k)+x(k)}, \\ \Delta y(k) &= -r_2(k)y(\sigma(k)) + \frac{b(k)x(k)y(k)}{c(k)+x(k)}, \end{aligned} \tag{28}$$

where Δ is forward difference,

$$r_1(k) = 10 + 2\cos 100\pi k,\ r_2(k) = 5 + 3\sin 100\pi k,\ a(k) = 0.04 + 0.02\cos 100\pi k,$$

https://doi.org/10.3390/sym18010045

$b(k) = 3 + \cos 100\pi k,\ c(k) = 0.1 \times 10^{-5} + 0.05 \times 10^{-5} \sin 100\pi k,\ k(k) = 2 \times 10^{-5} + 10^{-5} \cos 100\pi k.$

By simple calculation, we have

$$r_1^+ = 12,\ r_1^- = 8,\ r_2^+ = 8,\ r_2^- = 3,\ a^+ = 0.06,\ a^- = 0.02,\ b^+ = 4,$$

$$b^- = 2,\ c^+ = 0.15 \times 10^{-5},\ c^- = 0.05 \times 10^{-5},\ k^+ = 3 \times 10^{-5},\ k^- = 10^{-5}.$$

$$\omega = 0.02,\ \mu_1 \approx 4.5,\ \mu_2 \approx 10,\ \rho_1 \approx 0.82,\ \rho_2 \approx 1.22,\ \rho_3 \approx 0.9,\ \rho_4 \approx 1.1,\ \lambda \approx 0.67.$$

Choosing $r = 17,\ R = 17.5$, *we obtain*

$$\mu_2\rho_4\omega\left(2r_2^+ - \frac{b^-\lambda^2 r}{c^+ + 1}\right) \approx 0.65 < \lambda \text{ and } \mu_2\rho_3\omega(2r_2^+ - b^+)\lambda \approx 1.68 > 1.$$

Then, all conditions of Theorem 1 hold, so system (28) has a positive periodic solution. The simulation of the positive periodic solution to system (28) is given as Figure 2. It follows from Figure 2 that the solution of system (28) is positive periodic.

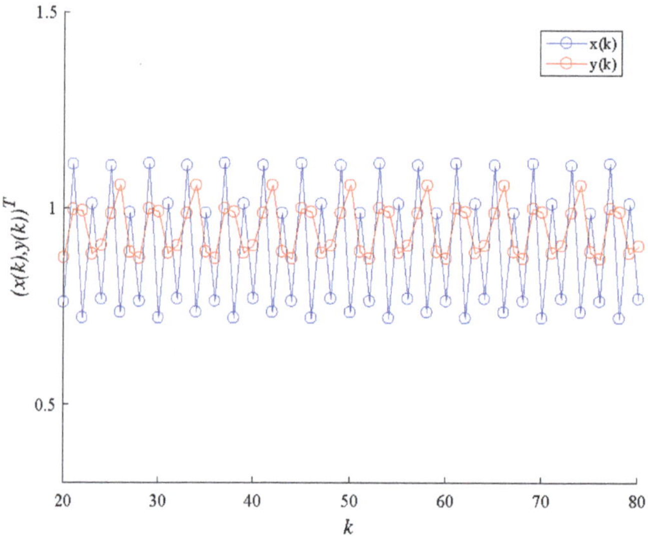

Figure 2. Positive periodic solution to system (28).

5. Conclusions

In practical systems, the variation in the parameters of such systems is not always continuous. Therefore, studying the dynamic behavior of systems on time scales has important value. In this paper, some criteria are established for the existence of positive periodic solutions for system (2). In future research, we will focus on more complex phytoplankton–zooplankton models, including pulse models, random models, and so on. The theoretical and numerical results in the present paper show the following:

- The prerequisite for the existence of positive periodic solutions in system (2) is that the verification operator F is strict-set-contractive. In this article, we verify that operator F is strict-set-contractive under the condition that the parameters of system (2) satisfy simple conditions. The set-contractive theorem has important applications in nonlinear systems, and its development has promoted the research and development of nonlinear systems, with a large number of achievements emerging, see [26–30]. This article extends the application of the compression theorem to time-scale dynamical

https://doi.org/10.3390/sym18010045

systems and obtains the existence conditions of positive periodic solutions under simple conditions. For more recent references of dynamic equations, see [31–37].

- From Figures 1 and 2, it can be observed that under the condition of satisfying Theorem 1, system (2) has both continuous and discrete positive periodic solutions. This study expands the scope of research on phytoplankton–zooplankton systems and deepens researchers' understanding and recognition of the system.
- Considering the practical significance of phytoplankton–zooplankton systems, the solution of system (2) must be positive. In order to obtain the existence of positive solutions, we constructed a suitable Banaach space P and verified that the operators defined on it are reasonable. Lemma 5 provides a rigorous proof. Of course, we can also use other methods to study the periodic solutions of system (2), such as topological theory, critical point theorem, etc. In future work, we will consider the application of these methods in studying system (2).

Author Contributions: Conceptualization, Y.L.; methodology, Y.L.; writing—original draft, F.Z.; validation, F.Z.; writing—review and editing, F.Z. All authors have read and agreed to the published version of the manuscript.

Funding: This research received no external funding.

Data Availability Statement: The original contributions presented in this study are included in the article. Further inquiries can be directed to the corresponding author.

Acknowledgments: The authors would like to acknowledge the reviewers for their valuable suggestions.

Conflicts of Interest: The authors declare no conflicts of interest.

References

1. Chattopadhayay, J.; Sarkar, R.; Mandal, S. Toxin producing plankton may act as a biological control for planktonic blooms filed study and mathematical modeling. *J. Theoret. Biol.* **2002**, *215*, 333–344. [CrossRef] [PubMed]
2. Abdllaoui, A.; Chattopadhyay, J.; Arino, O. Comparisons, by models, of some basic mechanisms acting on the dynamics of the zooplanktontoxic phytoplankton systems. *Math. Model. Methods Appl. Sci.* **2002**, *12*, 1421–1451. [CrossRef]
3. Odum, E. *Fundamentals of Ecology*; Saunders: Philadelphia, PA, USA, 1971.
4. Sarkar, R.; Chattopadhyay, J. The role of environmental stochasticity in a toxic phytoplankton-non-toxic phytoplankton zooplankton system. *Environmetrics* **2003**, *14*, 775–792. [CrossRef]
5. Chattopadhyay, J.; Sarkar, R.; Abdllaoui, A. A delay differential equation model on harmful algal blooms in the presence of toxic substances. *IMA J. Math. Appl. Med. Biol.* **2002**, *19*, 137–161. [CrossRef]
6. Buskey, E.; Hyatt, C. Effects of the Texas (USA) brown tide alga on planktonic grazers. *Marine Ecol. Prog. Ser.* **1995**, *126*, 285–292. [CrossRef]
7. Saha, T.; Bandyopadhyay, M. Dynamical analysis of toxin producing Phytoplankton-Zooplankton interactions. *Nonlinear Anal. Real World Appl.* **2009**, *10*, 314–332. [CrossRef]
8. Sarkar, R.; Pal, S.; Chattopadhyay, J. Role of two producing plankton and their effect on phytoplankton-zooplankton system: A mathematical study supported by experimental findings. *Biosystems* **2005**, *80*, 11–23. [CrossRef]
9. Chen, Z.; Tian, Z.; Zhang, S.; Wei, C. The stationary distribution and ergodicity of a stochastic phytoplankton-zooplankton model with toxin-producing phytoplankton under regime switching. *Phys. A* **2020**, *537*, 122728. [CrossRef]
10. Zhao, Y.; Yuan, S.; Zhang, T. Stochastic periodic solution of a non-autonomous toxic-producing Phytoplankton allelopathy model with environmental fluctuation. *Commun. Nonlinear* **2017**, *44*, 266–276. [CrossRef]
11. Zhang, J.; Wang, S.; Kong, X. Effects of toxin delay on the dynamics of a Phytoplankton Zooplankton model. *Phys. A* **2018**, *505*, 1150–1162. [CrossRef]
12. Liu, C.; Wang, L.; Zhang, Q.; Yan, Y. Dynamical analysis in a bioeconomic Phytoplankton Zooplankton system with double time delays and environmental stochasticity. *Phys. A* **2017**, *482*, 682–698. [CrossRef]
13. Kaufmann, E.; Raffoul, Y. Periodic solutions for a neutral nonlinear dynamical equation on a time scale. *J. Math. Anal. Appl.* **2006**, *319*, 315–325. [CrossRef]
14. Bohner, M.; Peterson, A. *Dynamic Equations on Time Scales, an Introduction with Applications*; Birkhäuser: Boston, MA, USA, 2001.
15. Smart, D. *Fixed Points Theorems*; Cambridge University Press: Cambridge, UK, 1980.
16. Cac, N.; Gatica, J. Fixed point theorems for mappings in ordered Banach spaces. *J. Math. Anal. Appl.* **1979**, *71*, 547–557. [CrossRef]

https://doi.org/10.3390/sym18010045

17. Lu, S. Existence of periodic solutions for a p-Laplacian neutral functional differential equation. *Nonlinear Anal.* **2009**, *70*, 231–243. [CrossRef]
18. Gao, F.; Lu, S.; Zhang, W. Periodic Solutions For $p-$laplacian Neutral Lienard Equation with a Sign-variable Coefficient. *J. Frankl. Inst.* **2009**, *1*, 57–64. [CrossRef]
19. Liu, B. Periodic solutions of a nonlinear second-order differential equation with deviating argument. *J. Math. Anal. Appl.* **2005**, *309*, 313–321. [CrossRef]
20. Guo, C.; Xu, Y. Existence of periodic solutions for a class of second order differential equation with deviating argument. *J. Appl. Math. Comput.* **2008**, *28*, 425–433. [CrossRef]
21. Wang, G.; Cheng, S. A priori bounds for periodic solutions of a delay Rayleigh equation. *Appl. Math. Lett.* **1999**, *12*, 41–44. [CrossRef]
22. Hammad, H.; Aydi, H.; Kattan, D. New Contributions to Fixed Point Techniques with Applications for Solving Fractional and Differential Equations. *Qual. Theory Dyn. Syst.* **2024**, *23*, 71. [CrossRef]
23. Proinov, P. Fixed point theorems for generalized contractive mappings in metric spaces. *J. Fixed Point Theory Appl.* **2020**, *22*, 2020. [CrossRef]
24. Mehmood, N.; Ahmad, N. Existence results for fractional order boundary value problem with nonlocal non-separated type multi-point integral boundary conditions. *AIMS Math.* **2019**, *5*, 385–398. [CrossRef]
25. Pant, A.; Pant, R. Fixed points and continuity of contractive maps. *Filomat* **2017**, *31*, 3501–3506. [CrossRef]
26. Agarwal, R.; Meehan, M.; O'Regan, D. *Fixed Point Theory and Applications*; Cambridge University Press: Cambridge, UK, 2001.
27. Chang, T.; Huang, Y.; Jeng, J. Fixed point theorems for multi-functions in S-KKM class. *Nonlinear Anal.* **2001**, *44*, 1007–1017. [CrossRef]
28. Chen, Y. Fixed points for convex continuous mappings in topological vector spaces. *Proc. Am. Math. Soc.* **2001**, *129*, 2157–2162. [CrossRef]
29. Petryshyn, W. Fixed point theorems for various classes of 1-set-contractive and 1-ball-contractive mappings in Banach spaces. *Trans. Am. Math. Soc.* **1973**, *182*, 323–352.
30. Tan, K.; Yuan, X. Random fixed-point theorems and approximation in cones. *J. Math. Anal. Appl.* **1994**, *185*, 378–390. [CrossRef]
31. Kostić, M.; Koyuncuoğlu, H.C.; Raffoul, Y.N. Positive periodic solutions for certain kinds of delayed q-difference equations with biological background. *Ann. Funct. Anal.* **2024**, *15*, 5. [CrossRef]
32. Agrawal, D.; Abbas, S. Existence of periodic solutions for a class of dynamic equations with multiple time varying delays on time scales. *Qual. Theory Dyn. Syst.* **2024**, *23*, 32. [CrossRef]
33. Lin, J.; Xu, C.; Zhao, Y.; Deng, Q. Hopf bifurcation and controller design for a predator-prey model with double delays. *AIP Adv.* **2025**, *15*, 075329. [CrossRef]
34. Lin, J.; Xu, C.; Zhao, Y.; Pang, Y.; Liu, Z.; Shen, J. Bifurcation and control of a predator-prey system with two time delays. *J. Appl. Anal. Comput.* **2026**, *16*, 807–859. [CrossRef]
35. Cui, M.; Lv, Y.; Zhang, Q. Periodic solutions of an NPZ model with periodic delay and space heterogeneity. *J. Math. Anal. Appl.* **2024**, *539*, 128549. [CrossRef]
36. Abd, H.M.; Naji, R.K. The impact of fear and harvesting on plankton-fish system dynamics incorporating harmful phytoplankton in the contaminated environment. *Commun. Math. Biol. Neurosci.* **2022**, *2022*, 92. [CrossRef]
37. Yang, H. Global dynamics of a diffusive phytoplankton-zooplankton model with toxic substances effect and delay. *Math. Biosci. Eng.* **2022**, *19*, 6712–6730. [CrossRef] [PubMed]

https://doi.org/10.3390/sym18010045

symmetry

MDPI

Article

Stability Analysis of Biological Systems Under Threshold Conditions

Jannat E Mahbuba and Xiang-Sheng Wang *

Department of Mathematics, University of Louisiana at Lafayette, Lafayette, LA 70503, USA;
jannat-e-.mahbuba1@louisiana.edu
* Correspondence: xswang@louisiana.edu

Abstract: In biological models exhibiting symmetric interactions within each compartmental group, threshold dynamics are typically governed by a key parameter known as the basic reproduction number R_0. The stability of an equilibrium often hinges on whether R_0 is greater than or less than one. However, general results for stability at the critical threshold—when R_0 equals one—remain scarce. In this paper, we establish two theorems to analyze the stability of both trivial and boundary equilibria under this threshold condition. Our results provide explicit expressions for the threshold parameters in terms of partial derivatives of the nonlinear reaction function, making them readily applicable to a wide range of biological systems.

Keywords: stability; biological systems; threshold dynamics; basic reproduction number; equilibrium

1. Introduction

In many biological systems exhibiting symmetry in birth and death rates across subpopulations, one should define the basic reproduction number based on the Jacobian matrix obtained by linearizing the system about an equilibrium point. For instance, consider a multigroup or multistage ecological model.

$$u'(t) = f(u(t)), \tag{1}$$

where $u(t) \in \mathbb{R}_+^n$ denotes the population densities at $t \geq 0$, and $f \in C^2(\mathbb{R}_+^n, \mathbb{R}^n)$ with $f(0) = 0$. The Jacobian matrix of the system about the trivial equilibrium 0 is given by

$$A = f'(0) \in \mathbb{R}^{n \times n}. \tag{2}$$

Assume that A is cooperative: all off-diagonal entries of A are non-negative. Furthermore, assume that A is irreducible: there does not exist a permutation matrix $P \in \mathbb{R}^{n \times n}$ such that $P^T AP$ is a block upper triangular matrix, or equivalently, for any $j, k = 1, \cdots, n$, there exists m such that the (j, k) entry of A^m is nonzero, namely, $(A^m)_{jk} \neq 0$. Let

$$A = F - V \tag{3}$$

be a regular splitting Section 3.6 of ref. [1] in the sense that $F \in \mathbb{R}_+^{n \times n}$ is a non-negative matrix containing the birth/growth rates of the species and the transition/development rates between different groups/stages, and $V \in \mathbb{R}^{n \times n}$ is an invertible matrix that includes the death/removal rates of species with a non-negative inverse matrix $V^{-1} \in \mathbb{R}_+^{n \times n}$. We can define the basic reproduction number as the spectral radius of the next-generation matrix FV^{-1}; that is,

$$R_0 := \rho(FV^{-1}) = \rho(V^{-1}F); \tag{4}$$

see [2,3]. It is well known that the following threshold dynamics holds:

(i) if $R_0 < 1$, then the spectral bound $s(A)$ is negative and the trivial equilibrium 0 is locally asymptotically stable;
(ii) if $R_0 > 1$, then $s(A) > 0$ and the trivial equilibrium 0 becomes unstable.

The biological interpretation of this result is that the species will survive if the basic reproduction number R_0 exceeds the threshold value 1 and will be extinct if $R_0 < 1$. A natural question is what if $R_0 = 1$. Will the trivial equilibrium 0 be stable or unstable under the threshold condition when the basic reproduction number is equal to one? The objective of this work is to provide a criterion for the stability of 0 under threshold conditions. Note that if $R_0 = 1$ then $s(A) = 0$ is the principal eigenvalue of A with a non-trivial and non-negative eigenvector $u_0 \in \mathbb{R}^n_+$. In this case, the linearized system $u'(t) = Au(t)$ possesses infinitely many equilibrium points cu_0 with $c \geq 0$. Thus, a linear approximation is not sufficient to determine the stability of 0 for the original system. To resolve this issue, we shall consider the second-order approximation of the function f and investigate the normal form of (1) in the center manifold of the equilibrium point 0.

In many applications, in particular for disease models or predator-prey systems, we shall linearize the system about the disease-free equilibrium or predator-free equilibrium to define the basic reproduction number R_0. We will also investigate the stability of the boundary equilibrium point under the threshold condition $R_0 = 1$.

Throughout this paper, we say a vector (or matrix) is non-negative if each component of the vector (or matrix) is non-negative. We use $\mathbb{R}^n_+$ and $\mathbb{R}^{n\times n}_+$ to denote the sets of non-negative (column) vectors and non-negative square matrices, respectively. We say a vector (or matrix) is positive if each component of the vector (or matrix) is positive. Given $f \in C^2(\mathbb{R}^n_+, \mathbb{R}^n)$, the first-order (Fréchet) derivative of f is denoted as $f' \in C^1(\mathbb{R}^n_+, \mathbb{R}^{n\times n})$ such that

$$f'_{ij}(x) = \frac{\partial f_i}{\partial x_j}(x),$$

for any $x \in \mathbb{R}^n_+$ and $i, j = 1, \cdots, n$. For each component $f_i \in C^2(\mathbb{R}^n, \mathbb{R})$, the second-order (Fréchet) derivative of f_i is denoted as $f''_i \in C(\mathbb{R}^n_+, \mathbb{R}^{n\times n})$ such that

$$f''_{ijk}(x) = \frac{\partial^2 f_i}{\partial x_j \partial x_k}(x),$$

for any $x \in \mathbb{R}^n_+$ and $i, j, k = 1, \cdots, n$. For any square matrix $M \in \mathbb{R}^{n\times n}$, the spectral radius $\rho(M)$ is defined as the maximum of the absolute values of its eigenvalues, while the spectral bound $s(M)$ is the maximum of the real parts of its eigenvalues. For any $x \in \mathbb{R}^n$ and $\varepsilon > 0$, we defined $B_\varepsilon(x)$ the open ball of all vectors whose Euclidean distance to x is less than ε.

For a mathematical model in biological systems, we provide a rigorous definition for the local asymptotic stability of the trivial equilibrium or a boundary equilibrium.

Definition 1. *Consider the system (1) with $f \in C(\mathbb{R}^n_+, \mathbb{R}^n)$ and an equilibrium point $\bar{u} \in \mathbb{R}^n_+$ satisfying $f(\bar{u}) = 0$. Assume that $\mathbb{R}^n_+$ is positively invariant; that is, $u(0) \in \mathbb{R}^n_+$ implies $u(t) \in \mathbb{R}^n_+$ for all $t \geq 0$. We say $\bar{u}$ is locally asymptotically stable (in $\mathbb{R}^n_+$) if the following conditions are satisfied:*

1. *(stability) For any $\varepsilon > 0$ there exists $\delta > 0$ such that $u(0) \in B_\delta(\bar{u}) \cap \mathbb{R}^n_+$ implies $u(t) \in B_\varepsilon(\bar{u})$ for all $t \geq 0$.*

2. *(attractivity) There exists $\delta > 0$ such that $u(0) \in B_\delta(\bar{u}) \cap \mathbb{R}^n_+$ implies that $u(t) \to \bar{u}$ as $t \to \infty$.*

We say $\bar{u}$ is unstable if there exists $\varepsilon > 0$ such that for any $\delta > 0$, we can find an initial value $u(0) \in B_\delta(\bar{u}) \cap \mathbb{R}^n_+$ and a time $t_1 \geq 0$ such that $u(t_1) \notin B_\varepsilon(\bar{u})$.

Remark 1. *Comparing with the traditional definition of local asymptotic stability of an equilibrium, we have used $B_\delta(\bar{u}) \cap \mathbb{R}^n_+$, instead of $B_\delta(\bar{u})$, in Definition 1. If $\bar{u}$ is an interior equilibrium with positive components, then it is unnecessary to make this modification because $B_\delta(\bar{u}) \subset \mathbb{R}^n_+$ for sufficiently small $\delta > 0$. However, if $\bar{u}$ is the trivial equilibrium or a boundary equilibrium with some components being zero, then we should replace $B_\delta(\bar{u})$ with $B_\delta(\bar{u}) \cap \mathbb{R}^n_+$. This is because, in biological systems, we are only interested in the non-negative solutions.*

2. Stability of Trivial Equilibrium

In this section, we consider the system (1) with the following biologically reasonable assumptions:

(A1) $f \in C^2(\mathbb{R}^n_+, \mathbb{R}^n)$ with $f(0) = 0$.

(A2) $\mathbb{R}^n_+$ is positively invariant; that is, $u(0) \in \mathbb{R}^n_+$ implies $u(t) \in \mathbb{R}^n_+$ for all $t \geq 0$.

(A3) $A = f'(0) \in \mathbb{R}^{n\times n}$ is cooperative and irreducible.

(A4) There exists a regular splitting $A = F - V$, where $F \in \mathbb{R}^{n\times n}_+$ is non-negative and V is invertible with a non-negative inverse $V^{-1} \in \mathbb{R}^{n\times n}_+$.

The following lemma plays a crucial role in the proof of our theorem.

Lemma 1. *Consider a scalar equation*

$$y'(t) = h(y(t)), \tag{5}$$

where $h \in C^2(\mathbb{R}_+)$ with $h(0) = 0$ and $h'(0) = 0$. Then 0 is locally asymptotically stable (in $\mathbb{R}_+$) if $h''(0) < 0$ and unstable if $h''(0) > 0$.

Proof. It is readily seen from $f(0) = 0$ that $\mathbb{R}_+$ is positively invariant; that is, $y(0) \geq 0$ implies $y(t) \geq 0$ for all $t \geq 0$.

If $h''(0) < 0$, then there exist $\alpha > 0$ and $\delta > 0$ such that $h''(y) \leq -2\alpha$ for all $y \in [0, \delta]$. By Taylor expansion, we obtain

$$h(y) = \frac{h''(\xi)}{2} y^2 \leq -\alpha y^2,$$

for all $y \in [0, \delta]$, where $\xi \in [0, y]$ depends on y. If $y(0) \in (0, \delta]$, then

$$y'(0) = h(y(0)) \leq -\alpha y(0)^2 < 0.$$

The positive invariance of $\mathbb{R}_+$ implies that $y(t) > 0$ for all $t \geq 0$. We claim that $y'(t) < 0$ for all $t \geq 0$. If not, there exists $t_1 > 0$ such that $y'(t) < 0$ for all $t \in [0, t_1)$ and $y'(t_1) = 0$. Hence, we obtain $0 < y(t_1) < y(0) \leq \delta$, which implies

$$y'(t_1) = h(y(t_1)) \leq -\alpha y(t_1)^2 < 0,$$

a contradiction to $y'(t_1) = 0$. Therefore, we have proved that if $y(0) \in (0, \delta]$, then $y(t)$ is always positive and strictly decreasing in t. Denote

$$c := \lim_{t\to\infty} y(t) \in [0, \delta].$$

It follows from

$$0 = \lim_{t \to \infty} y'(t) = h(c) \leq -\alpha c^2 \leq 0$$

that $c = 0$. Thus, 0 attracts the interval $[0, \delta]$. Moreover, since the interval $[0, \alpha]$ is positively invariant for any $\varepsilon \in (0, \delta)$, 0 is locally asymptotically stable.

Now we assume $h''(0) > 0$. A similar application of the continuity of h'' and Taylor expansion guarantees the existence of two small positive numbers $\beta > 0$ and $\sigma > 0$ such that

$$h(y) \geq \beta y^2,$$

for all $y \in [0, \sigma]$. For any $\varepsilon > 0$, we choose $y(0) = \min\{\varepsilon, \sigma\} > 0$ and prove by contradiction that $y(t_2) > \sigma$ for some $t_2 > 0$. Assume $y(t) \leq \sigma$ for all $t \geq 0$. The positive invariance of R_+ implies $y(t) > 0$ for all $t \geq 0$. Hence,

$$y'(t) = h(y(t)) \geq \beta y(t)^2,$$

for all $t \geq 0$. Solving the above differential inequality yields

$$\frac{1}{y(0)} - \frac{1}{y(t)} \geq \beta t.$$

The left-hand side is bounded by $1/y(0)$ while the right-hand side can be arbitrarily large. This leads to a contradiction. Therefore, 0 is unstable. □

Remark 2. *In Lemma 1, we say 0 is locally asymptotically stable (in $\mathbb{R}_+$) when it satisfies the conditions given in Definition 1. Note that if $f''(0) < 0$, then 0 attracts solutions from the interval $(0, \delta)$ for sufficiently small $\delta > 0$ while repelling those in the interval $(-\varepsilon, 0)$ for sufficiently small $\varepsilon > 0$. This phenomenon is called semi-stable or half-stable in some literature or textbooks [4]. However, since we are only interested in the non-negative solutions in biological systems, it is more convenient and common to say that 0 is locally asymptotically stable (in $\mathbb{R}_+$); see Remark 1.*

Now, we are ready to state our first main theorem.

Theorem 1. *Consider the system* (1) *under the assumptions (A1)–(A4). Define $R_0 = \rho(FV^{-1}) = \rho(V^{-1}F)$. If $R_0 = 1$, then we have $s(A) = 0$ and it is a simple eigenvalue of A with a positive left eigenvector $\alpha \in \mathbb{R}^n$ and a positive right eigenvector $\beta \in \mathbb{R}^n$ such that*

$$\alpha^T A = 0, \;\; A\beta = 0, \;\; \alpha^T \beta = 1.$$

Denote

$$\lambda := \sum_{i=1}^{n} \sum_{j=1}^{n} \sum_{k=1}^{n} \alpha_i f''_{ijk}(0) \beta_j \beta_k.$$

Then the trivial equilibrium 0 is locally asymptotically stable (in $\mathbb{R}^n_+$) if $\lambda < 0$ and unstable if $\lambda > 0$.

Proof. By (A4), the matrix FV^{-1} is non-negative. Hence, the Perron–Frobenius theorem implies that $R_0 = \rho(FV^{-1}) = 1$ is an eigenvalue of FV^{-1} with a non-negative left eigenvector $\alpha \in \mathbb{R}^n_+$; namely,

$$\alpha^T FV^{-1} = R_0 \alpha^T.$$

From $R_0 = 1$, we have $\alpha^T F = \alpha^T V$ and hence

$$\alpha^T A = \alpha^T (F - V) = 0.$$

Since A is cooperative by (A3), there exists $c > 0$ such that $B := cI + A$ is non-negative. The above equation shows that $c > 0$ is an eigenvalue of B with a non-negative left eigenvector c. Again, by Perron–Frobenius theorem, $c = \rho(B)$ is a simple eigenvalue of B and c is a positive left eigenvector. Consequently, 0 is a simple eigenvector of A. If $\mu \in \mathbb{C}$ is any eigenvalue of A, then $\mu + c$ is an eigenvalue of B and $|\mu + c| \leq c$. Therefore, we have $\mathrm{Re}(\mu + c) \leq c$ and $\mathrm{Re}\,\mu \leq 0$; namely, $s(A) = 0$.

Now, we restrict the dynamics of (1) to the center manifold that is locally represented by

$$w = \alpha^T u = \alpha_1 u_1 + \cdots + \alpha_n u_n.$$

Assume $u_i = \beta_i w + O(w^2)$. Then we have from (1) and Taylor expansion

$$w' = \sum_{i=1}^{n} \alpha_i f_i(u) = \sum_{i=1}^{n} \sum_{j=1}^{n} \alpha_i f'_{ij}(0) \beta_j w + O(w^2).$$

Recall that $A = f'(0)$ and $\alpha^T A = 0$, the first/linear term on the right-hand side of the above equation vanishes. Hence, we have $w' = O(w^2)$. To determine the coefficient of the quadratic term, we shall make use of (1) and Taylor expansion again to obtain for each $i = 1, \cdots, n$,

$$u'_i = f_i(u) = \sum_{j=1}^{n} f'_{ij}(0) \beta_j w + O(w^2).$$

From $u_i = \beta_i w + O(w^2)$ and $w' = O(w^2)$, we have $u'_i = O(w^2)$. Hence, the first/linear term on the right-hand side of the above equation should be zero; that is,

$$\sum_{j=1}^{n} f'_{ij}(0) \beta_j = 0, \;\; i = 1, \cdots, n.$$

This implies that $\beta = (\beta_1, \cdots, \beta_n)^T \in \mathbb{R}^n$ is a right eigenvector of A with respect to the eigenvector 0. From non-negativeness of u and positiveness of α, we obtain $w \geq 0$. Hence, we shall choose β to be positive. Moreover, since $w = \alpha^T u = \alpha^T \beta w + O(w^2)$, the left eigenvector α and the right eigenvector β are normalized by the condition $\alpha^T \beta = 1$.

Finally, we obtain from (1) and $f \in C^2(\mathbb{R}^n_+, \mathbb{R}^n)$ that

$$w' = \sum_{i=1}^{n} \alpha_i f_i(u) = \frac{1}{2} \sum_{i=1}^{n} \sum_{j=1}^{n} \sum_{k=1}^{n} \alpha_i f''_{ijk}(0) \beta_j \beta_k w^2 + o(w^2).$$

The result is a direct application of Lemma 1 and the equivalence of the dynamics of (1) and its restriction on the center manifold [5,6]. □

Remark 3. *In real applications, the normalization condition $\alpha^T \beta = 1$ can be released because any multiplication by a positive constant does not affect the sign of the stability parameter λ.*

3. Stability of Boundary Equilibrium

In this section, we consider the following system

$$u'(t) = f(u(t), v(t)), \tag{6}$$

$$v'(t) = g(u(t), v(t)), \tag{7}$$

where $u(t) \in \mathbb{R}^n_+$, $v(t) \in \mathbb{R}^m_+$, $f \in C^2(\mathbb{R}^{n+m}_+, \mathbb{R}^n)$ and $g \in C^2(\mathbb{R}^{n+m}_+, \mathbb{R}^m)$. Assume $(0, \bar{v}) \in \mathbb{R}^{n+m}_+$ is a boundary equilibrium such that $f(0, \bar{v}) = 0$ and $g(0, \bar{v}) = 0$. Denote the partial derivative of f with respect to u and v at the boundary equilibrium $(0, \bar{v})$ by

$$A = D_u f(0, \bar{v}) \in \mathbb{R}^{n \times n}, \quad B = D_v f(0, \bar{v}) \in \mathbb{R}^{n \times m} \tag{8}$$

such that

$$A_{ij} = \frac{\partial f_i}{\partial u_j}(0, \bar{v}), \quad i, j = 1, \cdots, n, \tag{9}$$

and

$$B_{ip} = \frac{\partial f_i}{\partial v_p}(0, \bar{v}), \quad i = 1, \cdots, n, \ p = 1, \cdots, m. \tag{10}$$

Denote the partial derivative of g with respect to u and v at the boundary equilibrium $(0, \bar{v})$ by

$$C = D_u g(0, \bar{v}) \in \mathbb{R}^{m \times n}, \quad D = D_v g(0, \bar{v}) \in \mathbb{R}^{m \times m} \tag{11}$$

such that

$$C_{pi} = \frac{\partial g_p}{\partial u_i}(0, \bar{v}), \quad p = 1, \cdots, m, \ i = 1, \cdots, n, \tag{12}$$

and

$$D_{pq} = \frac{\partial g_p}{\partial v_q}(0, \bar{v}), \quad p, q = 1, \cdots, m. \tag{13}$$

Similarly to Assumptions (A1)–(A4), we make the following assumptions.

(B1) $f \in C^2(\mathbb{R}^{n+m}_+, \mathbb{R}^n)$ and $g \in C^2(\mathbb{R}^{n+m}_+, \mathbb{R}^m)$ with $f(0, \bar{v}) = 0$, where $\bar{v} \in \mathbb{R}^m_+$.
(B2) $\mathbb{R}^{n+m}_+$ is positively invariant; that is, $u(0) \in \mathbb{R}^n_+$ and $v(0) \in \mathbb{R}^m_+$ implies $u(t) \in \mathbb{R}^n_+$ and $v(t) \in \mathbb{R}^m_+$ for all $t \geq 0$.
(B3) $A = D_u f(0, \bar{v}) \in \mathbb{R}^{n \times n}$ is cooperative and irreducible.
(B4) There exists a regular splitting $A = F - V$, where $F \in \mathbb{R}^{n \times n}_+$ is non-negative and V is invertible with a non-negative inverse $V^{-1} \in \mathbb{R}^{n \times n}_+$.

In addition to (B1)–(B4), we also assume that

(B5) $B = D_v f(0, \bar{v}) = 0 \in \mathbb{R}^{n \times m}$; namely,

$$\frac{\partial f_i}{\partial v_p}(0, \bar{v}) = 0,$$

for any $i = 1, \cdots, n$ and $p = 1, \cdots, m$.

(B6) $D = D_v g(0, \bar{v}) \in \mathbb{R}^{m \times m}$ is invertible.

Our second main theorem is presented below.

Theorem 2. *Consider the system (6) and (7) under the assumptions (B1)–(B6). Define $R_0 = \rho(FV^{-1}) = \rho(V^{-1}F)$. If $R_0 = 1$, then we have $s(A) = 0$ and it is a simple eigenvalue of A with a positive left eigenvector $\alpha \in \mathbb{R}^n$ and a positive right eigenvector $\beta \in \mathbb{R}^n$ such that*

$$\alpha^T A = 0, \quad A\beta = 0, \quad \alpha^T \beta = 1.$$

Denote $\delta := -D^{-1}C\beta \in \mathbb{R}^m$ and

$$\lambda := \sum_{i=1}^{n} \alpha_i \Bigg[\sum_{j=1}^{n} \sum_{k=1}^{n} \frac{\partial^2 f_i}{\partial u_j \partial u_k}(0, \bar{v}) \beta_j \beta_k + 2 \sum_{j=1}^{n} \sum_{p=1}^{m} \frac{\partial^2 f_i}{\partial u_j \partial v_p}(0, \bar{v}) \beta_j \delta_p + \sum_{p=1}^{m} \sum_{q=1}^{m} \frac{\partial^2 f_i}{\partial v_p \partial v_q}(0, \bar{v}) \delta_p \delta_q \Bigg].$$

Then the boundary equilibrium $(0, \bar{v})$ is locally asymptotically stable (in $\mathbb{R}^n_+$) if $\lambda < 0$ and unstable if $\lambda > 0$.

Proof. Similarly as in the proof of Theorem 1, we can show that $s(A) = 0$ and it is a simple eigenvalue of A with a positive left eigenvector $\alpha \in \mathbb{R}^n$ such that $\alpha^T A = 0$.

Now, we restrict the dynamics of (6) and (7) to the center manifold that is locally represented by

$$w = \alpha^T u = \alpha_1 u_1 + \cdots + \alpha_n u_n,$$

with $u_i = \beta_i w + O(w^2)$ for $i = 1, \cdots, n$ and $v_p = \bar{v}_p + \delta_p w + O(w^2)$ for $p = 1, \cdots, m$. Applying the Taylor expansion to (6) yields

$$u_i' = \sum_{j=1}^{n} \frac{\partial f_i}{\partial u_j}(0, \bar{v}) u_j + \sum_{p=1}^{m} \frac{\partial f_i}{\partial v_p}(0, \bar{v})(v_p - \bar{v}_p) + O(w^2).$$

By (B3), we have $D_u f(0, \bar{v}) = A$. By (B5), we have $D_v f(0, \bar{v}) = 0$. It then follows from $\alpha^T A = 0$ and $w = \alpha^T u$ that

$$w' = \sum_{i=1}^{n} \alpha_i u_i' = O(w^2).$$

A combination of $u_i = \beta_i w + O(w^2)$ and the above two equations gives

$$\sum_{j=1}^{n} \frac{\partial f_i}{\partial u_j}(0, \bar{v}) \beta_j = 0, \quad i = 1, \cdots, n.$$

This implies that $\beta = (\beta_1, \cdots, \beta_n)^T \in \mathbb{R}^n$ is a right eigenvector of A with respect to the eigenvector 0. We choose β to be positive and normalize it such that $\alpha^T \beta = 1$.

Next, we apply the Taylor expansion to (7) and find

$$v_p' = \sum_{i=1}^{n} \frac{\partial g_p}{\partial u_i}(0, \bar{v}) u_i + \sum_{q=1}^{m} \frac{\partial g_p}{\partial v_q}(0, \bar{v})(v_q - \bar{v}_q) + O(w^2).$$

Since $u_i = \beta_i w + O(w^2)$ and $v_q = \bar{v}_q + \delta_q w + O(w^2)$, we rewrite the above equation as

$$v_p' = \sum_{i=1}^{n} \frac{\partial g_p}{\partial u_i}(0, \bar{v}) \beta_i w + \sum_{q=1}^{m} \frac{\partial g_p}{\partial v_q}(0, \bar{v}) \delta_q w + O(w^2).$$

In view of $v_p = \bar{v}_p + \delta_p w + O(w^2)$ and $w' = O(w^2)$, the left-hand side of the above equation is of order $O(w^2)$. Hence, the linear term on the right-hand side of the above equation vanishes, that is,

$$\sum_{i=1}^{n} \frac{\partial g_p}{\partial u_i}(0, \bar{v}) \beta_i + \sum_{q=1}^{m} \frac{\partial g_p}{\partial v_q}(0, \bar{v}) \delta_q = 0,$$

for all $p = 1, \cdots, m$. On account of the definitions of matrices C and D in (11), the above system can be written in matrix form:

$$C\beta + D\delta = 0.$$

By (B6), D is invertible and we have

$$\delta = -D^{-1} C \beta.$$

Finally, we obtain from (6) and $f \in C^2(\mathbb{R}_+^{n+m}, \mathbb{R}^n)$ that

$$\begin{aligned} w' =& \sum_{i=1}^{n} \alpha_i f_i(u,v) \\ =& \frac{1}{2}\sum_{i=1}^{n} \alpha_i \Bigg[\sum_{j=1}^{n}\sum_{k=1}^{n} \frac{\partial^2 f_i}{\partial u_j \partial u_k}(0,\bar{v})\beta_j\beta_k + 2\sum_{j=1}^{n}\sum_{p=1}^{m} \frac{\partial^2 f_i}{\partial u_j \partial v_p}(0,\bar{v})\beta_j\delta_p \\ &+ \sum_{p=1}^{m}\sum_{q=1}^{m} \frac{\partial^2 f_i}{\partial v_p \partial v_q}(0,\bar{v})\delta_p\delta_q \Bigg] w^2 + o(w^2). \end{aligned}$$

Since the dynamics of (6) and (7) is equivalent to the dynamics of its restriction on the center manifold [5,6], we obtain our desired result from a direct application of Lemma 1. □

Remark 4. *Similar as in Remark 3, we may release the normalization condition $\alpha^T\beta = 1$ in real applications. It is also noted that Theorem 1 is a special case of Theorem 2 if we set $m = 0$.*

4. Applications

We consider the age structure model of a biological species that exhibits asymmetry between the immature and mature population densities, denoted by u_1 and u_2, respectively. The dynamics of these two compartments are governed by the equations

$$u_1'(t) = \frac{r u_2(t)}{1 + u_2(t)/H} - d_1 u_1(t) - \sigma u_1(t), \tag{14}$$

$$u_2'(t) = \sigma u_1(t) - d_2 u_2(t), \tag{15}$$

where r is the intrinsic birth rate, σ is the maturation rate, and d_1 and d_2 are the death rates of immature and mature population, respectively. Note that asymmetry is introduced by assuming different death rates for the immature and mature groups. The nonlinear birth function is modeled by the Holling type function $ru_2/(1 + u_2/H)$, which is a decreasing function of the mature population u_2, where H denotes the density of mature population when the birth rate is reduced to half the intrinsic birth rate $r/2$. Denote the right-hand side of the above system by a vector-valued function $f \in C^2(\mathbb{R}_+^2, \mathbb{R}^2)$. Linearizing the above system about the trivial equilibrium $0 \in \mathbb{R}^2$, we obtain the Jacobian matrix

$$A = f'(0) = \begin{pmatrix} -d_1 - \sigma & r \\ \sigma & -d_2 \end{pmatrix}.$$

We use the regular splitting $A = F - V$, where

$$F := \begin{pmatrix} 0 & r \\ 0 & 0 \end{pmatrix}$$

is the matrix of birth, while

$$V := \begin{pmatrix} d_1 + \sigma & 0 \\ -\sigma & d_2 \end{pmatrix}$$

is the matrix of death and maturation. Hence, the basic reproduction number R_0 is defined as the spectral radius of the next-generation matrix

$$FV^{-1} = \begin{pmatrix} r\sigma/[(d_1+\sigma)d_2] & r/d_2 \\ 0 & 0 \end{pmatrix};$$

that is,

$$R_0 = r \cdot \frac{\sigma}{d_1 + \sigma} \cdot \frac{1}{d_2},$$

where r is the intrinsic birth rate, $\sigma/(d_1 + \sigma)$ is the probability of maturation, and $1/d_2$ is the average lifespan of the mature population. It is easily seen that (A1)–(A4) are satisfied. Now, we assume that $R_0 = 1$, that is, $r\sigma = (d_1 + \sigma)d_2$. The spectral bound of the Jacobian matrix A is 0 and it is an eigenvalue associated with a positive left eigenvector $\alpha = (d_2, r)^T$ and a positive right eigenvector $\beta = (d_2, \sigma)^T$. As mentioned in Remark 3, we do not need to normalize the inner product $\alpha^T\beta$. A simple calculation gives

$$f''_{2jk}(0) = 0, \ \ j = 1,2, \ k = 1,2,$$

and

$$f''_{111}(0) = f''_{112}(0) = f''_{121}(0) = 0,$$

and

$$f''_{122}(0) = -\frac{r}{H}.$$

Consequently,

$$\lambda = \sum_{i=1}^{2}\sum_{j=1}^{2}\sum_{k=1}^{2} \alpha_i f''_{ijk}(0)\beta_j\beta_k = \alpha_1 f''_{122}\beta_2^2 = -\frac{d_2\sigma^2 r}{H} < 0.$$

Based on Theorem 1, we have the following result.

Proposition 1. *If $R_0 = 1$, then the trivial equilibrium $0 \in \mathbb{R}^2$ of the system* (14) *and* (15) *is locally asymptotically stable in $\mathbb{R}^2_+$.*

The above result is illustrated in Figure 1.

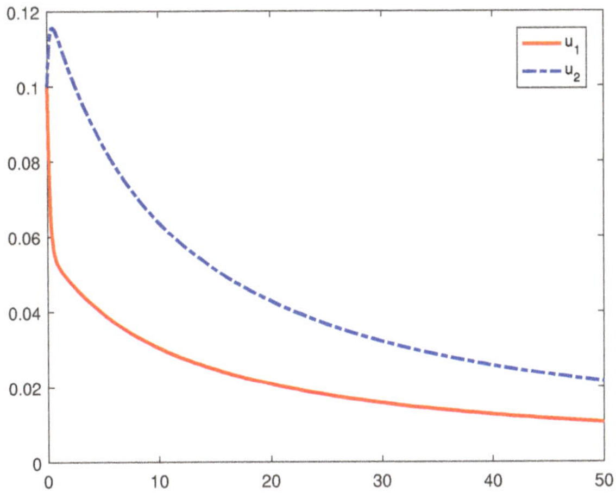

Figure 1. The trivial equilibrium 0 of the system (14) and (15) is locally asymptotically stable for $R_0 = 1$. The model parameters are chosen as $H = 1$, $r = 2$, $d_1 = 2$, $\sigma = 2$, $d_2 = 1$.

Next, we consider the infectious disease model with four compartments: susceptible (S), exposed (E), infectious (I) and recovered (R) populations. The dynamical system is given by

$$S'(t) = b - d_S S(t) - h(S(t), I(t)) + \eta R(t), \tag{16}$$
$$E'(t) = h(S(t), I(t)) - \sigma E(t) - d_E E(t), \tag{17}$$
$$I'(t) = \sigma E(t) - d_I I(t) - \gamma I(t), \tag{18}$$
$$R'(t) = \gamma I(t) - d_R R(t) - \eta R(t), \tag{19}$$

where b is the birth rate, d_S, d_E, d_I, and d_R are the death rates that characterize the asymmetry among the four compartmental groups, and $h \in C^2(\mathbb{R}^2_+, \mathbb{R}_+)$ is the nonlinear function of infection satisfying

$$h(x_1, 0) = h(0, x_2) = 0,$$

for any $x_1, x_2 \in \mathbb{R}^+$. For convenience, we denote the partial derivatives of h as

$$h_j(x) = \frac{\partial h}{\partial x_j}(x), \ \ h_{jk}(x) = \frac{\partial^2 h}{\partial x_j \partial x_k}(x)$$

for $j = 1, 2$, $k = 1, 2$, and $x = (x_1, x_2)^T \in \mathbb{R}^+_2$. Clearly,

$$h_1(x_1, 0) = h_{11}(x_1, 0) = 0$$

for any $x_1 \geq 0$. The progression rate from exposed to infectious is denoted by σ, while the recovery rate is γ. We also denote by η the rate of immunity loss. The disease-free equilibrium is given by $E_0 = (\bar{S}, 0, 0, 0)$, where $\bar{S} = b/d_S$. We choose $n = 2$ and $m = 2$, and define

$$u(t) = \begin{pmatrix} E(t) \\ I(t) \end{pmatrix} \in \mathbb{R}^2_+, \ v(t) = \begin{pmatrix} S(t) \\ R(t) \end{pmatrix} \in \mathbb{R}^2_+.$$

Hence, the infectious disease model (16)–(19) is equivalent to (6) and (7) with

$$f(u, v) = \begin{pmatrix} h(v_1, u_2) - (\sigma + d_E) u_1 \\ \sigma u_1 - (d_I + \gamma) u_2 \end{pmatrix},$$
$$g(u, v) = \begin{pmatrix} b - d_S v_1 - h(v_1, u_2) + \eta\, v_2 \\ \gamma u_2 - (d_R + \eta) v_2 \end{pmatrix}.$$

The boundary equilibrium is $(0, \bar{v})$, with $\bar{v} = (\bar{S}, 0) \in \mathbb{R}^2_+$. A simple calculation gives

$$A = D_u f(0, \bar{v}) = \begin{pmatrix} -(\sigma + d_E) & h_2(\bar{S}, 0) \\ \sigma & -(d_I + \gamma) \end{pmatrix} \in \mathbb{R}^{2\times 2},$$
$$B = D_v f(0, \bar{v}) = 0 \in \mathbb{R}^{2\times 2},$$
$$C = D_u g(0, \bar{v}) = \begin{pmatrix} 0 & -h_2(\bar{S}, 0) \\ 0 & \gamma \end{pmatrix} \in \mathbb{R}^{2\times 2},$$
$$D = D_v g(0, \bar{v}) = \begin{pmatrix} -d_S & \eta \\ 0 & -(d_R + \eta) \end{pmatrix} \in \mathbb{R}^{2\times 2}.$$

Now, we introduce the regular splitting $A = F - V$, where

$$F = \begin{pmatrix} 0 & h_2(\bar{S}, 0) \\ 0 & 0 \end{pmatrix}$$

is the matrix of infection, and

$$V = \begin{pmatrix} \sigma + d_E & 0 \\ -\sigma & d_I + \gamma \end{pmatrix}$$

is the matrix of transition and death. The basic reproduction number is defined as the spectral radius of the next-generation matrix

$$R_0 = \rho(FV^{-1}) = \rho(V^{-1}F) = h_2(\bar{S},0) \cdot \frac{\sigma}{\sigma + d_E} \cdot \frac{1}{d_I + \gamma}, \tag{20}$$

where $h_2(\bar{S},0)$ is the transmission rate, $\sigma/(\sigma + d_E)$ is the probability of progression from exposed to infectious, and $1/(d_I + \gamma)$ is the average infectious duration. It is easily seen that (B1)–(B6) are satisfied.

If $R_0 = 1$, then $h_2(\bar{S},0)\sigma = (\sigma + d_E)(d_I + \gamma)$ and $s(A) = 0$ is a simple eigenvalue of A with a positive left eigenvector $\alpha = (\sigma, \sigma + d_E)^T$ and a positive right eigenvector $\beta = (d_I + \gamma, \sigma)^T$. As commented in Remark 4, it is unnecessary to normalize the inner product $\alpha^T\beta$. A simple calculation gives

$$\delta = -D^{-1}C\beta = \begin{pmatrix} 1/d_S & \eta/[d_S(d_R + \eta)] \\ 0 & 1/(d_R + \eta) \end{pmatrix} \begin{pmatrix} -h_2(\bar{S},0)\sigma \\ \gamma\sigma \end{pmatrix} = \begin{pmatrix} \delta_1 \\ \delta_2 \end{pmatrix},$$

where

$$\delta_1 = \frac{\eta\gamma\sigma}{d_S(d_R + \eta)} - \frac{h_2(\bar{S},0)\sigma}{d_S}, \quad \delta_2 = \frac{\gamma\sigma}{d_R + \eta}.$$

Next, we evaluate the non-zero partial derivatives

$$\frac{\partial^2 f_1}{\partial u_2^2}(0, \bar{v}) = h_{22}(\bar{S},0),$$

and

$$\frac{\partial^2 f_1}{\partial v_1 \partial u_2}(0, \bar{v}) = h_{12}(\bar{S},0).$$

Finally, we compute

$$\lambda = \alpha_1[h_{22}(\bar{S},0)\beta_2^2 + 2h_{12}(\bar{S},0)\delta_1\beta_2] = \sigma^3\left[h_{22}(\bar{S},0) + 2h_{12}(\bar{S},0)\frac{\eta\gamma - h_2(\bar{S},0)(d_R + \eta)}{d_S(d_R + \eta)}\right].$$

An application of Theorem 2 gives the following result.

Proposition 2. *Assume $R_0 = 1$. Denote a threshold parameter*

$$\xi := d_S(d_R + \eta)h_{22}(\bar{S},0) + 2[\eta\gamma - h_2(\bar{S},0)(d_R + \eta)]h_{12}(\bar{S},0).$$

The boundary equilibrium $E_0 = (\bar{S},0,0,0) \in \mathbb{R}^4$ of system (16)–(19) is locally asymptotically stable (in $\mathbb{R}^4_+$) if $\xi < 0$ and unstable if $\xi > 0$.

Proof. Note that

$$\lambda d_S(d_R + \eta) = \xi\sigma^3.$$

The signs of λ and ξ are the same. Hence, the results follow from a direct application of Theorem 2. □

Corollary 1. *Assume $h_{12}(\bar{S},0) > 0$ and $h_{22}(\bar{S},0) \leq 0$. If $R_0 = 1$, then the boundary equilibrium $E_0 = (\bar{S},0,0,0) \in \mathbb{R}^4$ of system (16)–(19) is locally asymptotically stable in $\mathbb{R}^4_+$.*

Proof. Since $\eta < d_R + \eta$ and

$$h_2(\bar{S},0) = \frac{(\sigma + d_E)(d_I + \gamma)}{\sigma} > \gamma,$$

we obtain $\xi < 0$. The result then follows from a direct application of Proposition 2. □

Remark 5. *The condition in Corollary 1 is satisfied by many commonly used disease transmission functions $h(S,I)$, including the mass-action/bilinear function cSI, the standard incidence function $cSI/(S+I)$, the Holling type function $cSI/(1+aI)$, and the media impacted function $cSIe^{-mI}$; see [7,8].*

We consider the following air pollution model [9]

$$\begin{aligned}
G'(t) =& \Lambda - aG(t)P(t) + b_4C(t) - \mu G(t), && (21)\\
P'(t) =& aG(t)P(t) - b_1P(t) + b_3C(t), && (22)\\
C'(t) =& b_1P(t) - (b_2 + b_3)C(t), && (23)
\end{aligned}$$

where $G(t)$, $P(t)$, and $C(t)$ denote the general air class, the polluted air class, and the clean air class, respectively. The pollution-free equilibrium is given by $E_0 = (\bar{G},0,0)$, where $\bar{G} = \Lambda/\mu$. According to [9] (Theorem 3), E_0 is locally asymptotically stable if $R_0 < 1$ and unstable if $R_0 > 1$, where R_0 is the basic reproduction number defined as

$$R_0 = \frac{a\bar{G}(b_2 + b_3)}{b_1 b_2} \qquad (24)$$

We choose $n = 2$ and $m = 1$, and define

$$u(t) = \begin{pmatrix} P(t) \\ C(t) \end{pmatrix} \in \mathbb{R}^2_+, \quad v(t) = G(t) \in \mathbb{R}^1_+.$$

Consequently, the air pollution model (21)–(23) can be rewritten as (6) and (7) with

$$\begin{aligned}
f(u,v) =& \begin{pmatrix} avu_1 - b_1u_1 + b_3u_2 \\ b_1u_1 - (b_2 + b_3)u_2 \end{pmatrix},\\
g(u,v) =& \Lambda - avu_1 + b_4u_2 - \mu v.
\end{aligned}$$

The boundary equilibrium is $(0,\bar{v})$, where $\bar{v} = \bar{G} = \Lambda/\mu$. It is easy to verify that

$$A = D_u f(0,\bar{v}) = \begin{pmatrix} a\bar{v} - b_1 & b_3 \\ b_1 & -(b_2 + b_3) \end{pmatrix}$$

has a regular splitting $A = F - V$ with

$$F = \begin{pmatrix} a\bar{v} & 0 \\ 0 & 0 \end{pmatrix}, \quad V = \begin{pmatrix} b_1 & -b_3 \\ -b_1 & b_2 + b_3 \end{pmatrix}.$$

A simple calculation gives the explicit formula of the basic reproduction number $R_0 = \rho(FV^{-1})$ as in (24), which is consistent with Section 3.3 of ref. [9]

If $R_0 = 1$, then $a\bar{v}(b_2 + b_3) = b_1 b_2$ and $s(A) = 0$ is a simple eigenvalue of A with a positive left eigenvector $\alpha = (b_2 + b_3, b_3)^T$ and a positive right eigenvector $\beta = (b_2 + b_3, b_1)^T$. Furthermore, we compute

$$\delta = -[D_v g(0,\bar{v})]^{-1}[D_u g(0,\bar{v})]\beta = -\frac{(-a\bar{v}s.\ b_4)}{-\mu}\begin{pmatrix} b_2 + b_3 \\ b_1 \end{pmatrix} = \frac{b_1(b_4 - b_2)}{\mu}.$$

The only non-zero second-order partial derivative of f is

$$\frac{\partial^2 f_1}{\partial u_1 \partial v}(0,\bar{v}) = a.$$

Hence, we obtain

$$\lambda = 2\alpha_1 a \beta_1 \delta = \frac{2ab_1(b_2 + b_3)^2(b_4 - b_2)}{\mu}.$$

Proposition 3. *Assume $R_0 = 1$. The boundary equilibrium $E_0 = (\bar{G}, 0, 0) \in \mathbb{R}^3$ of system* (21)–(23) *is locally asymptotically stable (in $\mathbb{R}^3_+$) if $b_4 < b_2$ and unstable if $b_4 > b_2$.*

Proof. Since the sign of λ coincides with that of $b_4 - b_2$, the conclusion follows directly from Theorem 2. □

Remark 6. *Note that $\lambda = 0$ if $b_4 = b_2$. Theorem 2 is not applicable in this critical case. It would be interesting and more challenging to extend our results to the general models when both $R_0 = 1$ and $\lambda = 0$ hold.*

5. Conclusions and Discussion

In this work, we establish a simple criterion for determining the stability of biological equilibrium when the basic reproduction number equals one. We examine two distinct scenarios based on whether the equilibrium is trivial or located on the boundary. By applying the center manifold theorem, we reduce the original dynamical system to a scalar equation that preserves the local dynamics. For each case, we derive an explicit expression for the threshold parameter in terms of the partial derivatives of the nonlinear reaction term evaluated at the equilibrium. Our results have broad applications in the stability analysis of ecological and epidemiological models.

It is important to note a limitation in applying our results. When $R_0 = 1$, we define a threshold parameter λ based on second-order approximations of the nonlinear system. We prove that the relevant equilibrium is locally asymptotically stable for $\lambda < 0$ and unstable for $\lambda > 0$. However, the critical case $\lambda = 0$ remains unresolved. Third-order or even higher-order approximations of the nonlinear system are required to derive the normal form equation. The scenario where both $R_0 = 1$ and $\lambda = 0$ hold simultaneously is left for future study.

Author Contributions: Both authors make equal contributions to the research work. All authors have read and agreed to the published version of the manuscript.

Funding: This research was funded by the Louisiana Board of Regents Support Fund under contract No. LEQSF(2022-25)-RD-A-26.

Data Availability Statement: The original contributions presented in this study are included in the article. Further inquiries can be directed to the corresponding author.

Conflicts of Interest: The authors declare no conflicts of interest.

References

1. Varga, R.S. *Matrix Iterative Analysis*; Prentice-Hall: Englewood Cliffs, NJ, USA, 1962.
2. Diekmann, O.; Heesterbeek, J.A.P.; Metz, J.A.J. On the definition and the computation of the basic reproduction ratio R_0 in models for infectious diseases in heterogeneous populations. *J. Math. Biol.* **1990**, *28*, 365–382. [CrossRef] [PubMed]
3. van den Driessche, P.; Watmough, J. Reproduction numbers and sub-threshold endemic equilibria for compartmental models of disease transmission. *Math. Biosci.* **2002**, *180*, 29–48. [CrossRef] [PubMed]
4. Strogatz, S.H. *Nonlinear Dynamics and Chaos: With Applications to Physics, Biology, Chemistry, and Engineering*, 2nd ed.; CRC Press: Boca Raton, FL, USA, 2018.
5. Carr, J. *Applications of Center Manifold Theory*; Springer: New York, NY, USA; Berlin/Heidelberg, Germany, 1981.
6. Wiggins, S. *Introduction to Applied Nonlinear Dynamical Systems and Chaos*; Texts in Appl. Math. 5; Springer: New York, NY, USA, 1990.
7. Brauer, F.; Castillo-Chavez, C. *Mathematical Models in Population Biology and Epidemics*; Springer: New York, NY, USA, 2000.
8. Cui, J.; Sun, Y.; Zhu, H. The impact of media on the control of infectious diseases. *J. Dynam. Differ. Equ.* **2008**, *20*, 31–53. [CrossRef] [PubMed]
9. Aakash, M.; Gunasundari, C.; Athithan, S.; Kumar, G.S.; Meetei, M.Z.; Orsud, M.A. Modelling Air Pollution Dynamics and Mitigation Strategies: A Mathe-matical Approach. *Contemp. Math.* **2025**, *6*, 3454–3471. [CrossRef]

symmetry

MDPI

Article

Modeling the Digestion Process by a Distributed Delay Differential System

Junli Liu [1,2,*], Zhenghua Guo [1,2] and Hui Guo [1,2]

[1] School of Science, Xi'an Polytechnic University, Xi'an 710048, China; 230811033@stu.xpu.edu.cn (Z.G.); guohui1014@163.com (H.G.)
[2] Xi'an International Science and Technology Cooperation Base for Big Data Analysis and Algorithms, Xi'an 710048, China
* Correspondence: jlliu2008@126.com

Abstract: We modified the work of Wang and Zou, where both the costs and benefits of fear effects were considered, and a constant time delay was used to represent the biomass conversion time from prey to predator. In our work, we assumed that the digestion delay is not a constant, but rather follows a specific distribution. The delay was modeled using a general kernel function, and a more general functional response function was also employed. Then, we established an integral–differential model with distributed time delays. We show that there exists a delay-dependent threshold that determines the system's dynamics and the presence of coexistence equilibrium. In the absence of coexistence equilibrium, both populations tend toward extinction, or only the prey population survives. Conversely, when coexistence equilibrium exists, the system persists. Four kernel functions were considered to explore the effect of fear levels and time delays on population dynamics. We found that an increase in the fear level of the prey may alter the system dynamics from periodic oscillations to stability. Furthermore, our findings indicate that a fear effect-related functional response has great influence in shaping the model's dynamics. These results indicate that ignoring time delay or fear effects, or the inappropriate use of kernel functions, may lead to inaccurate prediction results of the model. We want to point out that, when we investigate a pair of purely imaginary roots of the characteristic equation at the coexistence equilibrium, we just need to consider one of them due to the symmetry.

Keywords: fear effect; distributed delay; stability; periodic solution

1. Introduction

Recently, people have been paying more attention to the indirect effect (such as the fear effect) between predators and prey [1–3]. To study prey anti-predation behaviors in response to predators, Wang et al. [4] developed a system of ordinary differential equations with a functional response of Holling types I and II [5]. In Wang and Zou [6], prey consists of immature and mature stages, assuming that adult prey can adjust their behavior according to the surrounding environment, then a delay differential equation is proposed to study the interplay between the fear effect and the maturation delay of prey. Later, the model in [4] was extended by Wang and Zou [7] to a delay differential equations model by incorporating the benefits of fear effects, that is, the prey's anti-predation response will reduce the change in the prey being caught by the predators. In this model, a constant delay is used to represent the time needed for the digestion of the predator. Sasmal and Takeuchi [8] used a model with anti-predation and a group defense of prey against predation to study the stability and Hopf bifurcation. Hossain et al. [9] introduced an eco-epidemiological model, where it was assumed that the fear effect decreases the reproductive rate of the prey and the transmission between susceptible prey and infected prey. Mishra and Upadhyay [10] formulated a partial differential equation model in a continuous state space to study the stability and Hopf-bifurcation, where the fear effect has a stabilizing effect on the instability induced by the cross-diffusion and spot patterns. Ma and Meng [11] used the same type of model to consider the fear effect and predator cannibalism. Li [12] proposed a diffusive Leslie–Gower model with a both-density-dependent fear effect, they discussed the global steady-state bifurcation near the homogeneous steady state, and they discussed the stability and the structure of the bifurcated spatially inhomogeneous steady-state solutions. Their results show that, when the fear level of the prey is moderate, complex spatial dynamic patterns are manifested, while, for high or low levels of fear, the system will tend to stabilize to be a uniform distribution in space. Cong et al. [13] developed a three-species food chain model to investigate the impact of fear. This model includes the prey and the middle predator and the top predator populations, where the cost and benefit of anti-predator behaviors are both included. They studied the dissipativity of the system and performed analysis on the existence and stability of equilibria. Numerical simulations show that the predators' fear effect can transform the system from chaotic dynamics to a stable state. Li and Zou [14] formulated a patch model to investigate the fear effect, and they considered not only cost, but also the benefit of the anti-predation response of the prey. The analysis of the model shows that dispersal will enhance the co-persistence of the prey on both patches. Numerical simulations imply the existence of an optimal anti-predation response level. Panday et al. [15] considered the difference of an anti-predator strategy for the juvenile and adult stages of the prey by a predator–prey model with an age structure. It was assumed that adult prey only adapt group defense as an anti-predator strategy, where an anti-predator sensitivity parameter is introduced to interlink both cost and benefit of group defense. It was found that a fear-induced stage-structured model exhibits rich dynamics. Liu et al. [16] proposed a fractional-order predator–prey system affected by fear effects and toxic substances with the function response of Holling type II. They explored the local stability of the equilibria and the Hopf bifurcation of the system. Based on their numerical simulations, they concluded that toxic substances have a significant impact on the stability of the system. Li et al. [17] proposed and analyzed a Leslie–Gower predator–prey model with a ratio-dependent type functional response, which incorporates both the Allee effect and fear effect on prey. They showed that the system undergoes saddle-node bifurcation, degenerate Hopf bifurcation, and Bogdanov–Takens bifurcation of codimension 2, and it exhibits two limit cycles.

In the real world, the time it takes for a predator to digest its food is not a constant, rather it follows some kind of distribution. Inspired by the studies of [4,6,7], in the present paper, we replace the discrete time delay with general distributed time delays and then we formulate an integral-differential equation, where our purpose is to analyze the model's dynamical behavior, explore how the fear effects and the kernel distributions impact the dynamics of the model, and compare the effects of different kernel functions on the model prediction results.

In Section 2, we will propose a model with general kernel distributions and address the well posedness of the model. We show that there are, at most, three equilibria. In Section 3, it is shown that, when the coexistence equilibrium is absent, both the extinction equilibrium and the predator-free equilibrium are globally asymptotically stable. Then, we consider the persistence of the model in Section 4. In Section 5, we consider the case when the coexistence equilibrium is present. We then assume the functional response is Holling type I and perform local stability analysis for the coexistence equilibrium with general kernel distributions. To obtain more information about the coexistence equilibrium, we then consider the gamma, delta, and the uniform distributions as delay kernels. After this, we show that Hopf bifurcations could occur at the coexistence equilibrium. In Section 6, we perform some numerical simulations to demonstrate how different forms of distribution impact the dynamical behavior of the model. We conclude with some discussions in the final part.

2. Model Formulation

We denote by $u(t)$ and $v(t)$ the number of prey and predators, respectively. And we assume that the time needed for the biomass transfer from prey to predator is not fixed, but, instead, is distributed with a kernel function $h(s)$ that satisfies

$$h(s) \geq 0, \quad \int_0^{\infty} h(s)ds = 1.$$

We define the mean delay as $\tau = \int_0^{\infty} sh(s)ds$. As mentioned in [18], if the current state of the model system only depends on the history of the system over a finite interval of past times, it was assumed that there exists a constant $L > 0$, so that $h(s) = 0$ for $s \in [L, \infty)$. If the current state of the model system depends on all past times, then $L = \infty$ is taken and $h(s) > 0$ is allowed for all $s \geq 0$. In our present work, we follow these assumptions.

When the predator is absent, it was assumed that the prey grows according to a logistic law. For the prey population, we assumed that its natural birth rate is r and the natural death rate is d, and the crowding effect in the prey is represented by au^2. Considering the fear of the prey to the predators, the reproduction rate of the prey will be reduced to $rf(k,v)$, where $f(k,v)$ is used to account for the anti-predation of the prey and $k > 0$ refers to the level of fear. Also, due to the fear effects, the prey will reduce foraging activity, which, in turn, lowers the risk of being captured by predators; thus, the functional response $g(k,u)$ is a monotonically decreasing function with respect to the level of fear k and v. Here, we assume that $g(k,u)$ depends on the prey only. Based on these assumptions, we propose the following differential equations:

$$\begin{cases} \dfrac{du(t)}{dt} = f(k,v(t))ru(t) - du(t) - au^2(t) - g(k,u(t))v(t), \\ \dfrac{dv(t)}{dt} = c\int_0^{\infty} g(k,u(t-s))v(t-s)e^{-ms}h(s)ds - mv(t). \end{cases} \tag{1}$$

Here, c is the biomass transform efficiency, m is the death rate of the predators, and e^{-ms} is referred as the "discounting" factor. The term $g(k,u(t-s))v(t-s)e^{-ms}$ in System (1) represents the number of prey at time t that were consumed at time $t-s$. It follows that the integral term in the second equation of System (1) is the predators at time t produced by all those prey individuals that were caught at previous times to t.

Following Wang and Zou [7], we make the following biologically meaningful assumptions for functions $f(k,v)$ and $g(k,u)$:

(A1) $f(k,0) = f(0,v) = 1, \dfrac{\partial f}{\partial k} < 0, \dfrac{\partial f}{\partial v} < 0, \lim_{k\to\infty} f(k,v) = \lim_{v\to\infty} f(k,v) = 0;$

(A2) $g(k,0) = 0, \dfrac{\partial g}{\partial k} < 0, \lim_{k\to\infty} g(k,u) = 0,$ for $u > 0, g(k,u) > 0, \dfrac{\partial g}{\partial u} > 0;$

(A3) For each fixed k, there is a positive real number u^*, which is related to k, such that

$$\begin{cases} g(k,u) < \dfrac{m}{c\int_0^{\infty} F(s)ds} & \text{if } u < u^*, \\ g(k,u) > \dfrac{m}{c\int_0^{\infty} F(s)ds} & \text{if } u > u^*, \end{cases} \tag{2}$$

where $F(s) = e^{-ms}h(s)$.

There are some typical functional response functions that satisfy Hypotheses (A2) and (A3), such as the functional response of Holling type I, II, and III, that is, $g(k,u) = \rho(k)u$, $g(k,u) = \rho(k)\frac{pu}{1+qu}$, and $g(k,u) = \rho(k)\frac{pu^2}{1+qu^2}$, respectively, where p and q are positive constants, $\rho(k)$ is positive and decreases as k increases, and $\rho(k) \to 0$ as $k \to \infty$.

We state the following lemma that is used to determine the existence and uniqueness of solution for System (1) (this lemma is from Theorem 2 in Driver [19]).

Lemma 1. *Let t_0 be a given finite number, and let α and γ be given numbers such that $-\infty \leq \alpha \leq t_0 < \gamma \leq \infty$. And let D be a given domain (a connected open set) in E^n, which is a Euclidean space of n dimensions.*

We consider the delay–differential system

$$y'(t) = F(t, y(\cdot)) \ for \ t_0 < t < \gamma,$$

where $F(t, \psi(\cdot))$ is a functional defined and takes values in E^n whenever $t \in [t_0, \gamma)$ and $\psi \in C([\alpha, t] \to D)$. Let the functional $F(t, \psi(.))$ be (i) continuous in t and (ii) locally Lipschitz with respect to ψ, and let φ be any member of $C([\alpha, t] \to D)$. Then, there is a number $h > 0$ such that a unique solution, $y(t) = y(t; t_0, \varphi)$, exists for $\alpha \leq t < t_0 + h$.

In the following, we consider the initial data $\phi = (\phi_1, \phi_2)$ for System (1) to be in BC^2_+, which is the set of positive, bounded continuous functions on $(-\infty, 0]$. The well posedness of System (1) is presented below.

Theorem 1. *For any initial data $\phi \in BC^2_+$, Model (1) has a unique solution, which is bounded and non-negative as long as it exists. Furthermore, we have $0 \leq \limsup_{t\to\infty} u(t) \leq \frac{r-d}{a}$, $0 \leq \limsup_{t\to\infty} v(t) \leq \frac{c(r-d+m)^2}{4am} \int_0^\infty F(s)ds$. If, in addition, $\phi_i(\theta) > 0$ for $\theta \leq 0$, $i = 1, 2$, then the solution is strictly positive for all $t > 0$.*

Proof. Note that the right hand side of System (1) is continuous in t. We can show that the right hand side is locally Lipschitz with respect to $\phi \in BC^2_+$. Then, from Lemma 1 , there is $\sigma > 0$, such that (1) has a unique solution for $t \in (0, \sigma)$. If $\phi_1(0) = 0$, we have $u(t) = 0$, and $\phi_1(0) > 0$ implies that $u(t) > 0$ for $0 < t < \sigma$. To show that positive initial data give positive solutions, suppose that $v(t)$ is zero for the first time at $t^\natural > 0$. Then, $v'(t^\natural) \leq 0$ and $v(t) > 0$, for $t \in (0, t^\natural)$, by (1), we have

$$0 \geq v'(t^\natural) = c \int_0^{+\infty} g(k, u(t^\natural - s))v(t^\natural - s)F(s)ds > 0,$$

which is a contradiction.

Non-negativity of $v(t)$ for $t \in (0, \sigma)$ follows as $v'(t) \geq -mv(t)$. As $\dfrac{du(t)}{dt} \leq ru(t) - du(t) - au^2(t)$, then $\limsup_{t\to\infty} u(t) \leq \frac{r-d}{a}$.

We then show that the solutions remain bounded for $\phi \in BC^2_+$. Denote $V(t) = v(t) + c\int_0^\infty u(t-s)F(s)ds$, then, by (A1), we have

$$\begin{aligned} V' &= c\int_0^\infty [f(k, v(t-s))ru(t-s) - du(t-s) - au^2(t-s)]F(s)ds - mv(t) \\ &\leq c\int_0^\infty [(r-d)u(t-s) - au^2(t-s)]F(s)ds - mv(t) \\ &= c\int_0^\infty [(r-d+m)u(t-s) - au^2(t-s)]F(s)ds - mV(t) \\ &\leq \frac{c(r-d+m)^2}{4a} \int_0^\infty F(s)ds - mV(t). \end{aligned} \tag{3}$$

Therefore, we obtain $\limsup_{t\to\infty} V(t) \leq \frac{c(r-d+m)^2}{4am} \int_0^\infty F(s)ds$, and, consequently, the boundedness of $v(t)$ now follows immediately and $\sigma = \infty$ applies. □

System (1) always has an extinction equilibrium $P_0 = (0,0)$, and when $r > d$, then the predator-free equilibrium $P_1 = (\frac{r-d}{a}, 0)$ exists, which means only when the growth rate is greater than the death rate can the prey population can survive; otherwise, it will become extinct. We denote the coexistence equilibrium by $P^* = (u^*, v^*)$, where u^* is described in Assumption (A3), we have

$$g(k, u^*) = \frac{m}{c\int_0^\infty F(s)ds}, \tag{4}$$

and v^* is the positive real roots of the following equation:

$$F(k, v) = f(k, v)r - d - au^* - \frac{g(k, u^*)}{u^*}v = 0. \tag{5}$$

By (A1), $F(k, 0) = r - d - au^*$ and $F(k, +\infty) = -\infty$, $\frac{\partial F}{\partial v} < 0$. If so, then v^* exists if and only if $F(k, 0) > 0$, namely

$$r > d + au^* \text{ or } u^* < \frac{r-d}{a}. \tag{6}$$

By Assumption (A2) and Equality (4), then (6) has the following equivalent form:

$$m < cg\left(k, \frac{r-d}{a}\right) \int_0^\infty F(s)ds. \tag{7}$$

3. Global Stability of P_0 and P_1

When linearizing System (1) at P_0, then the characteristic equation's eigenvalues are found to be $r - d$ and $-m$; hence, for $r < d$, P_0 exhibits local asymptotic stability, and it is a saddle point that is unstable for $r > d$. In the case when $r < d$, a much stronger result is formulated.

Theorem 2. *If $r \leq d$, then $P_0 = (0,0)$ is globally asymptotically stable.*

Proof. Let $L(t) = u(t) + \frac{1}{c}v(t) + \int_0^\infty F(s)\left(\int_{t-s}^t g(k, u(\theta))v(\theta)d\theta\right)ds$, then

$$\begin{aligned} L'(t) &= f(k, v(t))ru(t) - du(t) - au^2(t) - \tfrac{m}{c}v(t) \\ &\quad -(1 - \textstyle\int_0^\infty F(s)ds)g(k, u(t))v(t) \\ &\leq (r-d)u(t) - au^2(t) - \tfrac{m}{c}v(t) \leq 0. \end{aligned} \tag{8}$$

It should be noted that $L'(t) = 0$ occurs only when $u(t) = v(t) = 0$. By applying LaSalle's invariance principle, the expected result is derived. □

When $r > d$, then linearizing System (1) at $P_1 = (\frac{r-d}{a}, 0)$ gives the characteristic equation

$$(\lambda + r - d)\left(\lambda + m - cg\left(k, \frac{r-d}{a}\right)\int_0^\infty e^{-\lambda s}F(s)ds\right) = 0. \tag{9}$$

It is clear that there is one root $d - r < 0$ for the characteristic equation, and the other roots of this equation are governed by the equation

$$\lambda + m - cg\left(k, \frac{r-d}{a}\right)\int_0^\infty e^{-\lambda s}F(s)ds = 0. \tag{10}$$

This equation can be regarded as the characteristic equation of

$$\frac{dx(t)}{dt} = cg\left(k, \frac{r-d}{a}\right) \int_0^\infty x(t-s)F(s)ds - mx(t). \tag{11}$$

By Lemma 1 of [20] that if $m > cg\left(k, \frac{r-d}{a}\right) \int_0^\infty F(s)ds$, that is, (7) is reversed, then the trivial solution $x = 0$ of (11) is locally asymptotically stable; if (7) holds, then the$x = 0$ of (11) is unstable. We conclude that P_1 is locally asymptotically stable only when P^* does not exit.

The following theorem demonstrates that the local stability of P_1 leads to its global stability.

Theorem 3. *If $r > d$ and (7) is reversed and let $\phi_1(0) > 0$, then*

$$\lim_{t\to\infty} (u(t), v(t)) = \left(\frac{r-d}{a}, 0\right).$$

Proof. Since $m > cg\left(k, \frac{r-d}{a}\right) \int_0^\infty F(s)ds$, then, if $\varepsilon > 0$ is chosen small enough, we have

$$m > cg\left(k, \frac{r-d}{a} + \varepsilon\right) \int_0^\infty F(s)ds.$$

Theorem 1 gives $\limsup_{t\to\infty} u(t) \le \frac{r-d}{a}$. Then, there is some $t_0 > 0$, for $t > t_0$, where $u(t) \le \frac{r-d}{a} + \varepsilon$. Note that

$$\begin{aligned}
&\int_0^\infty g(k, u(t-s))v(t-s)F(s)ds \\
=& \int_0^{t-t_0} g(k, u(t-s))v(t-s)F(s)ds + \int_{t-t_0}^\infty g(k, u(t-s))v(t-s)F(s)ds \\
\le& g\left(k, \tfrac{r-d}{a} + \varepsilon\right) \int_0^{t-t_0} v(t-s)F(s)ds + \int_{t-t_0}^\infty g(k, u(t-s))v(t-s)F(s)ds.
\end{aligned}$$

The boundedness of $u(t)$ and $v(t)$ for $t \in \mathbb{R}$ results in $\int_{t-t_0}^\infty g(k, u(t-s))v(t-s)F(s)ds \to 0$ as $t \to \infty$. If so, then by (1), we have

$$\frac{dv(t)}{dt} \le cg\left(k, \frac{r-d}{a} + \varepsilon\right) \int_0^\infty v(t-s)F(s)ds - mv(t).$$

Again, by the comparison theorem and Lemma 1 of [20], we obtain $\lim_{t\to\infty} v(t) = 0$. Then, the equation for $u(t)$ tends to $u'(t) = ru(t) - du(t) - au^2(t)$ with $u(0) = \phi_1(0) > 0$; thus, $\lim_{t\to\infty} u(t) = \frac{r-d}{a}$. This proves the theorem. □

Theorem 3 suggests that the global stability of $P_1 = (\frac{r-d}{a}, 0)$ is equivalent to the reversal of (7). In other words, if the coexistence equilibrium $P^* = (u^*, v^*)$ exists, then P_1 is unstable.

4. Permanence

By the proof of Theorem 3, when $v(t) \to 0$ as $t \to \infty$, then $u(t) \to \frac{r-d}{a}$ as $t \to \infty$ if $r > d$ and $\phi_1(0) > 0$. Then, the following lemma holds.

Lemma 2. *If $r > d$, then, for any solution $(u(t), v(t))$ of (1) with $\phi_1(0) > 0$, there is no solution that converges to $P_0 = (0, 0)$.*

Lemma 3. *If $r > d + au^*$, then, for any solution $(u(t), v(t))$ of (1) with $\phi_i(\theta) > 0$ for $\theta \le 0$, $i = 1, 2$, there is no solution that converges to $P_1 = (\frac{r-d}{a}, 0)$.*

Proof. By Theorem 1, $v(t) > 0$ for $t > 0$. If there is a sequence $\{t_n\}$, which is monotonically increasing, and $\lim_{n\to\infty} t_n = \infty$, then $v(t_n) \geq v(t_{n+1})$, $v'(t_n) \leq 0$, and, for $t \in [0, t_n)$, we have $v(t) \geq v(t_n)$. Since $r > d + au^*$, then $\frac{r-d}{a} - \delta > u^*$ for some $\delta > 0$; thus, $g\left(k, \frac{r-d}{a} - \delta\right) > g(k, u^*) = \frac{m}{c\int_0^\infty F(s)ds}$. We can find $T_0 > 0$ to be large enough, such that

$$\int_{T_0}^{\infty} F(s)ds < \frac{m}{c}\left(\frac{1}{g(k,u^*)} - \frac{1}{g\left(k, \frac{r-d}{a} - \delta\right)}\right). \tag{12}$$

For any $l \in [0, T_0)$, let n be large, such that $t_n - l > 0$, then $v(t_n - l) > v(t_n)$. Suppose that $(u(t), v(t)) \to P_1$ as $t \to \infty$, then $u(t_n - l) > \frac{r-d}{a} - \delta$ for all $l \in [0, T_0)$ and sufficiently large n, it is yielded that

$$\begin{aligned} v'(t_n) &= c\int_0^\infty g(k, u(t_n - s))v(t_n - s)F(s)ds - mv(t_n) \\ &\geq c\int_0^{T_0} g(k, u(t_n - s))v(t_n)F(s)ds - mv(t_n) \\ &> v(t_n)\left(cg(k, \tfrac{r-d}{a} - \delta)\int_0^{T_0} F(s)ds - m\right) > 0, \end{aligned} \tag{13}$$

which contradicts the fact that $v'(t_n) \leq 0$. □

Lemma 4. *If $r > d$ and $(u(t), v(t))$ is a solution of (1) with $\phi_1(0) > 0$, then*

$$\limsup_{t\to\infty} u(t) \geq \min\left\{\frac{r-d}{a}, u^*\right\}.$$

Proof. Denote $u^\infty = \limsup_{t\to\infty} u(t)$ and $v^\infty = \limsup_{t\to\infty} v(t)$. Suppose that $u^\infty < \min\{\frac{r-d}{a}, u^*\}$. Applying the fluctuation method, there exists a sequence of times $\{t_n\}$ such that $t_n \to \infty$ as $n \to \infty$, $\lim_{n\to\infty} v(t_n) = v^\infty$, and $\lim_{n\to\infty} v'(t_n) = 0$. It is clear that, for any $\varepsilon > 0$, there exists some $T_1 > 0$, such that $u(t) < u^\infty + \varepsilon$ and $v(t) < v^\infty + \varepsilon$ holds for $t \geq T_1$. We can let n be large enough, such that $t_n > T_1$, and then we have $u(t_n - l) < u^\infty + \varepsilon$ and $v(t_n - l) < v^\infty + \varepsilon$ for $l \in [0, t_n - T_1]$. As such, we obtain

$$\begin{aligned} &\int_0^\infty g(k, u(t_n - s))v(t_n - s)F(s)ds \\ &= \int_0^{t_n - T_1} g(k, u(t_n - s))v(t_n - s)F(s)ds + \int_{t_n - T_1}^\infty g(k, u(t_n - s))v(t_n - s)F(s)ds \\ &\leq g(k, u^\infty + \varepsilon)(v^\infty + \varepsilon)\int_0^{t_n - T_1} F(s)ds + \int_{t_n - T_1}^\infty g(k, u(t_n - s))v(t_n - s)F(s)ds. \end{aligned}$$

Since $g(k, u(t))v(t)$ is bounded for $t \in \mathbb{R}$, then the second integral approaches to 0 as $n \to \infty$. Thus, when n is large, we have

$$\int_0^\infty g(k, u(t_n - s))v(t_n - s)F(s)ds \leq g(k, u^\infty + \varepsilon)(v^\infty + \varepsilon)\int_0^\infty F(s)ds$$

and

$$0 = v'(t_n) \leq cg(k, u^\infty + \varepsilon)(v^\infty + \varepsilon)\int_0^\infty F(s)ds - mv^\infty.$$

Then, if we let $\varepsilon \to 0^+$, we obtain the inequality

$$0 \leq cg(k, u^\infty)v^\infty \int_0^\infty F(s)ds - mv^\infty. \tag{14}$$

Since $u^\infty < u^*$, then $g(k, u^\infty) < g(k, u^*) = \frac{m}{c\int_0^\infty F(s)ds}$. Inequality (14) leads to $v^\infty = 0$; hence, $\lim_{t\to\infty} v(t) = 0$. Then, by (1), $u(t) \to \frac{r-d}{a}$ as $t \to \infty$, we have a contradiction to $u^\infty < \frac{r-d}{a}$. As such, the theorem is completed. □

Lemma 5. *If $P^* = (u^*, v^*)$ exists, and $\phi_i(\theta) > 0$ for $\theta \leq 0$, $i = 1, 2$, then there exists some $\eta > 0$, such that $v^\infty > \eta$.*

Proof. Denote $u_\infty = \liminf_{t\to\infty} u(t)$ and $v_\infty = \liminf_{t\to\infty} v(t)$. Applying the Laplace transform to $v(t)$ yields

$$(\lambda + m)\mathcal{L}[v(t)] = v(0) + c\mathcal{L}[g(k,u(t))v(t)] \int_0^\infty e^{-\lambda s}F(s)ds$$
$$+c\int_0^\infty e^{-\lambda t}\int_t^\infty g(k,u(t-s))v(t-s)F(s)dsdt,$$

where $\lambda > 0$ is the transform variable. There is $\gamma > 0$, such that $u(t) \geq u_\infty - \gamma > 0$ for $t \geq 0$. Then, $\mathcal{L}[g(k,u(t))v(t)] \geq g(k,u_\infty - \gamma)\mathcal{L}[v(t)]$ and $\lambda + m \geq cg(k,u_\infty - \gamma)\int_0^\infty e^{-\lambda s}F(s)ds$. If we let $\lambda, \gamma \to 0^+$, we have $cg(k,u^*)\int_0^\infty F(s)ds = m \geq cg(k,u_\infty)\int_0^\infty F(s)ds$. By Assumption (A2), we obtain

$$u_\infty \leq u^*. \tag{15}$$

By Theorem 4 of [18], we can show that there is $\epsilon > 0$, such that $u_\infty > \epsilon$. Then, $\frac{\epsilon}{2} < u(t) < \frac{r-d}{a} + \epsilon$ for all $t \geq T_2$, with $T_2 > 0$ being a constant. Let $M = \max_{u\in[\frac{\epsilon}{2},\frac{r-d}{a}+\epsilon]}\{\frac{g(k,u)}{u}\}$. Since P^* exists, that is, $u^* < \frac{r-d}{a}$, then, if $\varepsilon > 0$ is to be chosen small enough, we have

$$u^* < \frac{1}{a}(f(k,\varepsilon)r - d - M\varepsilon). \tag{16}$$

If there is $\phi \in BC_+^2$ and $\phi_i(\theta) > 0$ for $\theta \leq 0$, $i = 1, 2$, such that $v^\infty < \frac{\varepsilon}{2}$, then, when t is large, $v(t) < \varepsilon$; hence, by System (1) and (A1), we obtain

$$\frac{du}{dt} \geq f(k,\varepsilon)ru - du - au^2 - \varepsilon Mu.$$

Therefore, $u_\infty \geq \frac{1}{a}(f(k,\varepsilon)r - d - \varepsilon M)$, which is a contradiction of (15) and (16). □

The uniform persistence of System (1) follows from Theorem 5 of [18].

Theorem 4. *If the hypotheses in Lemma 5 hold, then a constant $\kappa > 0$ exists, such that $u_\infty \geq \kappa$ and $v_\infty \geq \kappa$.*

5. Stability of P^*

To discuss the local stability of $P^* = (u^*, v^*)$, we let $g(k,u)$ be linear about u, specifically, $g(k,u) = \rho(k)u$. Then, we observe that $u^* = \frac{m}{c\rho(k)\int_0^\infty F(s)ds}$ and v^* can be solved from the equation

$$f(k,v^*)r - d - au^* - \rho(k)v^* = 0. \tag{17}$$

Then, the characteristic equation at P^* is

$$\begin{aligned} G(\lambda) &:= \lambda^2 + (m + au^*)\lambda + mau^* \\ &-c\rho(k)u^*\int_0^\infty e^{-\lambda s}F(s)ds\left[\lambda + au^* - \rho(k)v^* + rv^*\frac{\partial f(k,v^*)}{\partial v}\right] = 0. \end{aligned} \tag{18}$$

Note that $G(0) = m\left(\rho(k)v^* - rv^*\frac{\partial f(k,v^*)}{\partial v}\right) > 0$, implying that 0 is not a solution of $G(\lambda) = 0$.

Using similar arguments as those in the proof of Lemma 3 and Theorem 3 of [18], the following theorem can be established.

Theorem 5. *If $r > d + au^*$, then P^* exists and there are no positive real roots for (18). Furthermore, if $A < u^* < \frac{r-d}{a}$, then P^* is locally asymptotically stable, where $A = \frac{1}{a}\left(\rho(k)v^* - au^* - rv^*\frac{\partial f(k,v^*)}{\partial v}\right)$.*

To find more information about the dynamics for the case when P^* exists, and to compare the dynamics of the system with different distributions, we will consider four distributions: the gamma distribution, with the weak kernel and the strong kernel variants; the delta distribution; and the uniform distribution. These were chosen since they are widely used in the literature and because they have different types of support.
The weak kernel [20–24] can be expressed as follows:

$$h(s) = \alpha e^{-\alpha s},\ \alpha > 0.$$

The strong kernel [20,22–24] can be expressed as follows:

$$h(s) = \alpha^2 s e^{-\alpha s},\ \alpha > 0.$$

The delta kernel [20,24,25] can be expressed as follows:

$$h(s) = \delta(s - \tau).$$

The uniform distribution can be expressed as follows [20,21]:

$$h(s) = \begin{cases} \frac{\rho_1}{\tau}, & s \in \left[\tau(1 - \frac{1}{2\rho_1}), \tau(1 + \frac{1}{2\rho_1})\right],\ \rho_1 \geq 0.5, \\ 0, & \text{otherwise}. \end{cases}$$

5.1. The Weak Kernel

In this case, the characteristic equation at P^* reduces to

$$G_1(\lambda) := \lambda^3 + A_1\lambda^2 + A_2\lambda + A_3 = 0, \tag{19}$$

with $u^* = \frac{m(m+\alpha)}{c\alpha\rho(k)}$, $A_1 = A_1(\alpha) = 2m + \alpha + au^* > 0$, $A_2 = A_2(\alpha) = au^*(2m + \alpha) > 0$, and $A_3 = A_3(\alpha) = mv^*(m + \alpha)\left(\rho(k) - r\frac{\partial f(k,v^*)}{\partial v}\right) > 0$. Let $H_1(\alpha) = A_1(\alpha)A_2(\alpha) - A_3(\alpha)$. If $H_1(\alpha) = 0$, for a certain $\alpha = \alpha_0$, then (19) admits a pair of purely imaginary roots, $\lambda_{1,2} = \pm i\omega_0$, $\omega_0 = \sqrt{A_2(\alpha_0)}$, and the third root of (19) is $\lambda_3 = -A_1(\alpha_0) < 0$. Direct computation yields

$$\frac{d(Re\lambda)}{d\alpha}|_{\alpha=\alpha_0} = -\frac{1}{2(A_2 + A_1^2)}\frac{dH_1}{d\alpha}|_{\alpha=\alpha_0}. \tag{20}$$

Theorem 6. *If $H_1(\alpha) > 0$, then P^* is locally stable. If $\frac{dH_1}{d\alpha}|_{\alpha=\alpha_0} \neq 0$, then System (1) undergoes Hopf bifurcation at P^* when α passes through α_0.*

5.2. The Strong Kernel

The characteristic Equation (18) becomes

$$G_2(\lambda) := \lambda^4 + B_1\lambda^3 + B_2\lambda^2 + B_3\lambda + B_4 = 0, \tag{21}$$

with $u^* = \frac{m(m+\alpha)^2}{c\alpha^2\rho(k)}$, $B_1 = B_1(\alpha) = 3m + 2\alpha + au^* > 0$, $B_2 = B_2(\alpha) = (m + \alpha)(3m + \alpha + 2au^*) + mau^* > 0$, and $B_3 = B_3(\alpha) = au^*(m + \alpha)(3m + \alpha) > 0$, $B_4 = B_4(\alpha) = mv^*(m + \alpha)^2\left(\rho(k) - r\frac{\partial f(k,v^*)}{\partial v}\right) > 0$. It is clear that $B_1(\alpha)B_2(\alpha) - B_3(\alpha) > 0$. We then denote $H_2(\alpha) = B_1(\alpha)B_2(\alpha)B_3(\alpha) - B_3^2(\alpha) - B_1^2(\alpha)B_4(\alpha)$. If $H_2(\alpha) = 0$, for a certain $\alpha = \alpha_0$, then (21) possess a pair of simple roots, $\lambda_{1,2} = \pm i\omega_1$, with $\omega_1 = \sqrt{\frac{B_3(\alpha_0)}{B_1(\alpha_0)}}$, and the other two roots of (21) are λ_3 and λ_4, which have negative real parts. Direct computation gives

$$\frac{d(Re\lambda)}{d\alpha}|_{\alpha=\alpha_0} = -\frac{B_1}{2(B_3B_1^3 + (B_1B_2 - 2B_3)^2)}\frac{dH_2}{d\alpha}|_{\alpha=\alpha_0}. \tag{22}$$

Theorem 7. *If $H_2(\alpha) > 0$, then P^* is locally stable. If $\frac{dH_2}{d\alpha}|_{\alpha=\alpha_0} \neq 0$, then System (1) undergoes Hopf bifurcation at P^* when α passes through α_0.*

5.3. The Delta Kernel

For this case, System (1) reduces to a differential system with a discrete delay:

$$\begin{cases} \dfrac{du(t)}{dt} = f(k, v(t))ru(t) - du(t) - au^2(t) - g(k, u(t))v(t), \\ \dfrac{dv(t)}{dt} = cg(k, u(t-\tau))v(t-\tau)e^{-m\tau} - mv(t). \end{cases} \tag{23}$$

For System (23), the characteristic Equation (18) is

$$G_3(\lambda) := \lambda^2 + (m + au^*)\lambda + mau^* + me^{-\lambda\tau}(D - \lambda) = 0, \tag{24}$$

where $u^* = \frac{me^{m\tau}}{c\rho(k)}$, $D = -au^* + \rho(k)v^* - rv^*\frac{\partial f(k,v^*)}{\partial v}$. Clearly, when $\tau = 0$, P^* is locally stable. If (24) has a purely imaginary root $\lambda = i\omega$, then $G_3(i\omega) = 0$, and it follows that $G_3(-i\omega) = \overline{G_3(i\omega)} = 0$; hence, $-i\omega$ is also a root of (24). According to the symmetry, we only need to take into account $\lambda = i\omega$ with $\omega > 0$, and then ω satisfies

$$H(\omega, \tau) = \omega^4 + (au^*)^2\omega^2 + m^2((au^*)^2 - D^2) = 0 \tag{25}$$

and

$$\begin{cases} \sin\omega\tau = \frac{-\omega^3 + (mau^* + (m + au^*)D)\omega}{m(\omega^2 + D^2)}, \\ \cos\omega\tau = \frac{(m + au^* + D)\omega^2 - mau^*D}{m(\omega^2 + D^2)}. \end{cases} \tag{26}$$

Since $au^* + D > 0$, then, only when $au^* < D$, (25) has a unique positive root given by $\omega = \omega_2 = (\frac{1}{2}(-(au^*)^2 + \sqrt{\Delta}))^{\frac{1}{2}}$, with $\Delta = (au^*)^4 - 4m^2((au^*)^2 - D^2)$. Let $\zeta(\tau) \in [0, 2\pi]$ be the solution of (26), namely

$$\begin{cases} \sin\zeta(\tau) = \frac{-\omega^3 + (mau^* + (m + au^*)D)\omega}{m(\omega^2 + D^2)}, \\ \cos\zeta(\tau) = \frac{(m + au^* + D)\omega^2 - mau^*D}{m(\omega^2 + D^2)}. \end{cases}$$

According to [26], we denote

$$S_n(\tau) = \tau - \frac{\zeta(\tau) + 2n\pi}{\omega_2(\tau)},\ n \in \mathbb{N}_0 := \{0, 1, 2, \cdots\},\ \tau \in (0, \tau_1), \tag{27}$$

where τ_1 is determined by the inequality $au^* < D$. Note that $i\omega_2(\check{\tau})$ is a root of (24), which is equivalent to $S_n(\check{\tau}) = 0$ for some $n \in \mathbb{N}_0$. Since $H'_\omega(\omega, \tau) = 4\omega^3 + 2(au^*)^2\omega > 0$ for $\omega > 0$, then the following theorem follows from Theorem 4.1 of [26].

Theorem 8. *If, for some $n \in \mathbb{N}_0$, there is $\check{\tau} \in (0, \tau_1)$, such that $S_n(\check{\tau}) = 0$, then (24) has a pair of purely imaginary roots $\pm i\omega_2(\check{\tau})$. Denote*

$$\varrho(\check{\tau}) = \text{sign}\left\{ \frac{d\text{Re}\lambda}{d\tau}|_{\lambda=i\omega_2(\check{\tau})} \right\} = \text{sign}\left\{ \frac{dS_n(\tau)}{d\tau}|_{\tau=\check{\tau}} \right\}. \tag{28}$$

Then, $\pm i\omega_2(\check{\tau})$ crosses the imaginary axis from left to right if $\varrho(\check{\tau}) = 1$ and from right to left if $\varrho(\check{\tau}) = -1$.

5.4. The Uniform Distribution

In this case, the characteristic Equation (18) reduces to

$$G_4(\lambda) := \lambda^2 + (m + au^*)\lambda + mau^* + m^2 e^{-\lambda\tau}(D - \lambda)\frac{e^{\frac{(\lambda+m)\tau}{2\rho_1}} - e^{-\frac{(\lambda+m)\tau}{2\rho_1}}}{(\lambda + m)\left(e^{\frac{m\tau}{2\rho_1}} - e^{-\frac{m\tau}{2\rho_1}}\right)} = 0, \tag{29}$$

where $u^* = \frac{m^2\tau e^{m\tau}}{c\rho_1\rho(k)\left(e^{\frac{m\tau}{2\rho_1}} - e^{-\frac{m\tau}{2\rho_1}}\right)}$. The theoretical analysis is difficult since (29) is a transcendental equation.

6. Numerical Explorations

As in Wang and Zou [7], we let $g(k, u) = \rho(k)u$, $\rho(k) = \frac{1}{1+c_1 k}$, and $f(k, v) = \frac{1}{1+c_2 kv}$. We take the parameter values as

$$r = 1, c_1 = 1, c_2 = 1, d = 0.1, a = 0.1, c = 4, m = 0.5, \tag{30}$$

where $c_1 = c_2 = 1$ are taken from [7], and the values of other parameters are biologically acceptable. All the simulations are carried out in MATLAB R2020b, which was produced by MathWorks, a company headquartered in Natick, Massachusetts, USA. The numerical method we use is the Euler method.

For the strong kernel case, we fix $\alpha = 10$. Solving the equation $m = cg\left(k, \frac{r-d}{a}\right)\int_0^\infty F(s)ds$ gives $k = 64.3061$. If $k > 64.3061$, Theorem 3 shows that $P_1 = (9, 0)$ is globally asymptotically stable (see Figure 1a for $k = 65$). When $k < 64.3061$, $P_1 = (9, 0)$ becomes unstable, and there is a unique coexistence equilibrium P^*. If we take $k = 10$, then $P^* = (1.5159, 0.263)$ and the inequality $A < u^* < \frac{r-d}{a}$ holds, and then, by Theorem 5 , $P^* = (1.5159, 0.263)$ is locally asymptotically stable (see Figure 1b).

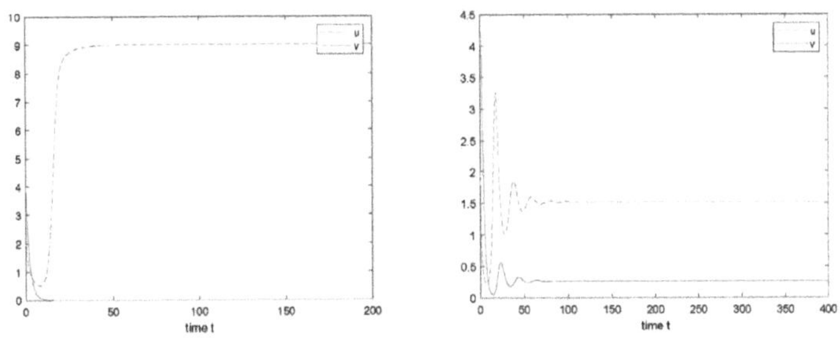

(a) (b)

Figure 1. The solution trajectories of System (1), with $\alpha = 10$, in the strong kernel case. (**a**) For $k = 65$, the prey persists but the predator dies out. The initial condition is as follows: $(u(\theta), v(\theta)) = (2, 4)$ for $\theta \in (-\infty, 0]$. (**b**) When $k = 10$, both species persist, and they will then stabilize in a stable level. The initial condition is as follows: $(u(\theta), v(\theta)) = (2, 4)$ for $\theta \in (-\infty, 0]$.

If we let $k = 1$, then solving $H_2(\alpha) = B_1(\alpha)B_2(\alpha)B_3(\alpha) - B_3^2(\alpha) - B_1^2(\alpha)B_4(\alpha) = 0$, we obtain $\alpha_0 = 0.29$ and $\frac{dH_2}{d\alpha}|_{\alpha=\alpha_0} = -6.8539 < 0$, which means $\frac{d(Re\lambda)}{d\alpha}|_{\alpha=\alpha_0} > 0$. When α passes through 0.29, the coexistence equilibrium P^* will loses its stability and periodic solutions will appear. As shown in Figure 2a and Figure 2b, we let $\alpha = 0.2$ and $\alpha = 0.4$, respectively, and these figures demonstrate that $(u(t), v(t))$ switches from stable to periodic oscillation. Bifurcation diagrams in terms of α and k are depicted in Figure 3a and Figure 3b, respectively. Note that, for the strong kernel, the mean delay $\tau = \frac{2}{\alpha}$; thus, Figure 3a shows that a periodic solution occurs for a small τ, and then the solution becomes stable as τ increases, where two populations coexist. Finally, the predator becomes extinct for a large τ. As shown in Figure 3b, the system is unstable at first, which shows periodic oscillation, and when we increased the strength of the fear, we observed that the system became stable around the coexistence equilibrium. Therefore, high levels of fear can stabilize the steady state.

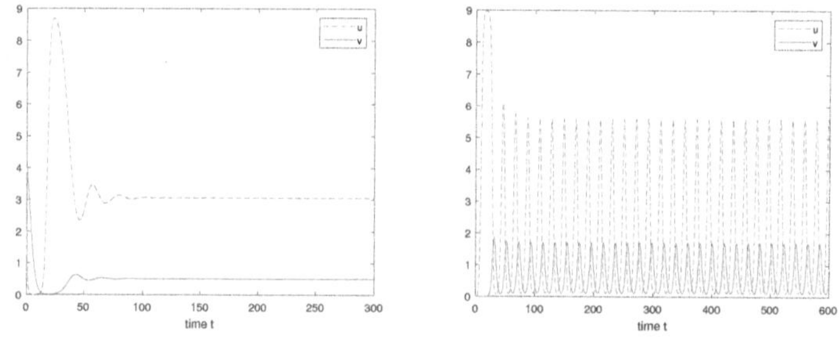

(a) (b)

Figure 2. The solution trajectories of System (1), with $k = 1$, in the strong kernel case. (**a**) For $\alpha = 0.2$, the coexistence equilibrium was stable. The initial condition is as follows: $(u(\theta), v(\theta)) = (2, 4)$ for $\theta \in (-\infty, 0]$. (**b**) When $\alpha = 0.4$, a periodic solution occurs. The initial condition is as follows: $(u(\theta), v(\theta)) = (0.01, 0.001)$ for $\theta \in (-\infty, 0]$.

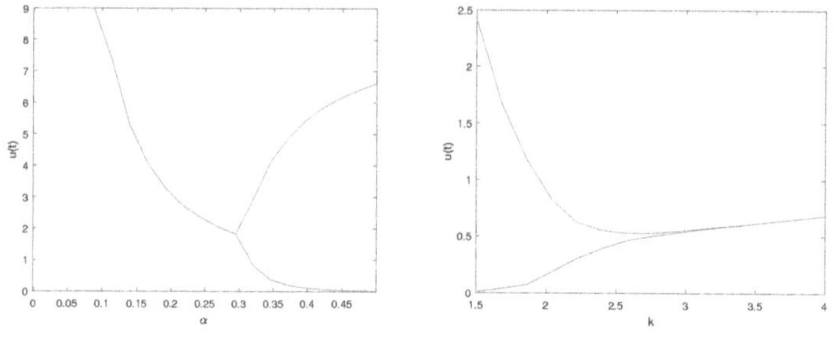

(a) (b)

Figure 3. Bifurcation diagram of the prey versus α and k in the strong kernel case. (**a**) The prey species can be understood as a function of α when $k = 1$ and α varies from 0.01 to 0.5. (**b**) The prey species can be understood as a function of k when $\alpha = 10$ and k varies from 1.5 to 4.

For the delta kernel, we let the parameter τ vary from 0.05 to 5. The corresponding solution trajectories of System (1) are depicted in Figure 4. It can be found from Figure 4 that the coexistence equilibrium P^* exists and is stable when $\tau = 0.05$, and, as τ increases, periodic oscillations can occur with $\tau = 2$, where the oscillations become damped when $\tau = 5$, and P^* can regain stability. For a large τ, the predator species will die out. Figure 4 shows that stability switches can occur as the τ varies. As shown in Figure 5a, we give the relation between $S_0(\tau)$, $S_1(\tau)$, and τ for $\tau \in [0, 4.6]$ and $k = 1$. We find that $S_0(\tau)$ has two

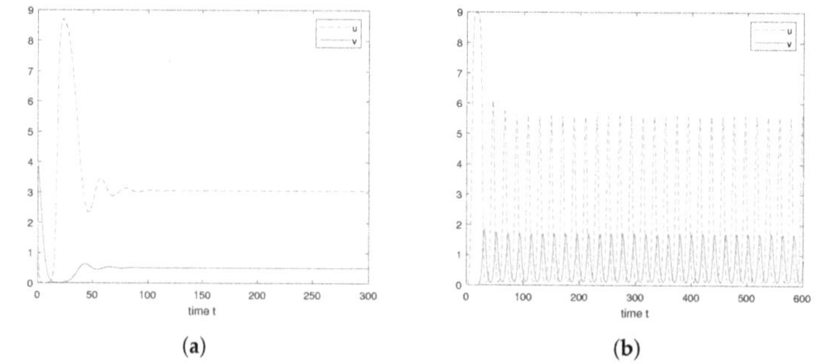

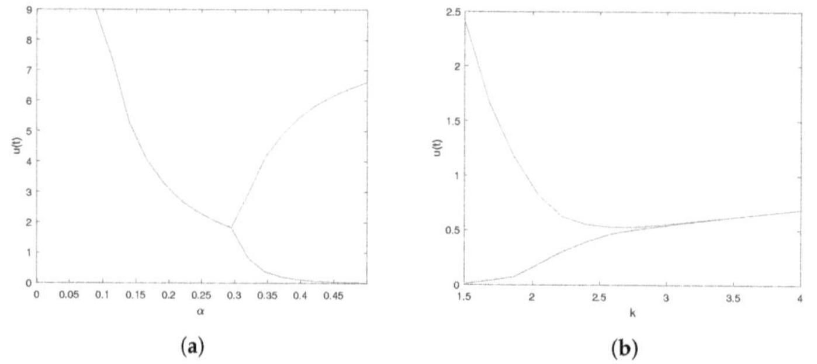

positive zeros: $\tau_1^* = 0.083$ and $\tau_2^* = 4.48$. At τ_1^* and τ_2^*, stability switches occur, and P^* is stable for $\tau \in [0, \tau_1^*) \cup (\tau_2^*, 4.6]$. Then, it is unstable for $\tau \in (\tau_1^*, \tau_2^*)$. These results are in agreement with Figure 4. A bifurcation diagram with respect to parameter k is presented in Figure 5b. We point out that, in Wang and Zou [7] with a functional response of Holling type I, when P^* exists, it is always unstable if τ is greater than some critical value. Since, for the weak kernel case with uniform distribution, their numerical simulations results are similar to the strong kernel and the delta kernel, respectively; as such, we omitted their numerical results.

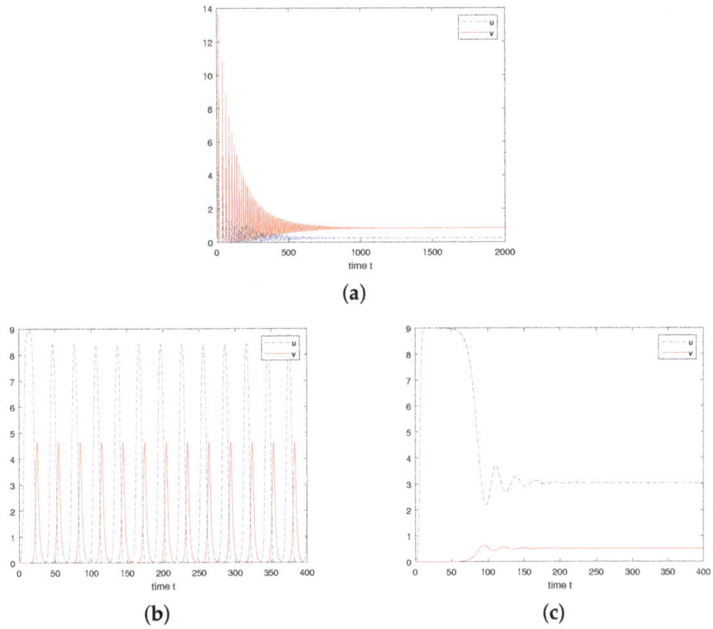

Figure 4. The solution trajectories of System (1) in the delta kernel case when τ varies. (**a**) $\tau = 0.05$. The initial condition is as follows: $(u(\theta), v(\theta)) = (0.05, 0.01)$ for $\theta \in [-0.05, 0]$. (**b**) $\tau = 2$. The initial condition is as follows: $(u(\theta), v(\theta)) = (0.05, 0.01)$ for $\theta \in [-2, 0]$. (**c**) $\tau = 5$. The initial condition is as follows: $(u(\theta), v(\theta)) = (0.05, 0.01)$ for $\theta \in [-5, 0]$.

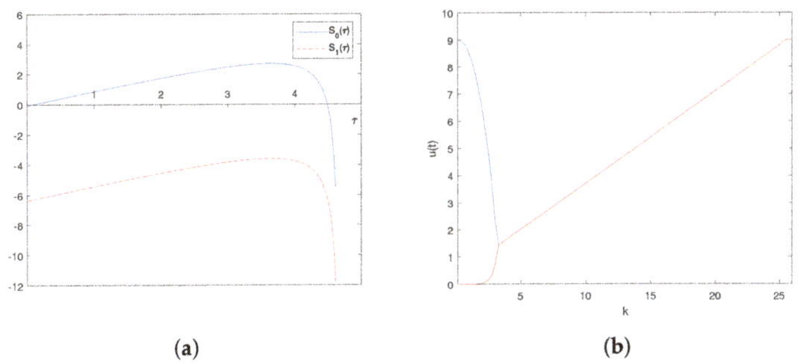

Figure 5. Graphs of the stability switch in terms of time delay τ and k in the delta kernel case. (**a**) Graphs of $S_0(\tau)$ and $S_1(\tau)$. Here, $k = 1$ and τ vary from 0 to 4.6. (**b**) The prey species as a function of k. Here, $\tau = 2$ and k varies from 0 to 26.

If the functional response is Holling type II, i.e., $g(k, u) = \frac{pu}{(1+c_1 k)(1+qu)}$, then, by taking the delta delay kernel, for example, when $p = 0.5, q = 0.6$, we set $k = 1$ and keep the other parameters as those in (30). Then, if $\tau = 0$, there is a periodic solution (see Figure 6a), and the periodic solution disappears when τ increases to 1.5 (see Figure 6b). A bifurcation diagram of $u(t)$ versus τ is depicted in Figure 7.

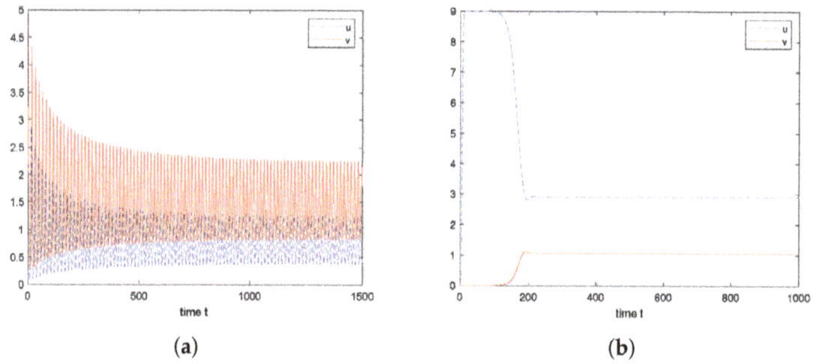

Figure 6. The solution trajectories of System (1) for a functional response of Holling type II. (**a**) $\tau = 0$. The initial condition is as follows: $(u(0), v(0)) = (0.05, 0.01)$. (**b**) $\tau = 1.5$. The initial condition is as follows: $(u(\theta), v(\theta)) = (0.05, 0.01)$ for $\theta \in [-1.5, 0]$.

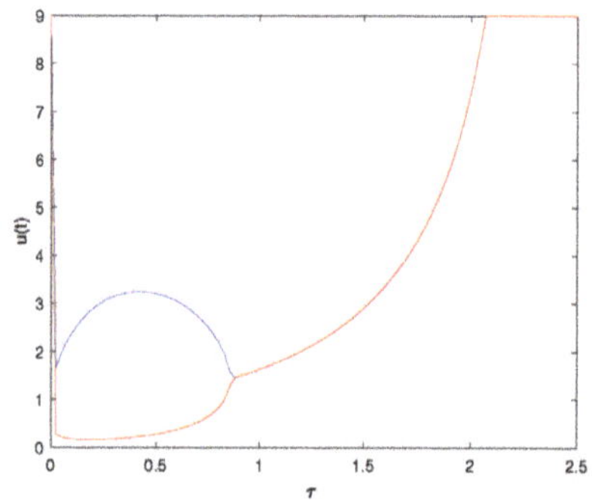

Figure 7. A bifurcation diagram of the prey versus τ for a functional response of Holling type II. Here, $k = 1$ and τ varies from 0 to 2.5. All the other parameter values are given in (30).

7. Discussion

In this work, we modify the existing predator–prey models with the fear effect by introducing distributed delay. We assumed that, if the prey is captured, the time required for biomass transfer from the prey to the predator is not fixed; instead, it follows some distribution. Then, we proposed a differential system with distributed delay, where the functional response is a relatively general function, which is increasing with respect to the prey.

For the model with a general kernel function, we proved its well posedness, such as the positivity and boundedness of solutions. We discussed the global stability of the extinction equilibrium P_0 and the predator-free equilibrium P_1, which is the uniform persistence of the system. More precisely, we showed that, if the birth rate of the prey is no greater than the death rate, then both species die out; conversely, if the coexistence equilibrium P^* does not exist, then P_1 is globally stable, that is, only the prey survives if P^* exists, P_1 loses stability, and the solutions persist.

If we assume that the functional response is Holling type I, then, for a general delay kernel, we obtained criteria for the local asymptotic stability of P^*. Due to the introduction of distributed delays, depending on the forms of delay kernels, the characteristic equation of the coexistence steady state P^* may differ significantly. For the weak kernel and the strong kernel, the characteristic equations are polynomials, while it is a transcendental equation for the delta kernel or uniform distribution. For the weak kernel and the strong kernel, as α varies, it is demonstrated that P^* will lose stability and a Hopf bifurcation occurs. For the delta kernel, we found that time delay τ can induce stability switches.

We performed numerical simulations for four particular distributions. For the weak kernel and the strong kernel, System (1) is stable for a small α, but it becomes unstable for a bigger α, where periodic orbits appear. For the delta delay distribution, System (1) displays rich dynamics, and it is found that intermediate delays will destabilize the coexistence equilibrium. However, small delays and large delays have a stabilizing effect. The dynamics of System (1) with a uniform distribution is similar to the delta distribution. For all the distributions that we considered, we showed that, for small values of fear level k, the system undergoes periodic oscillations, and, as k increases, the system gains stability. Biologically, this means that, if the level of the fear effect in prey is increased, then the populations of the prey and predator may have a state transition, i.e., from periodic oscillation to stability. The fear effects and delay kernels together affect the population dynamics of the model.

Our theoretical, as well as numerical, simulations results indicate that delays play important roles in the dynamics of the system. For a functional response of Holling type I without delay, if we further neglect the benefit of the fear effect, i.e., $g(k,u) = g(u)$, then System (1) reduces to an ordinary differential equation model that was proposed by Wang et al. [4], where periodic solutions do not appear. How the delay is incorporated into the model also impacts the dynamical behavior. If the delay is fixed as a constant, then System (1) becomes the System (8) shown in Wang and Zou [7] (except that our model has an extra delay dependent parameter $e^{-m\tau}$). In [7], when the coexistence equilibria exist, it is unstable for all $\tau > \tau_0$, namely large time delay always destabilize the system, which is opposite to our results. Figures 6 and 7 indicate that different functional responses also have a significant impact on model dynamics.

An extension of our model that considers the impact of seasonality would be an interesting study. Incorporating the age structure or nonlinear harvesting of the predator is also another interesting topic. These problems will be left for further investigation. Our method may be applicable or useful to analyze the dynamics of other population models with distributed delays. Applying our method for population models with spatial heterogeneity and temporal dependence may lead to incorrect statements.

Author Contributions: Formal analysis, methodology, and writing-original draft, J.L.; writing—review and editing, Z.G.; software, H.G. All authors have read and agreed to the published version of the manuscript.

Funding: This research was funded by the National Natural Science Foundation of China (grant number 11801431) and the Natural Science Basic Research Plan in Shaanxi Province of China (grant numbers 2024JC-YBMS-001 and 2022JM-023).

Data Availability Statement: Data are contained within the article.

Acknowledgments: We sincerely appreciate the reviewers for their careful reading and valuable comments. We thank them for all their efforts in perfecting this paper.

Conflicts of Interest: The authors declare no conflicts of interest.

References

1. Creel, S.; Christianson, D.; Liley, S.; Winnie, J.A., Jr. Predation risk affects reproductive physiology and demography of elk. *Science* **2007**, *315*, 960. [CrossRef] [PubMed]
2. Suraci, J.P.; Clinchy, M.; Dill, L.M.; Roberts, D.; Zanette, L.Y. Fear of large carnivores causes a trophic cascade. *Nat. Commun.* **2016**, *7*, 10698. [CrossRef]
3. Zanette, L.Y.; White, A.F.; Allen, M.C.; Clinchy, M. Perceived predation risk reduces the number of offspring songbirds produce per year. *Science* **2011**, *334*, 1398–1401. [CrossRef]

4. Wang, X.; Zanette, L.; Zou, X. Modelling the fear effect in predator-prey interactions. *J. Math. Biol.* **2016**, *73*, 1179–1204. [CrossRef]
5. Holling, C.S. The functional response of predators to prey density and its role in mimicry and population regulation. *Mem. Ent. Soc. Can.* **1965**, *97*, 1–60. [CrossRef]
6. Wang, X.; Zou, X. Modeling the fear effect in predator-prey interactions with adaptive avoidance of predators. *Bull. Math. Biol.* **2017**, *79*, 1325–1359. [CrossRef] [PubMed]
7. Wang, Y.; Zou, X. On a predator-prey system with digestion delay and anti-predation strategy. *J. Nonlinear Sci.* **2020**, *30*, 1579–1605. [CrossRef]
8. Sasmal, S.K.; Takeuchi, Y. Dynamics of a predator-prey system with fear and group defense. *J. Math. Anal. Appl.* **2020**, *481*, 123471. [CrossRef]
9. Hossain, M.; Pal, N.; Samanta, S. Impact of fear on an eco-epidemiological model. *Chaos Solitons Fractals* **2020**, *134*, 109718. [CrossRef]
10. Mishra, S.; Upadhyay, R.K. Strategies for the existence of spatial patterns in predator-prey communities generated by cross-diffusion. *Nonlinear Anal. Real World Appl.* **2020**, *51*, 103018. [CrossRef]
11. Ma, T.; Meng, X. Global analysis and Hopf-bifurcation in a cross-diffusion prey-predator system with fear effect and predator cannibalism. *Math. Biosic. Eng.* **2022**, *19*, 6040–6071. [CrossRef]
12. Li, Y. Global steady-state bifurcation of a diffusive Leslie-Gower model with both-density-dependent fear effect. *Commun. Nonlinear Sci. Numer. Simulat.* **2025**, *141*, 108477. [CrossRef]
13. Cong, P.; Fan, M.; Zou, X. Dynamics of a three-species food chain model with fear effect. *Commun. Nonlinear Sci. Numer. Simulat.* **2021**, *99*, 105809. [CrossRef]
14. Li, A.; Zou, X. Evolution and adaptation of anti-predation response of prey in a two-patchy environment. *Bull. Math. Biol.* **2021**, *83*, 59. [CrossRef]
15. Panday, P.; Pal, N.; Samanta, S.; Tryjanowski, P.; Chattopadhyay, J. Dynamics of a stage-structured predator-prey model: Cost and benefit of fear-induced group defense. *J. Theor. Biol.* **2021**, *528*, 110846. [CrossRef]
16. Liu, C.; Chen, Y.; Yu, Y.; Wang, Z. Bifurcation and stability analysis of a new fractional-order prey-predator model with fear effects in toxic injections. *Mathematics* **2023**, *11*, 4367. [CrossRef]
17. Li, Y.; He, M.; Li, Z. Dynamics of a ratio-dependent Leslie-Gower predator-prey model with Allee effect and fear effect. *Math. Comput. Simul.* **2022**, *201*, 417–439. [CrossRef]
18. Teslya, A.; Wolkowicz, G.S.K. Dynamics of a predator-prey model with distributed delay to represent the conversion process or maturation. *Differ. Equat. Dyn. Sys.* **2023**, *31*, 613–649. [CrossRef]
19. Driver, R.D. Existence and stability of solutions of a delay-differential system. *Arch. Ration. Mech. Anal.* **1962**, *10*, 401–426. [CrossRef]
20. Lin, C.J.; Wang, L.; Wolkowicz, G.S.K. An alternative formulation for a distributed delayed logistic equation. *Bull. Math. Biol.* **2018**, *80*, 1713–1735. [CrossRef]
21. Yuan, Y.; Blair, J. Threshold dynamics in an SEIRS model with latency and temporary immunity. *J. Math. Biol.* **2014**, *69*, 875–904. [CrossRef] [PubMed]
22. Wolkowicz, G.S.K.; Xia, H.; Wu, J. Global dynamics of a chemostat competition model with distributed delay. *J. Math. Biol.* **1999**, *38*, 285–316. [CrossRef]
23. Gourley, S.A.; Ruan, S. Spatio-temporal delays in a nutrient-plankton model on a finite domain: Linear stability and bifurcations. *Appl. Math. Comput.* **2003**, *145*, 391–412. [CrossRef]
24. Deng, J.; Shu, H.; Wang, L.; Wang, X.S. Viral dynamics with immune responses: Effects of distributed delays and Filippov antiretroviral therapy. *J. Math. Biol.* **2023**, *86*, 37. [CrossRef] [PubMed]
25. Shu, H.; Chen, Y.; Wang, L. Impacts of the cell-free and cell-to-cell infection modes on viral dynamics. *J. Dyn. Diff. Equat.* **2018**, *30*, 1817–1836. [CrossRef]
26. Beretta, E.; Kuang, Y. Geometric stability switch criteria in delay differential systems with delay dependent parameters. *SIAM J. Math. Anal.* **2002**, *33*, 1144–1165. [CrossRef]

symmetry

MDPI

Article

Diffusion Mechanisms for Both Living and Dying Trees Across 37 Years in a Forest Stand in Lithuania's Kazlų Rūda Region

Edmundas Petrauskas [1,2] and Petras Rupšys [1,2,3,*]

1 Faculty of Forest Sciences and Ecology, Vytautas Magnus University, 44248 Kaunas, Lithuania; edmundas.petrauskas@vdu.lt

2 Bioeconomy Research Institute, Vytautas Magnus University, 44248 Kaunas, Lithuania

3 Faculty of Informatics, Vytautas Magnus University, 44248 Kaunas, Lithuania

* Correspondence: petras.rupsys@vdu.lt

Abstract: This study aimed to examine changes in the number of live and dying trees in central Lithuanian forests over time. Results were obtained using stochastic differential equations combined with the normal copula function. The examination of each tree's individual size variables (height and diameter) showed that the mean values of dead or dying trees' size variables had significantly lower trajectories that were particularly pronounced in mature stands. According to the data set under examination, the tree mortality rate gradually declined with age, reaching approximately 7% after 10 years. Birch trees 60–70 years old were the first species to reach the 1% mortality rate, followed by spruce trees 70–80 years old and pine trees 80–90 years old. The Maple symbolic algebra system was used to implement all results.

Keywords: mortality; living and dying trees; probability density function; stochastic differential equation

1. Introduction

Theories that suggested a decline in resource usage efficiency and received significant support in the past were not accurately formalized mathematically. Much of that research was undertaken to determine the importance of specific tree size variables when analyzing the mortality rate in a forest stand that is not influenced by environmental perturbations [1]. Forest statisticians studied the equilibrium between a stand's tree sizes and stocking density. The fundamental idea discussed in modeling literature is that there is a relationship between the balance of mortality, stocking density, and stand growth after a forest stand's mortality has reached a plateau [2]. The main goal of this study was to provide a quantitative evaluation of changes in live and dying tree numbers over time (not static) according to different tree species in mixed-species and uneven-aged stands. A key factor driving changes in stands' spatial heterogeneity is the tree mortality phenomenon. When a stand is first established, thousands of seedlings are planted per hectare, and the evolution of unmanaged stands demonstrates that most trees in a stand naturally die due to competition [1,2]. The literature provides an extensive overview of the rates and causes of mortality at various stages of stand evolution; however, little research has addressed the dynamics of the number of dead or dying trees or how this process changes with age [1,3,4]. Assessing tree mortality factors and dynamics is among the most essential aspects of the proper use, conservation, and restoration of forest ecosystems. In boreal forests, tree mortality is mainly influenced by competition, age, disease, and random changes in the forest environment. In the early phases of forest development, competition is especially intense

https://doi.org/10.3390/sym17020213

as young trees fiercely compete for water, nutrients, and sunlight [5]. This study refers to dying and dead trees in a stand as forming the same class. Standing dead trees, which can take a long time to die, and fallen trees are both sources of clusters of dying trees. Even with the far-reaching effects of dead wood accumulation, our quantitative understanding of trees' ongoing mortality and the reduction in wood volume over longer periods is quite limited. As the value of the tree-level size variable in a stand and the demand for resources to support the growth process both increase, competition between neighboring trees arises, resulting in two processes occurring simultaneously: the process of each individual tree's natural mortality and the growth process of living tree size variables. The regular loss of trees due to mortality means that a stand's biomass at a particular age consists of the biomass of growing trees and dying trees. The forecasted mortality time of a particular tree depends on many fixed and random environmental factors, including location, species composition, air quality, and climate. The most common statistical model used to study individual tree and stand mortality is the logistic regression model. Annual survival logistic regression equations predict the probability that a tree will survive the following year. Consequently, it might be challenging to calculate annual survival probability using data that are routinely obtained at intervals longer than a year. The process-driven model presented in this study is dynamic and can be fitted with remeasurements in cycles of unequal periods. Age and tree-level size variables (diameter, height, crown base height, etc.) are the main drivers of tree mortality in a stand, making tree mortality a dynamic phenomenon [6–8].

Individual tree mortality occurs when a tree is recorded as dead, but it is not possible to determine the exact time and cause of death. A precise mathematical definition of the dynamic process of mortality in a forest stand requires repeated measurements of experimental plots, which are usually not large enough. Most models that explain forest mortality dynamics rely on databases that combine dendrochronologically derived information on individual tree age and radial growth with static data on the forest's structure and composition [9–11]. The dynamics of a region's forests can be characterized using tree mortality rates.

For the past 20 years, experimental plots have served as the foundation for the majority of ecosystem-scale studies on tree mortality in stands [12,13]. Long-term tree mortality trajectories would undoubtedly greatly improve our understanding of growth processes and increase our capacity for predicting stand development. However, long-term stand monitoring is expensive and time-consuming, which raises the problem of how to replace regression models used to simulate growth processes with more complex models that cover the whole age range of tree growth. Normal distribution with constant variance has long been central to building regression models for a wide range of values of modeled variables, but unfortunately, regression concepts are often applied to highly asymmetrical data [14–16].

This study proposed a dynamic model in all respects, defined by mixed-effects parameters and stochastic differential equations with unknown parameters estimated from repeated measurements on permanent experimental plots. Most current models of the mortality process are based on even-aged forest conditions, as they assume that mortality is simply calculated as the ratio of the mean annual mortality to the number of trees per hectare and requires uniform intervals of the remeasurement cycle throughout the time interval. These models, therefore, have two main limitations: (1) they may distort the actual underlying process, as it is continuous in time, which may lead to the misidentification of relationships, and (2) they have difficulty adjusting to non-uniform intervals in remeasurement cycles. Without a doubt, many phenomena that have been continually observed throughout time in domains like forestry, biology, and ecology have inherent uncertainty [17–20]. Stochastic differential equation models outperform deterministic models in these situations because they relate to stochastic processes that can capture both the unpredictability of the underlying trajectory and the deterministic trend [21,22]. Typically, random noise drives stochastic differential equations and is represented by the standard Brownian process [23,24]. Using Brownian motion to control a stochastic differential equation's trajectory is mathematically supported by the central limit theorem, which states that normal distribution is naturally found in "many" situations, namely as a case of a limit distribution. Therefore, to model biological processes without sufficient information about the shape of the probability distribution of the quantity being modeled, it is appropriate to define changes in the quantity over time using a stochastic differential equation constructed using a normal distribution [25]. Stochastic differential equations with fixed- and random-effect parameters have been used to predict tree-size components (diameter at breast height, height, crown base height, volume, etc.) using univariate or multivariate measurements. Because the modeled variable was dynamic, it was possible to analyze the dynamics of the current size increment as well as tree-level size variables in detail using models defined by stochastic differential equations [26,27]. For a long time, forest statisticians focused on modeling individual tree size variables (diameter, height, etc.) using sigmoidal regression models, as changes in plant development over time follow a sigmoidal pattern [28].

The development of model systems that describe the growth behavior of trees and stands has yielded a significant amount of knowledge. Fluctuations in the number of living and dying trees in a stand over time are described herein, taking into account the process-driven method's superiority and focusing on earlier research regarding stochastic differential equations and copula functions. This approach is superior to commonly applied static regression methods. Notably, in the past, the number of living trees was traditionally determined using the balancing regression equation between a stand's stocking density and tree sizes.

2. Methodology

The main goal of this study was to define the linkage between a tree's potentially occupied area and tree mortality processes to characterize more precisely the dynamics of the number of dead and living trees per hectare. Two methods were used in this study: (1) the dynamic of the individual tree size variable was described in the diffusion process' framework, and the corresponding exact transition probability density function was obtained; (2) density functions of individual tree size variables were combined using the normal copula function. In this paper, we present a mixed-effects 4-parameter Gompertz-type stochastic differential equation to define the dynamics of tree size variables. Fixed- and random-effect parameters were estimated using an approximate maximum likelihood procedure and an observed estimation dataset. The number of living and dead trees per hectare and their relationship to the mean tree diameter and occupied area in a stand were examined. Results are illustrated visually and statistically and were implemented using the Maple symbolic algebra system.

This paper presents a simulation framework for the tree mortality process in a forest stand using stochastic differential equations (SDEs) and the normal copula function. The number of living and dead trees per hectare and their relationship to a stand's mean diameter and height are examined. Transition probability density functions are derived in the exact form using the proposed mixed-effects parameters SDE framework, and parameter estimators for the diameter and occupied area are produced using an approximated maximum likelihood technique. In the next step, we estimate the dependence parameter of the two-dimensional copula density function. Finally, we define the number of live trees in the stand as the mean value of the random variable using the integration operation, as all densities with the corresponding parameter estimates are known, and using the derivative operation, we define the number of dying trees in the stand. This formalization also makes it possible to write formulas for volume and basal area calculations using an integration process, which may support foresters in assessing various management strategies. The framework was designed to make it as flexible as possible by allowing machine-learning resources to adapt in response to evolving conditions at any point, as depicted in Figure 1.

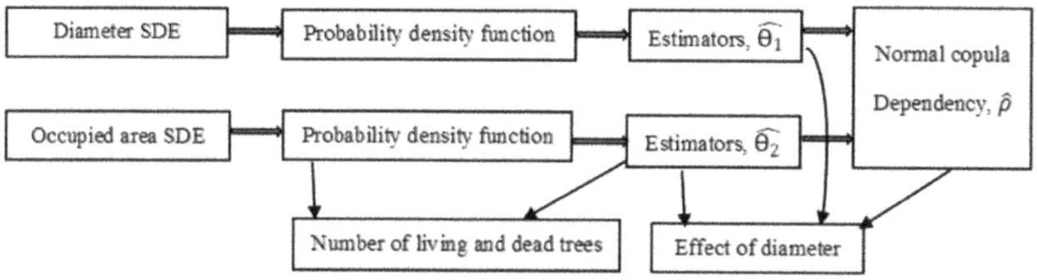

Figure 1. SDE algorithm flow chart visualization.

2.1. Stochastic Differential Equation Framework

The probability distribution of tree-level size variables is useful for defining the mean, mode, median, quantiles, and other numerical characteristics of tree-level and stand-level size attributes. The main tools for assessing tree or stand quantitative and qualitative characteristics are tree height and diameter distributions [29,30]. Classical, well-known distributions, including gamma, Weibull, normal, exponential, and others, are most frequently used by forest statisticians [31,32]. The main drawback of these distribution models is that they are not associated with trees' ages. Itô-type [23,33] stochastic differential equations, which describe diffusion processes, can be effectively used to determine the relationship between changes in a tree size variable and a tree's age or a stand's average age.

Vasicek, Gompertz, Bertalanffy, and gamma SDE growth models provide exact solution transition probability density functions. In this paper, we use a multiplicative form of noise and a one-dimensional mixed-effects 4-parameter Gompertz-type stochastic differential equation, separately defining the dynamics of the area occupied by the tree and those of the tree's diameter. Suppose that change rates in tree diameter at breast height $X^i_{1k}(t), i = 1, \ldots, M; k = 1, \ldots, n_{i1}$ (M is the number of plots and n_{i1} is the number of trees in the ith plot), and change rates in the occupied area $X^i_{2k}(t)$ are determined according to the Gompertz-type stochastic differential equation:

$$dX^i_{jk}(t) = \left(\left(\alpha_j + \varphi^i_j\right) - \beta_j ln\left(X^i_{jk}(t) - \gamma_j\right)\right)\left(X^i_{jk}(t) - \gamma_j\right)dt + \sqrt{\sigma_j}\left(X^i_{jk}(t) - \gamma_j\right)dW^i_{jk}(t), \quad (1)$$

where α_1 and α_2 are birth rate parameters, β_1 and β_2 are death rate parameters ($\alpha_1, \alpha_2 > 0$ and $\beta_1, \beta_2 > 0$), γ_1 and γ_2 are threshold parameters, σ_1 and σ_2 are volatility coefficients, and random effects $\varphi^i_1, \varphi^i_2, i = 1, \ldots, M$ have constant variances and zero means. They are independent, normally distributed random variables, respectively, $\varphi^i_1 \sim N(0; \sigma^2_{11})$ and $\varphi^i_2 \sim N(0; \sigma^2_{21})$. Moreover, φ^i_j is a random variable that is independent to $W^i_{jk}(t)$, and an initial condition takes the following form: if $t = t_0$, then $X^i_1(t_0) = x_{10}$, and $X^i_2(t_0) = x_{20} = \delta$ ($x_{10} > \gamma_1, x_{20} > \gamma_2$). The unknown fixed-effect parameters vectors $\theta_1 = \{\alpha_1, \beta_1, \gamma_1, \sigma_1\}$ and $\theta_2 = \{\alpha_2, \beta_2, \gamma_2, \sigma_2, \delta\}$ must be estimated.

After performing the process transformation $Y^i_{jk} = e^{\beta_j t} ln\left(X^i_{jk}(t) - \gamma_j\right), j = 1, 2$, we can derive the transition probability density function of the solution in the exact form. The solution of the 4-parameter Gompertz-type stochastic differential Equation (1) $X^i_{jk}(t) - \gamma_j$ has a lognormal distribution $LN_1\left(\mu^i_j\left(t\middle|\theta_j, \varphi^i_j\right); v_j(t|\theta_j)\right)$, $i = 1, \ldots, M$, with the mean

$\mu_j^i\left(t\middle|\theta_j,\varphi_j^i\right)$, the variance $v_j(t|\theta_j)$, $j = 1, 2$; $k = 1, \ldots, n_{ij}$, and the probability density function $f_j^i\left(x_{jk}, t\middle|\theta_j,\varphi_j^i\right)$, as follows:

$$\mu_j^i\left(t\middle|\theta_j,\varphi_j^i\right) = ln(x_{j0}-\gamma_j)e^{-\beta_j(t-t_0)}e^{-\beta_j(t-t_0)} + \frac{1}{\beta_j}\left(1-e^{-\beta_j(t-t_0)}\right)\left(\alpha_j+\varphi_j^i-\frac{\sigma_j}{2}\right), \quad (2)$$

$$v_j(t|\theta_j) = \frac{1-e^{-2\beta_j(t-t_0)}}{2\beta_j}\sigma_j, \quad (3)$$

$$f_j^i\left(x_j, t\middle|\theta_j,\varphi_j^i\right) = \frac{1}{\sqrt{2\pi v_j(t|\theta_j)}(x_j-\gamma_j)}exp\left(-\frac{\left(ln(x_j-\gamma_j)-\mu_j^i\left(t\middle|\theta_j,\varphi_j^i\right)\right)^2}{2v_j(t|\theta_j)}\right). \quad (4)$$

The dynamics of the mean, $m_j^i\left(t\middle|\theta_j,\varphi_j^i\right)$, median, $me_j^i\left(t\middle|\theta_j,\varphi_j^i\right)$, mode, $mo_j^i\left(t\middle|\theta_j,\varphi_j^i\right)$, qth quantile ($0 < q < 1$), $qm_j^i\left(t\middle|\theta_j,\varphi_j^i\right)$, and variance, $w_j^i\left(t\middle|\theta_j,\varphi_j^i\right)$, $i = 1, \ldots, M$, of the diameter are given by the following expressions:

$$m_j^i\left(t\middle|\theta_j,\varphi_j^i\right) = \gamma_j + exp\left(\mu_j^i\left(t\middle|\theta_j,\varphi_j^i\right) + \frac{1}{2}v_j(t|\theta_j)\right), \quad (5)$$

$$me_j^i\left(t\middle|\theta_j,\varphi_j^i\right) = \gamma_j + exp\left(\mu_j^i\left(t\middle|\theta_j,\varphi_j^i\right)\right), \quad (6)$$

$$mo_j^i\left(t\middle|\theta_j,\varphi_j^i\right) = \gamma_j + exp\left(\mu_j^i\left(t\middle|\theta_j,\varphi_j^i\right) - v_j(t|\theta_j)\right), \quad (7)$$

$$qm_j^i\left(t\middle|\theta_j,\varphi_j^i\right) = \gamma_j + exp\left(\mu_j^i\left(t\middle|\theta_j,\varphi_j^i\right) + \sqrt{v_j(t|\theta_j)}\Phi_q^{-1}(0;1)\right), \quad (8)$$

$$w_j^i\left(t\middle|\theta_j,\varphi_j^i\right) = exp\left(2\mu_j^i\left(t\middle|\theta_j,\varphi_j^i\right) + v_j(t|\theta_j)\right)\cdot(exp(v_j(t|\theta_j))-1). \quad (9)$$

2.2. *Bivariate Normal Copula*

Copula functions play an important role in linking one-dimensional probability distributions to multidimensional distributions of a particular form. That parameter estimates of tree diameter and occupied area stochastic differential Equation (1) may be obtained utilizing different samples highlights the benefit of employing the copula function method. Sklar's theorem makes this link possible [34]. The normal copula function has attracted particular attention because the normal probability distribution is widely used in agriculture, biology, engineering, economics, and finance. Let us define a normal two-dimensional copula function. The two-dimensional normal copula distribution function with correlation parameter $\rho \in (-1;1)$ is defined using Sklar's formula in the following form:

$$C(u,v;\rho) = \Phi_2\left(\Phi^{-1}(u), \Phi^{-1}(v);\rho\right), \quad (10)$$

where

$$\Phi(x) = \int_{-\infty}^{x}\varphi(z)dz,\ \varphi(x) = \frac{1}{\sqrt{2\pi}}e^{-\frac{x^2}{2}}, \quad (11)$$

$$\Phi_2(x,y;\rho) = \int_{-\infty}^{x}\int_{-\infty}^{y}\varphi_2(z_1,z_2;\rho)dz_1dz_2,\ \varphi_2(x,y;\rho) = \frac{1}{2\pi\sqrt{1-\rho^2}}e^{-\frac{x^2-2\rho xy+y^2}{2(1-\rho^2)}}. \quad (12)$$

The two-dimensional normal copula probability density function takes the following form:

$$c_2(u,v;\rho) = \frac{1}{\sqrt{1-\rho^2}}e^{-\frac{\rho^2(x^2+y^2)-2\rho xy}{2(1-\rho^2)}}, \quad (13)$$

where $x = \Phi^{-1}(u)$ and $y = \Phi^{-1}(v)$. The joint two-dimensional copula-type probability density function $f(x, y)$ is given as follows:

$$f(x_1, x_2) = c_2(F_1(x_1), F_2(x_2); \rho) f_1(x_1) f_2(x_2), \tag{14}$$

where $f_j(x_j)$ and $F_j(x_j)$, j = 1, 2 are the probability density and cumulative distribution functions of X_j, respectively.

The conditional probability density function of $X_j(t)$, j = 1, 2 at a given $(X_k(t) = x_k)$, $j \neq k$, is defined as follows:

$$f_{1|2}(x_1|x_2) = \frac{f(x_1, x_2)}{f_2(x_2)},\ f_{2|1}(x_2|x_1) = \frac{f(x_1, x_2)}{f_1(x_1)}. \tag{15}$$

2.3. *Semiparametric Maximum Pseudo-Likelihood Procedure*

Given that in the previous section we determined the exact transition probability density functions for tree diameter and occupied area and the two-dimensional normal copula function that connects them, we can directly apply the maximum likelihood method to estimate unknown parameters. The direct implementation of the one-step maximum likelihood method raises several numerical problems in optimizing the maximum log-likelihood function [35]. Naturally, estimating parameters using the maximum log-likelihood function can be divided into two steps.

In the first step, Equations (1) and (2) can be fitted to the diameter sample dataset $\left\{x^i_{11}, x^i_{12}, \ldots, x^i_{1n_{ij}}\right\}$ or occupied area sample dataset $\left\{x^i_{21}, x^i_{22}, \ldots, x^i_{2n_{ij}}\right\}$ at discrete times (ages) $\left\{t^i_1, t^i_2, \ldots, t^i_{n_{ij}}\right\}$ (n_{ij} is the number of observed trees of the ith plot for the jth variable, i = 1, 2, …, M) using the maximum likelihood procedure. The associated maximum log-likelihood function for the mixed-effects parameters takes the following form:

$$LL_j\left(\theta_j, \sigma_{j1}, \Psi_j\right) = \sum_{i=1}^{M} \int_{-\infty}^{+\infty} \left(\sum_{k=1}^{n_{ij}} ln\left(f^i_j\left(x^i_{jk}, t^i_k \middle| \theta_j, \varphi^i_j\right)\right) + ln\left(p\left(\varphi^i_j \middle| \sigma^2_{j1}\right)\right)\right) \cdot d\varphi^i_j,\ j = 1,\ 2, \tag{16}$$

where (θ_j, σ_{j1}) are fixed-effect parameters (the same for all plots), the normal density function of random effects is $p\left(\varphi^i_j \middle| \sigma^2_{j1}\right)$, and $\Psi_j = \left(\varphi^1_j, \varphi^2_j, \ldots, \varphi^M_j\right)$.

For mixed-effects parameters Models (1) and (2), the two-stage approximated maximum log-likelihood procedure takes the following form (j = 1, 2; i = 1, …, M):

$$LL_j(\theta_j, \sigma_{j1}, \hat{\Psi}_j) \approx \sum_{i=1}^{M} \left(g\left(\hat{\varphi}^i_j \middle| \theta^1\right) + \frac{1}{2} ln(2\pi) - \frac{1}{2} ln \left(det\left(\left[-\frac{\partial^2 g\left(\varphi^i_j | \theta_j\right)}{\partial\left(\varphi^i_j\right)^2} \right] \right) \Bigg|_{\varphi^i_j = \hat{\varphi}^i_j} \right) \right) \tag{17}$$

$$\hat{\varphi}^i_j = \underset{\varphi^i_j}{argmax} g\left(\varphi^i_j | \hat{\theta}_j\right), \tag{18}$$

where

$$g\left(\varphi^i_j | \theta_j\right) = \sum_{k=1}^{n_i} ln\left(f^i_j\left(x^i_{jk}, t^i_k \middle| \theta_j, \varphi^i_j\right)\right) + ln\left(p\left(\varphi^i_j \middle| \sigma^2_{j1}\right)\right), \tag{19}$$

and *argmax* is an operation that finds the argument that gives the maximum value from a target function.

The maximization of $LL_j\left(\theta_j, \sigma_{j1}, \Psi_j\right)$ is a two-stage optimization problem. The internal optimization step estimates the φ^i for every plot i = 1, …, M using Equation (18). The external optimization step maximizes $LL_j(\theta_j, \sigma_{j1}, \hat{\Psi}_j)$ after plugging $\hat{\varphi}^i_j$, i = 1, …, M into Equation (17).

In the second step, we estimate the density parameters of the two-dimensional copula density function defined using Equation (13) by maximizing the log-likelihood copula function defined as follows:

$$1(p) = \sum_{i=1}^{M} \sum_{k=1}^{n_{ij}} ln\left(c_2\left(\Phi^{-1}\left(F_1^i\left(x_{1k}^i, t_k^i\right)\right), \Phi^{-1}\left(F_2^i\left(x_{2k}^i, t_k^i\right)\right)\right)\right), \quad (20)$$

where $F_j^i\left(x_{jk}^i, t_k^i\right) = \int_{\gamma_j}^{x_{jk}^i} f_j^i\left(z, t_k^i \middle| \hat{\theta}_j, \hat{\varphi}_j^i\right)dz$ and Φ^{-1} is the inverse of a standard normal distribution.

2.4. Parameter Calibration

The main challenge in defining the dynamics of tree size variables comes from calibrating random effects to the new stand. Observed data from a new plot were used in this study to estimate random effects [36]. If there are no measurements of standing dead trees in a new plot, the random effects needed to define the dynamics of the dead tree size variables are equated to the corresponding random effects of the living trees. For a new plot, the random effects $\hat{\varphi}$ are defined in the following form [37]:

$$\hat{\varphi}_j = \underset{\varphi_j}{argmax}\left(\sum_{k=1}^{m} ln\left(f_j\left(x_{jk}, t_k \middle| \hat{\theta}_j, \varphi_j\right)\right) + ln\left(p\left(\varphi_j \middle| \hat{\sigma}_{j1}^2\right)\right)\right), \quad (21)$$

where the number of observed trees in a plot is denoted by m, $\{x_{j1}, x_{j2}, \ldots, x_{jm}\}, j = 1, 2$ (tree diameter or occupied area) is the newly observed dataset (measured plot) on fixed time values $\{t_1, t_2, \ldots, t_m\}$, $t_0 = 4$, and $f_j\left(x_{jk}, t_k \middle| \hat{\theta}, \varphi_j\right)$ is the log-normal density function defined using Equation (5). Estimated values of fixed-effect parameters for mixed-effects Models (1) and (2) are denoted by "hat" and are estimated separately for living and dead trees using an approximated maximum likelihood procedure described using Equations (17)–(19).

3. Material

3.1. Sample Collection

In this paper, we present 37 years of measurements from continued monitoring of permanent experimental plots. During the 1983–1987 period, 53 permanent experimental plots were installed in the forests of Lithuania's Kazlų Rūda region and measured between one and seven times at 2- to 37-year intervals. Figure A1 shows the location of the permanent experimental plots in the forests of the Kazlų Rūda region of Lithuania. The sampling method used rectangular plots that consisted of about 0.16–0.72 ha. The area covered by Scots pine (*Pinus sylvestris* L.) stands accounts for 63.8% of the particular allocation; Norway spruce (*Picea abies*) for 30.2%; silver birch (*Betula pendula Roth* and *Betula pubescens Ehrh.*) for 5.8%; and other stands for 0.2%. From 1983 to 2020, 58,829 live trees (36,689 pine, 18,738 spruce, 3270 birch, and 132 other species) were measured in 48 plots. During each measurement, the following were recorded for every sample tree: age, diameter at breast height, and tree position (x and y coordinates). The area occupied by a tree was determined by measuring each tree's location inside the plots and utilizing a Voronoi diagram [37]. Trees that fell out of measurement within 37 years were considered dead. Figure 2 shows the dynamics of the number of trees per ha depending on the stand's average age by tree species. A total of 16,857 trees (10,620 pine, 5049 spruce, 1104 birch, and 94 others) died in 48 plots from 1983 to 2020, which represents 28.7% of the sample population (58,829 trees). In most cases, we were unable to identify the causal agent, and death was not consistently associated with biotic or abiotic forest characteristics.

Notably, the data-gathering process design likely contributed to the uncertainty of model predictions. Most likely, number-of-trees-per-hectare models lacked precision because age was a complicated variable to control in these ongoing experiments. This was problematic, as only 10% of trees whose height was measured had their age measured; the remaining trees were evaluated based on an average age.

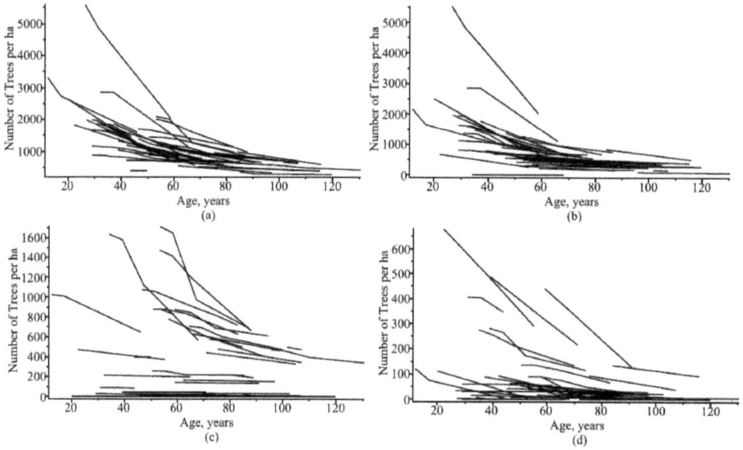

Figure 2. Dynamics of the number of observed trees per hectare: (**a**) all species; (**b**) Scots pine; (**c**) Norway spruce; and (**d**) silver birch.

3.2. Parameter Estimation

We used the semiparametric maximum likelihood method described above to find unknown parameters, where the diameter of the trees $\left\{x_{11}^i, x_{12}^i, \ldots, x_{1n_i}^i\right\}$ and the area occupied by the trees $\left\{x_{21}^i, x_{22}^i, \ldots, x_{2n_i}^i\right\}$ at a fixed point in time $\left\{t_1^i, t_2^i, \ldots, t_{n_i}^i\right\}$ were discretely measured for $i = 1, \ldots, M$ in $M = 48$ plots. Parameters of the stochastic differential Equation (1) were estimated separately for living and dead (dying) trees under four possible outcomes: all trees, Scots pine, Norway spruce, and silver birch. The results of the parameter estimation are summarized in Table 1. All parameters were statistically significant. The observed Fisher information matrix, which is the negative of the second derivative (the Hessian matrix) of the approximated maximum log-likelihood function, was used to estimate standard deviations [38].

Table 1. Parameter estimates for Equations (1) and (2) for living and dead trees.

Species	**Living Trees**						**Dead Trees**					
	α_1	β_1	γ_1	δ	σ_1	σ_{11}	α_1	β_1	γ_1	δ	σ_1	σ_{11}
Diameter, $\hat{\theta}_1$												
All	0.0904	0.0252	−6.3206	-	0.0051	0.0075	0.0904	0.0251	−3.4080	-	0.0059	0.0112
Pine	0.0815	0.0198	−20.0858	-	0.0008	0.0027	0.1043	0.0292	−7.3245	-	0.0021	0.0067
Spruce	0.0967	0.0296	−1.5744	-	0.0098	0.0102	0.1415	0.0564	−0.5799	-	0.0185	0.0233
Birch	0.1421	0.0427	−4.6322	-	0.0071	0.0159	0.4630	0.1865	0.0479	-	0.0504	0.0938
	α_2	β_2	γ_2	δ	σ_2	σ_{21}	α_2	β_2	γ_2	δ	σ_2	σ_{21}
Occupied area, $\hat{\theta}_2$												
All	0.0499	0.0139	−1.8124	1.6003	0.0075	0.0086	0.0586	0.0195	−0.8030	1.6003	0.0121	0.0118
Pine	0.0620	0.0177	−1.6587	1.6040	0.0079	0.0086	0.0486	0.0126	−1.1019	1.6040	0.0078	0.0099
Spruce	0.0559	0.0180	−0.8855	2.1216	0.0131	0.0103	0.0533	0.0176	−0.6102	2.1216	0.0148	0.0101
Birch	0.0581	0.0177	−2.0621	2.0168	0.0083	0.0093	0.1042	0.0408	−2.1966	2.0168	0.0134	0.0151

Equation (20) was used to estimate the parameter of dependence, $\hat{\rho}$, which yielded values of 0.2913 for all tree species, 0.2180 for pine, 0.2374 for spruce, and 0.1999 for birch.

4. Results and Discussion

4.1. Effect of Age on Mortality

Deadwood is generally classified according to its position in relation to the forest canopy as standing or fallen because the decay rate of standing deadwood can be much lower than that of fallen deadwood. In this study, each stand's standing and fallen dead trees were merged into a single class called dead (dying) trees. As trees age, stands naturally change into a phase of spontaneous decline in stem number in a process known as self-thinning. In forestry research, a complicated phenomenon like tree self-thinning is typically described mathematically as a power function between the number of trees per hectare (stand density) and tree size (e.g., mean diameter, volume, or biomass) [39–41]. This proposed power function is universal but dependent on species, age, and environmental conditions. Subsequent investigations by Yoda [3] and Mrad et al. [42] documented similar patterns relating to the time dependency of tree size and density. Modeling forest growth requires self-thinning equations to predict changes in stand density by tree species, age, and any combination of species or age. Using the stochastic differential Equation (1) for the dynamics of a tree's occupied area (j = 2), we defined the dynamics of the number of trees per ha for four outcomes: all tree species, pine species, spruce species, and birch species in a forest stand using the following equation:

$$Nl^i(t) = \frac{10{,}000}{m_2^i(t|\hat{\theta}_2, \hat{\varphi}_2^i)}, \; i = 1, \ldots M, \quad (22)$$

where estimates of fixed-effect parameters $\hat{\theta}_2$ are from living trees data in Table 1; and random effects $\hat{\varphi}_2^i$ are calibrated using Equation (21) or, in the case of a fixed-effect scenario, are set to the mean values, namely zero ($\hat{\varphi}_2^i = E\varphi_2^i = 0$).

We defined the dynamics of the number of trees per hectare of dead trees using the derivative operation, as follows:

$$Nd^i(t) = -10{,}000\frac{d}{dt}\left(\frac{1}{m_2^i(t|\hat{\theta}_2, \hat{\varphi}_2^i)}\right), \; i = 1, \ldots M, \quad (23)$$

where estimates of fixed-effect parameters $\hat{\theta}_2$ are taken from living trees data in Table 1; and random effects $\hat{\varphi}_2^i$ are calibrated using Equation (21) or, in the case of a fixed-effect scenario, are set to the mean values, namely zero ($\hat{\varphi}_2^i = E\varphi_2^i = 0$).

Tree mortality per hectare is often defined differently [43,44], so it makes sense to have a single measure of mortality. The absolute mortality rate per hectare derived from Equation (23) depends on the existing number of trees in the stand and is therefore not useful for mortality analysis when comparing stands with different initial numbers of trees. In this case, the relative mortality rate, or, in other words, the instantaneous dynamics of the relative mortality rate, is defined as the decrease in the number of trees per hectare compared to the current number of trees (using a percentage scale) in the following form:

$$Mr^i(t) = -\frac{d}{dt}\left(ln\left(Nl^i(t)\right)100 - \frac{d}{dt}\left(\frac{1}{m_2^i(t|\hat{\theta}_2, \hat{\varphi}_2^i)}\right) \cdot m_2^i\left(t\middle|\hat{\theta}_2, \hat{\varphi}_2^i\right)100, i = 1, 2, \ldots, M. \quad (24)$$

The relationship between relative mortality and logarithmic size characteristics, expressed in Equation (24), is commonly used in forestry, for example, to describe the relationship between the number of trees per hectare in a stand and tree size [25,45,46].

Figure 3 shows simulated trajectories of the number of trees per hectare of living and dead trees, along with observations, and dynamics of tree mortality in the stand are shown on a percentage scale. Figure 3a–c shows that thinning occurred at a high rate in stands up to 60 years of age, whereas in stands above 90 years of age, the rate was below 1%. Figure 3 also shows trends in the number of living and dead trees per ha in all mixed-species, uneven-aged stands in the region, ignoring the plot's characteristics (only fixed-effect parameters were used). Figure 4 visualizes analogous trajectories for Scots pine, Norway spruce, and silver birch species separately. In this region, Norway spruce had significantly lower relative mortality than other tree species, as seen by comparing Figure 4(p3,s3,b3).

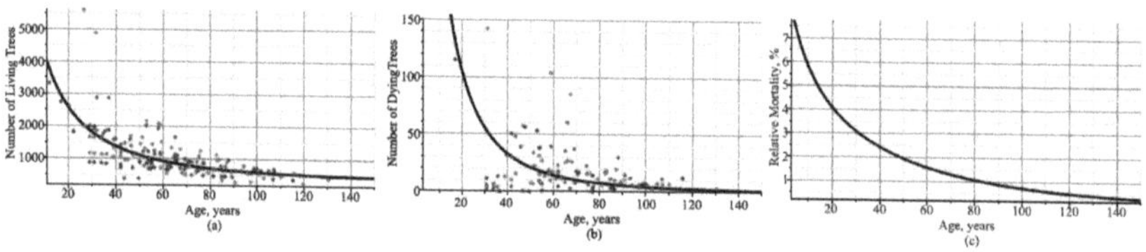

Figure 3. Trajectories of number of trees per 1 ha: (**a**) living trees; (**b**) dead trees; (**c**) dead–living trees ratio expressed as a percentage. Circles indicate observed values.

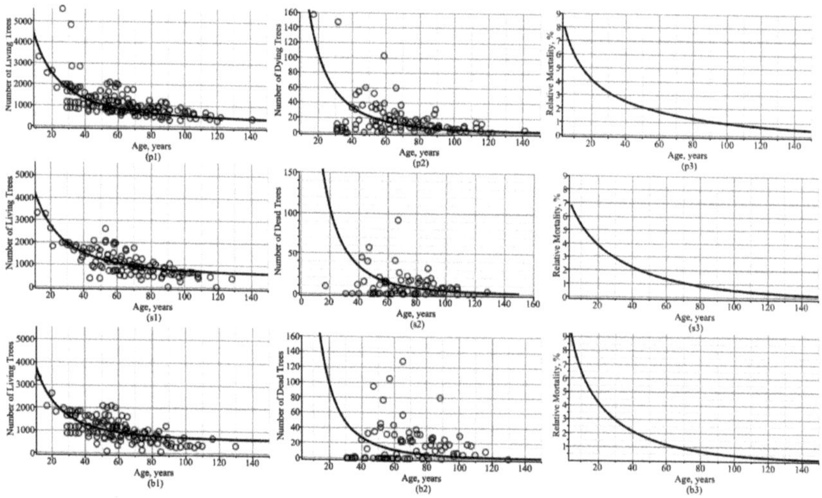

Figure 4. Trajectories of number of trees per 1 ha: (**p1**,**s1**,**b1**) living trees; (**p2**,**s2**,**b2**) dead trees; (**p3**,**s3**,**b3**) dead–living trees ratio expressed as a percentage; (**p1**,**p2**,**p3**) pine species; (**s1**,**s2**,**s3**) spruce species; (**b1**,**b2**,**b3**) birch species. Circles indicate observed values.

4.2. *Effect of Tree Size on Mortality*

Next, we analyze how the mean diameter of trees in a stand affects the number of trees per ha. To determine the conditional number of trees per hectare in relation to the mean diameter of trees in the stand, we use a copula-type two-dimensional probability density function of the tree diameter and the occupied area, which is defined using Equation (14) and an additional integration operation, as follows:

$$Nl^i(t|\,x_1) = 10{,}000\left[\int_0^{+\infty} x_2 f^i_{2|1}(t,\ x_2|x_1)dx_2\right]^{-1},\ i = 1,\ 2,\ \ldots M, \quad (25)$$

where conditional probability density function is defined as:

$$f_{2|1}^{i}(t,\ x_2|x_1) = c_2\left(F_1^i(x_1,t), F_2^i(x_2,t); \hat{\rho}\right) f_2^i\left(x_2, t \middle| \hat{\theta}_2, \hat{\varphi}_2^i\right), \tag{26}$$

and $F_j^i(x_j,t) = \int_0^{x_j} f_j^i\left(z, t \middle| \hat{\theta}_j, \hat{\varphi}_j^i\right) dz$; $j = 1, 2$; estimates of fixed-effect parameters $\hat{\theta}_j$ are taken from living trees data in Table 1; the parameter of dependence $\hat{\rho}$ is estimated using Equation (21) (for all tree species, 0.2913; for pine, 0.2180; for spruce, 0.2374; and for birch 0.1999); and random effects $\hat{\varphi}_j^i$ are calibrated using Equation (21) or, in the case of a fixed-effect scenario, are set to the mean values, namely zero ($\hat{\varphi}_j^i = E\varphi_j^i = 0$).

Next, we visually analyze whether the number of trees per hectare is affected by the mean diameter of a forest stand. For Figure 5, the number of trees per hectare was modeled by taking three different trajectories of tree diameter dynamics: the mean (defined using Equation (6)), the 5% quantile, and the 95% quantile (defined using Equation (9)). Figure 5 shows that a strong increase in the diameter trajectory significantly affected the dynamics of the number of trees per ha. In this context, it is appropriate to investigate the rates of increase and decrease in the number of trees per ha as a function of the rate of change in the trajectory of tree diameter in a forest stand. For this purpose, the mean tree diameter in the stand, as defined using Equation (6), was increased or decreased by 10%, 25%, and 50%, and the effect on the number of trees per ha is shown graphically in Figure 6. Increasing the mean stand diameter by 10%, 25%, and 50% would reduce the number of trees per hectare by more than 3.5%, 8%, and 14%, respectively, at an average stand age of 60 years (see Figure 6a). On the other hand, reducing the mean stand diameter by 10%, 25%, and 50% would increase the number of trees per hectare by more than 4%, 10%, and 24%, respectively, at an average stand age of 60 years (see Figure 6b). This confirms that thinning accelerates the increase in stand diameter and reduces the number of trees in the stand.

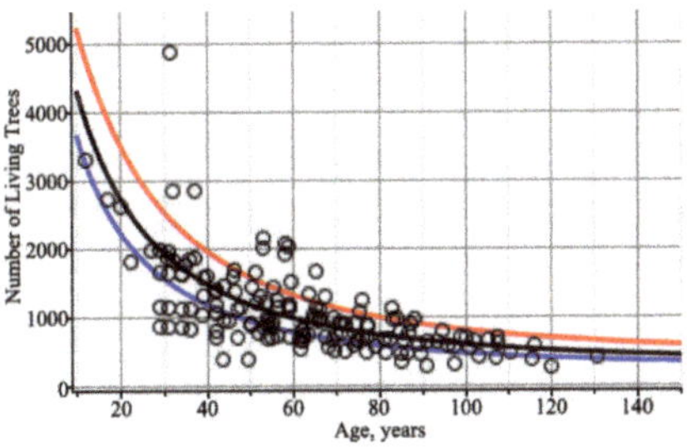

Figure 5. Dynamics of the number of trees per ha of living trees using different trajectories of tree diameter in a stand: mean diameter trend (black); the trend of the diameter's 5% quantile (red); the trend of the diameter's 95% quantile (blue). Circles indicate the observed dataset.

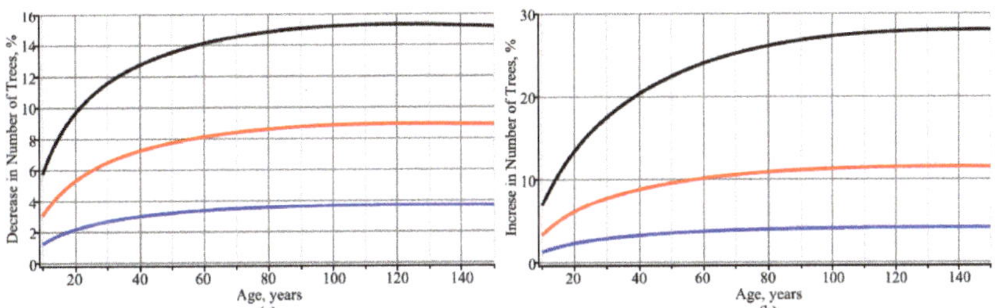

Figure 6. Percentage dynamics of decreases or increases in the number of trees per hectare: (**a**) mean increases in diameters of the stand's trees of 10% (blue), 25% (red), and 50% (black); (**b**) mean decreases in diameters of the stand's trees of 10% (blue), 25% (red), and 50% (black).

The analysis of the number of trees per hectare shown in Figures 4–6 was carried out using a fixed-effect scenario, i.e., random effects were equated to their mean values, which were zero under the previous assumption. The analysis of the dynamic of the number of trees per hectare under the mixed-effects scenario is presented below. For this purpose, estimates of fixed-effect parameters were taken from Table 1, and random effects were calibrated according to Equation (21). Figure 7 shows the dynamic of the number of trees per ha for living and dead trees and the dynamic of the relative mortality (dead–live trees ratio). Simulated trajectories of the number of trees per ha for all species of trees were in good agreement with the observed values for both living and dead trees, as shown in Figure 7(a1,p1,s1,b1) (for living trees) and Figure 7(a2,p2,s2,b2) (for dead trees). Notably, the tree mortality rate reached about 7% from the age of 10 years onwards and steadily decreased with age (see Figure 7(a3,p3,s3,b3)). Figure 7(a3,p3,s3,b3) shows that birch species (60–70 years old) reached the 1% mortality rate the fastest, followed by spruce species (70–80 years old) and then pine species (80–90 years old). In the case of pine species, the proportion of species in the species composition did not affect the mortality rate (see Figure 7(p3)). In contrast, birch species showed a higher mortality rate with a low proportion of birch species (see Figure 7(b3)).

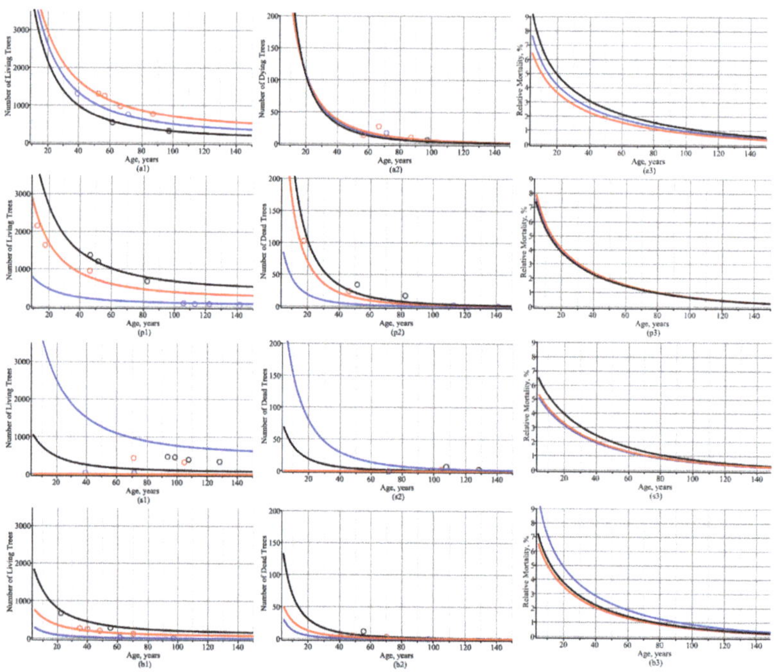

Figure 7. Trajectories of the number of trees per 1 ha for the mixed-effects scenario: (**a1**,**a2**,**a3**) all species of trees: the first stand consisted of 92% pine (P), 2% spruce (S), and 6% birch (B) (black), the second stand consisted of 14% P, 82% S, and 4% B (red), and the third stand consisted of 60% P, 3% S, and 37% B (blue); (**p1**,**p2**,**p3**) pine trees: the first stand consisted of 99% P, 0% S, and 1% B (black), the second stand consisted of 65% P, 31% S, and 4% B (red), and the third stand consisted of 18% P, 80% S, and 2% B (blue); (**s1**,**s2**,**s3**) spruce trees: the first stand consisted of 18% P, 80% S, and 2% B (black), the second stand consisted of 49% P, 48% S, and 3% B (red), and the third stand consisted of 60% P, 3% S, and 37% B (blue); (**b1**,**b2**,**b3**) birch trees: the first stand consisted of 37% P, 26% S, and 37% B (black), the second stand consisted of 84% P, 0% S, and 16% B (red), and the third stand consisted of 92% P, 2% S, and 6% B (blue); (**a1**,**p1**,**s1**,**b1**) living trees; (**a2**,**p2**,**s2**,**b2**) dead trees; (**a3**,**p3**,**s3**,**b3**) dead–living trees ratio, expressed as a percentage. Circles indicate observed values.

To understand the mechanisms underlying tree mortality, it is worthwhile to investigate further the relationship between stand size attributes (mean diameter, height, etc.) and the relative mortality between different tree species and environmental conditions. To find a link between relative mortality and mean size attributes, we used tree diameter, height, and occupied area as size proxies and investigated their relationship with relative mortality. It has been repeatedly observed in the literature that mortality rates have a general multivariate dependence on tree size attributes and various environmental factors [4,47]. The analysis of the dynamic of relative mortality's dependence on mean diameter and mean occupied area, shown in Figure 8, was carried out using a fixed-effect scenario; i.e., random effects were set to their mean values, which were assumed to be zero according to the previous assumption, estimates of fixed-effect parameters in Table 1 (living trees) were taken into account, and the mean trajectories of diameter and occupied area were calculated using Equation (5).

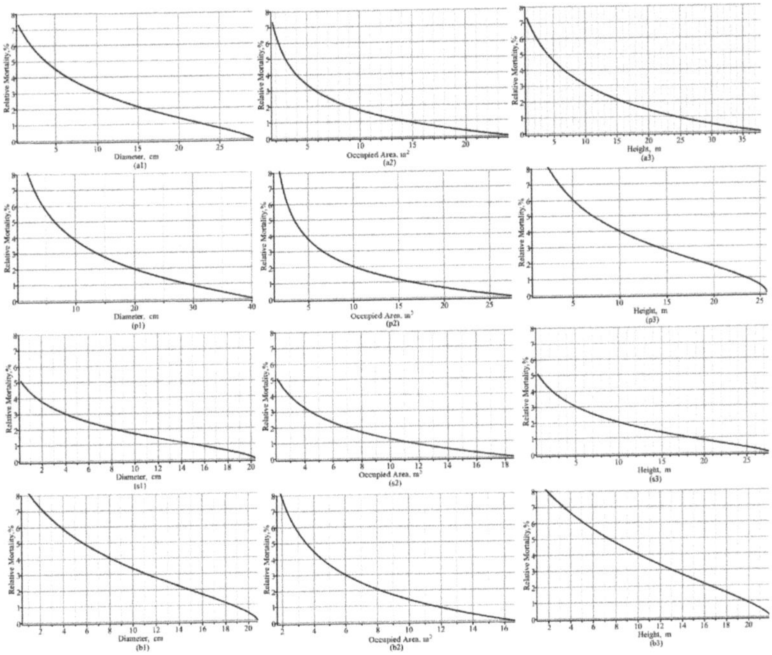

Figure 8. Dead–living trees ratios, expressed as percentages, for the fixed-effect scenario: (**a1**,**a2**,**a3**) all species of trees; (**p1**,**p2**,**p3**) pine species; (**s1**,**s2**,**s3**) spruce species; (**b1**,**b2**,**b3**) birch species; (**a1**,**p1**,**s1**,**b1**) dynamic of dead–living trees ratio versus mean diameter; (**a2**,**p2**,**s2**,**b2**) dynamic of dead–living trees ratio versus mean occupied area; and (**a3**,**p3**,**s3**,**b3**) dynamic of dead–living trees ratio versus mean height.

As Figure 8 shows, Norway spruce's relative mortality was the most likely to reduce, by up to 4%, when the mean diameter exceeded 1.5 cm or the occupied area exceeded 3 m^2. In addition, Norway spruce's relative mortality was reduced by up to 2% when the mean diameter exceeded 8 cm or the occupied area exceeded 6.5 m^2. The next most common species in terms of the rate of decline in relative mortality was silver birch, for which the relative mortality rate decreased by up to 4% when the mean diameter was greater than 8 cm or the occupied area was greater than 4.5 m^2. The relative mortality of silver birch decreased by up to 2% when the mean diameter exceeded 15 cm or when the occupied area exceeded 8 m^2. The smallest decreases in relative mortality were observed for Scots pine: 4% relative mortality occurred when the mean diameter exceeded 9 cm or the occupied area exceeded 4.5 m^2, and 2% relative mortality occurred when the mean diameter exceeded 19.5 cm or the occupied area exceeded 10 m^2.

Relative mortalities shown in Figure 8 reflect all stands in the Kazlų Rūda region and do not take into account the peculiarities of tree growth processes in a particular stand. To reflect the effects of individual stands on differences in relative mortality required a mixed-effects scenario to be applied. Figure 9 shows the relationship of relative mortality with the mean tree diameter and the mean area occupied in three different stands. Figure 9 also shows the dependence of the relative mortality dynamic on the mean diameter and the mean occupied area under a mixed-effects scenario; i.e., random effects were calibrated according to Equation (21), fixed-effect parameters from Table 1 (living trees) were used, and the mean trajectories of diameter, height, and occupied area were calculated according to Equation (5). The asymptotic values of mean diameter and mean occupied area for pine species are roughly illustrated in Figure 9: e.g., mean diameters were 32 cm (black in the first plot), 42 cm (red in the second plot), and 49 cm (blue in the third plot); and mean occupied areas were 23 m^2 (black in the first plot), 24 m^2 (red in the second plot), and 31 m^2 (blue in the third plot). Through analysis, we observed that the relative mortality was lower in the plot where asymptotic values of the explanatory variable (diameter or occupied area) were smaller. Therefore, Figure 9 indicates that the process of slowing down relative mortality is proportional to the increase in tree size attributes (mean diameter and occupied area). Figure 9 also shows that site characteristics such as tree species composition and soil type had the greatest influence on the relative mortality rate of birch trees and the least influence on pine trees. This shows that the Kazlų Rūda region, where these observations were made, had the most favorable conditions for pine species tree growth.

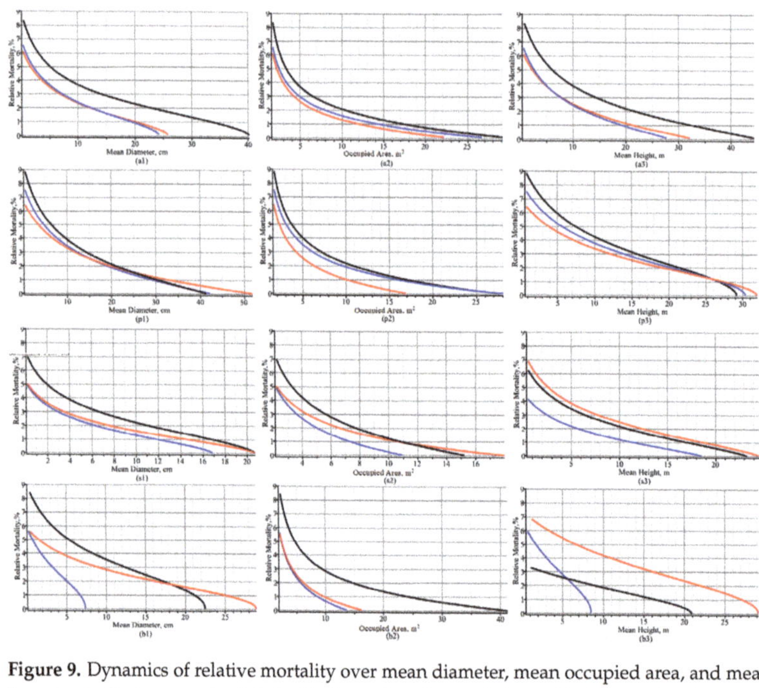

Figure 9. Dynamics of relative mortality over mean diameter, mean occupied area, and mean height for mixed-effects scenario: (**a1**,**a2**,**a3**) all species of trees; (**p1**,**p2**,**p3**) pine species; (**s1**,**s2**,**s3**) spruce species; (**b1**,**b2**,**b3**) birch species; (**p1**,**s1**,**b1**) dynamic of relative mortality versus mean diameter; (**p2**,**s2**,**b2**) dynamic of relative mortality versus mean occupied area; and (**p3**,**s3**,**b3**) dynamic of relative mortality versus mean height.

Table 2 presents the potential for forecasting the number of trees per hectare using the newly developed mixed-effects parameters model. It utilizes fixed-effect parameter estimates from Table 1 and random effects for the occupied area calibrated using Equation (21) and the observed datasets. The presented model showed high goodness-of-fit statistical measures for the number of trees per hectare of live tree predictions in this region. For example, the root mean square error (percentage root mean square errors) for all species and pine, spruce, and birch species were 171.6 (15.4%), 130.1 (16.6%), 101.4 (24.2%), and 22.0 (30.0%), respectively, and the coefficient of determination for all species and pine, spruce, and birch species were 94.4%, 96.9%, 94.6%, and 95.8%, respectively.

Table 2. Statistical measures * for the number of live trees per hectare model defined using Equation (22).

Tree Species	B (%)	AB (%)	RMSE (%)	R^2
All	131.963 (11.82)	133.167 (11.93)	171.593 (15.37)	0.9439
Pine	88.359 (11.25)	89.201 (11.36)	130.075 (16.56)	0.9691
Spruce	59.866 (14.30)	66.511 (15.89)	101.429 (24.23)	0.9457
Birch	3.292 (4.47)	13.651 (18.56)	22.028 (29.95)	0.9577

* Statistical measures: the mean bias, $B = \frac{1}{n}\sum_{i=1}^{n}\left(y_i - \hat{y}_i\right)$ (the percentage mean bias, $\%B = \frac{1}{n}\sum_{i=1}^{n}\frac{y_i - \hat{y}_i}{y_i} * 100$); the absolute mean bias, $AB = \frac{1}{n}\sum_{i=1}^{n}\left|y_i - \hat{y}_i\right|$ (the percentage absolute mean bias, $\%B = \frac{1}{n}\sum_{i=1}^{n}\left|\frac{y_i - \hat{y}_i}{y_i}\right| * 100$); the root mean square error, $RMSE = \sqrt{\frac{1}{n}\sum_{i=1}^{n}\left(y_i - \hat{y}_i\right)^2}$ (the percentage root mean square error, $\%RMSE = \sqrt{\frac{1}{n}\sum_{i=1}^{n}\left(\frac{y_i - \hat{y}_i}{y_i}\right)^2} * 100$); and the coefficient of determination, $R^2 = 1 - \frac{\sum_{i=1}^{n}\left(y_i - \hat{y}_i\right)^2}{\sum_{i=1}^{n}\left(y_i - \overline{y}\right)^2}$.

This paper suggests analyzing the instantaneous tree relative mortality in a forest stand using models based on stochastic differential equations. Higher predictability and interpretability are the primary benefits of newly developed stochastic differential equation models.

5. Conclusions

The main achievement of this study was the application of a 4-parameter Gompertz-type diffusion process to model tree mortality in mixed-species, uneven-aged stands. The normal copula function combined several diffusion processes and allowed the inclusion of not only age but also additional explanatory variables, such as tree diameter, height, crown base height, and crown width, to explain stand mortality. These newly derived probability density functions allow the formulation of equations describing the mean, quantile, and variance of the number of living and dead trees in mixed-species, uneven-aged forest stands.

Future work will focus on the derivation of multivariate distributions (e.g., diameter, height, and occupied area) with a general shape, which would allow the study of the basal area and volume and their increments of living and dead trees in a stand. To generate multivariate distributions, it is appropriate to use the copula method and stochastic differential equations.

Author Contributions: Conceptualization, E.P. and P.R.; Methodology, P.R.; Software, P.R.; Formal analysis, E.P. and P.R.; Data curation, E.P. and P.R.; Writing—original draft, P.R.; Writing—review & editing, E.P. and P.R.; Project administration, P.R. All authors have read and agreed to the published version of the manuscript.

Funding: This research was funded by the Horizon Europe Framework Programme (HORIZON) Teaming for Excellence (HORIZON-WIDERA-2022-ACCESS-01-two-stage), a creation of the Centre of Excellence in Smart Forestry "Forest 4.0", No. 101059985. This research was co-funded by FOREST 4.0: "Ekscelencijos centras tvariai miško bioekonomikai vystyti" (No. 10-042-P-0002).

Data Availability Statement: Original data presented in this study are included in the main text, and field data presented in this study are available on request from the corresponding author.

Acknowledgments: The authors are very grateful to the Lithuanian Association of Impartial Timber Scalers for the sample dataset.

Conflicts of Interest: The authors declare no conflict of interest.

Appendix A

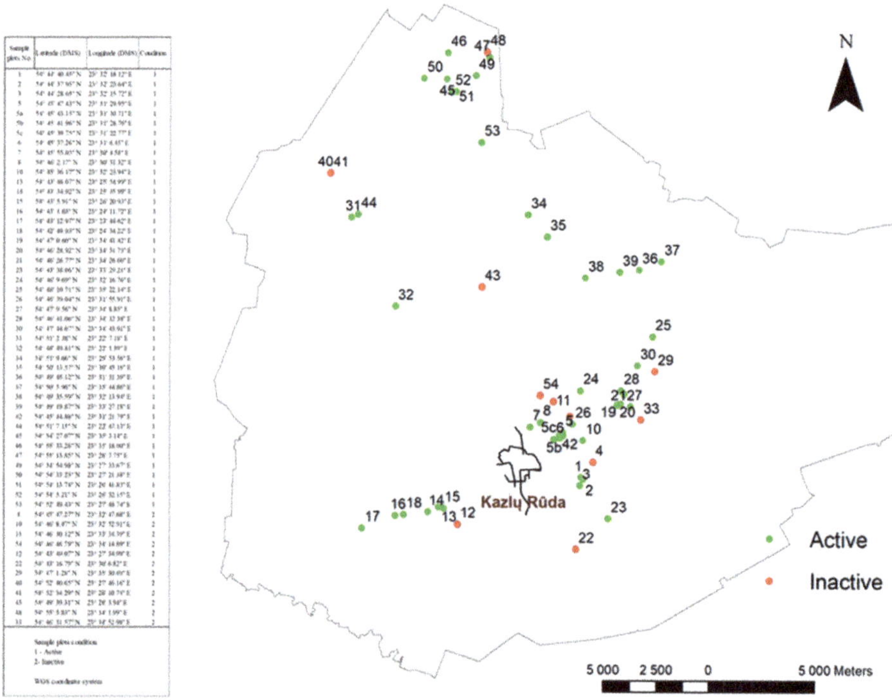

Figure A1. The study area location.

References

1. Del Río, M.; Oviedo, J.A.B.; Pretzsch, H.; Löf, M.; Ruiz-Peinado, R. A review of thinning effects on Scots pine stands: From growth and yield to new challenges under global change. *For. Syst.* **2017**, *26*, eR03S. [CrossRef]
2. Hutchings, M.J.; Budd, C.S.J. Plant self-thinning and leaf area dynamics in experimental and natural monocultures. *Oikos* **1981**, *36*, 319–325. [CrossRef]
3. Yoda, K. Self-thinning in overcrowded pure stands under cultivated and natural conditions (intraspecific competition among higher plants. *J. Biol. Osaka City Univ.* **1963**, *14*, 107–129.

4. Lalor, A.R.; Law, D.J.; Breshears, D.D.; Falk, D.A.; Field, J.P.; Loehman, R.A.; Triepke, F.J.; Barron-Gafford, G.A. Mortality thresholds of juvenile trees to drought and heatwaves: Implications for forest regeneration across a landscape gradient. *Front. For. Glob. Change* **2023**, *6*, 1198156. [CrossRef]
5. Morris, E. Self-thinning lines differ with fertility level. *Ecol. Res.* **2002**, *17*, 17–28. [CrossRef]
6. Dhakal, T.; Cho, K.H.; Kim, S.-J.; Beon, M.-S. Modeling decline of mountain range forest using survival analysis. *Front. For. Glob. Change* **2023**, *6*, 1183509. [CrossRef]
7. Rose, C.; Hall, D.; Shiver, B.; Clutter, M.; Borders, B. A Multilevel Approach to Individual Tree Survival Prediction. *For. Sci.* **2006**, *52*, 31–43. [CrossRef]
8. Tian, X.; Sun, S.; Mola-Yudego, B.; Cao, T. Predicting individual-tree growth using stand-level simulation, diameter distribution and Bayesian calibration. *Ann. For. Sci.* **2020**, *77*, 57. [CrossRef]
9. Fransson, P.; Brännström, A.; Franklin, O. A tree's quest for light—Optimal height and diameter growth under a shading canopy. *Tree Physiol.* **2021**, *41*, 1–11. [CrossRef] [PubMed]
10. Da Silva, B.G.; Demétrio, C.G.B.; Sermarini, R.A.; Molenberghs, G.; Verbeke, G.; Behling, A.; Marques, E.; Accioly, Y.; Figura, M.A. Height-Diameter Models: A Comprehensive Review with New Insights on Relationships to Generalized Linear Models and Differential Equations. *Int. For. Rev.* **2024**, *26*, 398–419. [CrossRef]
11. Gärtner, A.; Jönsson, A.M.; Metcalfe, D.B.; Pugh, T.A.M.; Tagesson, T.; Ahlström, A. Temperature and Tree Size Explain the Mean Time to Fall of Dead Standing Trees across Large Scales. *Forests* **2023**, *14*, 1017. [CrossRef]
12. Bradford, J.B.; Bell, D.M. A window of opportunity for climate-change adaptation: Easing tree mortality by reducing forest basal area. *Front. Ecol. Environ.* **2017**, *15*, 11–17. [CrossRef]
13. Rogers, B.M.; Solvik, K.; Hogg, E.H.; Ju, J.; Masek, J.G.; Michaelian, M.; Berner, L.T.; Goetz, S.J. Detecting early warning signals of tree mortality in boreal North America using multiscale satellite data. *Glob. Change Biol.* **2018**, *24*, 2284–2304. [CrossRef]
14. Rupšys, P. Understanding the Evolution of Tree Size Diversity within the Multivariate Nonsymmetrical Diffusion Process and Information Measures. *Mathematics* **2019**, *7*, 761. [CrossRef]
15. Alzaatreh, A.; Aljarrah, M.; Almagambetova, A.; Zakiyeva, N. On the Regression Model for Generalized Normal Distributions. *Entropy* **2017**, *23*, 173. [CrossRef] [PubMed]
16. Kohyama, T.S.; Potts, M.D.; Kohyama, T.I.; Kassim, A.R.; Ashton, P.S. Demographic properties shape tree size distribution in a Malaysian rain forest. *Am. Nat.* **2015**, *185*, 367–379. [CrossRef]
17. Hara, T. A stochastic model and the moment dynamics of the growth and size distribution in plant populations. *J. Theor. Biol.* **1984**, *109*, 173–190. [CrossRef]
18. Frank, S.A. An enhanced transcription factor repressilator that buffers stochasticity and entrains to an erratic external circadian signal. *Front. Syst. Biol.* **2023**, *3*, 1276734. [CrossRef]
19. Maliyoni, M.; Gaff, H.D.; Govinder, K.S.; Chirove, F. Multipatch stochastic epidemic model for the dynamics of a tick-borne disease. *Front. Appl. Math. Stat.* **2023**, *9*, 1122410. [CrossRef]
20. Mortoja, S.G.; Paul, A.; Panja, P.; Bhattacharya, S.; Mondal, S.K. Role Reversals in a Tri-Trophic Prey–Predator Interaction System: A Model-Based Study Using Deterministic and Stochastic Approaches. *Math. Comput. Appl.* **2024**, *29*, 3. [CrossRef]
21. Leander, J.; Lundh, T.; Jirstrand, M. Stochastic differential equations as a tool to regularize the parameter estimation problem for continuous time dynamical systems given discrete time measurements. *Math. Biosci.* **2014**, *251*, 54–62. [CrossRef] [PubMed]
22. Guo, W.; Ma, S.; Teng, L.; Liao, X.; Pei, N.; Chen, X. Stochastic differential equation modeling of time-series mining induced ground subsidence. *Front. Earth Sci.* **2023**, *10*, 1026895. [CrossRef]
23. Ito, K. On Stochastic Differential Equations. *Mem. Amer. Math. Soc.* **1951**, *4*, 1–51. [CrossRef]
24. Krikštolaitis, R.; Mozgeris, G.; Petrauskas, E.; Rupšys, P. A Statistical Dependence Framework Based on a Multivariate Normal Copula Function and Stochastic Differential Equations for Multivariate Data in Forestry. *Axioms* **2023**, *12*, 457. [CrossRef]
25. Ditlevsen, S.; Samson, A. Introduction to Stochastic Models in Biology. In *Stochastic Biomathematical Models*; Lecture Notes in Mathematics; Springer: Berlin/Heidelberg, Germany, 2013; Volume 2058.
26. Pouta, P.; Kulha, N.; Kuuluvainen, T.; Aakala, T. Partitioning of Space Among Trees in an Old-Growth Spruce Forest in Subarctic Fennoscandia. *Front. For. Glob. Change* **2022**, *5*, 817248. [CrossRef]
27. Rupšys, P.; Narmontas, M.; Petrauskas, E. A Multivariate Hybrid Stochastic Differential Equation Model for Whole-Stand Dynamics. *Mathematics* **2020**, *8*, 2230. [CrossRef]
28. Seo, Y.; Lee, D.; Choi, J. Developing and Comparing Individual Tree Growth Models of Major Coniferous Species in South Korea Based on Stem Analysis Data. *Forests* **2023**, *14*, 115. [CrossRef]
29. Güner, Ş.T.; Diamantopoulou, M.J.; Özçelik, R. Diameter distributions in Pinus sylvestris L. stands: Evaluating modelling approaches including a machine learning technique. *J. Forestry Res.* **2023**, *34*, 1829–1842. [CrossRef]
30. Räty, J.; Hietala, A.M.; Breidenbach, J.; Astrup, R. An analysis of stand-level size distributions of decay-affected Norway spruce trees based on harvester data. *Ann. For. Sci.* **2023**, *80*, 2. [CrossRef]

31. Fu, Y.; He, H.S.; Wang, S.; Wang, L. Combining Weibull distribution and k-nearest neighbor imputation method to predict wall-to-wall tree lists for the entire forest region of Northeast China. *Ann. For. Sci.* **2022**, *79*, 42. [CrossRef]
32. Sa, Q.; Jin, X.; Pukkala, T.; Li, F. Developing Weibull-based diameter distributions for the major coniferous species in Hei-longjiang Province, China. *J. Forestry Res.* **2023**, *34*, 1803–1815. [CrossRef]
33. Øksendal, B.K. An Introduction with Applications. In *Stochastic Differential Equations*; Springer: Berlin/Heidelberg, Germany, 2023.
34. Sklar, M. Fonctions de repartition an dimensions et leurs marges. *Publ. Inst. Statist. Univ. Paris* **1959**, *8*, 229–231.
35. Rupšys, P.; Mozgeris, G.; Petrauskas, E.; Krikštolaitis, R. A Framework for Analyzing Individual-Tree and Whole-Stand Growth by Fusing Multilevel Data: Stochastic Differential Equation and Copula Network. *Forests* **2023**, *14*, 2037. [CrossRef]
36. Ciceu, A.; Chakraborty, D.; Ledermann, T. Examining the transferability of height–diameter model calibration strategies across studies. *Forestry* **2023**, *2023*, cpad063. [CrossRef]
37. Rupšys, P.; Petrauskas, E. On the Construction of Growth Models via Symmetric Copulas and Stochastic Differential Equations. *Symmetry* **2022**, *14*, 2127. [CrossRef]
38. Efron, B.; Hinkley, D.V. Assessing the accuracy of the maximum likelihood estimator: Observed versus expected Fisher Information. *Biometrika* **1978**, *65*, 457–487. [CrossRef]
39. Reineke, L.H. Perfecting a stand-density index for even-aged forests. *J. Agric. Res.* **1933**, *46*, 627–630.
40. Neumann, M.; Adams, M.A.; Lewis, T. Native Forests Show Resilience to Selective Timber Harvesting in Southeast Queens-land, Australia. *Front. For. Glob. Change* **2021**, *4*, 750350. [CrossRef]
41. Tian, D.; Bi, H.; Jin, X.; Li, F. Stochastic frontiers or regression quantiles for estimating the self-thinning surface in higher di-mensions? *J. Forestry Res.* **2021**, *32*, 1515–1533. [CrossRef]
42. Mrad, A.; Manzoni, S.; Oren, R.; Vico, G.; Lindh, M.; Katul, G. Recovering the Metabolic, Self-Thinning, and Constant Final Yield Rules in Mono-Specific Stands. *Front. For. Glob. Change* **2020**, *3*, 62. [CrossRef]
43. McCune, B.; Cottam, G. The successional status of a southern Wisconsin oak woods. *Ecology* **1985**, *66*, 1270–1278. [CrossRef]
44. Sheil, D.; May, R.M. Mortality and recruitment rate evaluations in heterogeneous tropical forests. *J. Ecol.* **1996**, *84*, 91–100. [CrossRef]
45. Westoby, M. The Self-Thinning Rule. *Adv. Ecol. Res.* **1984**, *14*, 167–225.
46. Pavel, M.A.A.; Barreiro, S.; Tomé, M. The Importance of Using Permanent Plots Data to Fit the Self-Thinning Line: An Example for Maritime Pine Stands in Portugal. *Forests* **2023**, *14*, 1354. [CrossRef]
47. Gavrikov, V.L. A simple theory to link bole surface area, stem density and average tree dimensions in a forest stand. *Eur. J. For. Res.* **2014**, *133*, 1087–1109. [CrossRef]

symmetry

MDPI

Article

Optimal Harvesting Strategies for Timber and Non-Timber Forest Products with Nonlinear Harvesting Terms

Yaning Zhang, Lina Hao and Shan Zhang *

School of Mathematics and Statistics, Changchun University of Technology, Changchun 130012, China; zhangyaningjob@163.com (Y.Z.); haolina@ccut.edu.cn (L.H.)
* Correspondence: zhangshan9039@126.com

Abstract: Forest resources are renewable, and the rational exploitation and utilization of forest resources are not only conducive to sustainable development on a population scale, they can also lead to higher economic benefits. Based on the actual timber harvest problem, this paper establishes the joint harvest model of timber and non-timber with nonlinear harvest items. In the numerical simulation, by comparing the existing proportional harvest model, it is concluded that the optimal harvest strategy of nonlinear harvest items in this paper can obtain larger ecological benefits and be more conducive to the sustainable development of a population. Firstly, using the qualitative theory of ordinary differential equations, the dynamic behavior of the model is studied, and the existence and stability of the equilibrium point of the model are proven. Secondly, the optimal control solution is obtained by using the optimal control theory. Finally, the optimal harvesting strategy of timber and non-timber products is given based on the numerical simulation results, and a comparison of the effects of different parameters on the optimal harvest strategy, which provides a certain theoretical basis for the sustainable development of the ecological economy of forestry, is carried out.

Keywords: biomathematics model; nonlinear harvest; optimal control; non-timber forest products; sustainable timber harvest

1. Introduction

Population dynamics is one of the branches of biomathematics, which focuses on the quantitative, spatial, and structural dynamics of populations, and can be used to describe the dynamic relationships between populations and their environment and between populations and other populations, as well as to explain, predict, regulate, and control the developmental processes and trends of species [1]. The updating and development of biological population dynamics models have effectively contributed to human knowledge of biological systems. At present, many scholars have established mathematical models to judge and predict the stable development of populations, such as forestry, agriculture, fisheries, the integrated control and management of pests, etc., which have given us practical production knowledge [2–4].

Symmetry in mathematics and its applications are very broad fields. Geometric symmetry plays an important role in design, architecture, and mathematical proofing. Algebraic symmetry helps us better understand and solve a wide range of equations and algebraic problems. In this paper, some concepts of symmetry are referred to, and related journal articles solve some problems in the processing of differential equations [5].

The problem of the optimal control of ecosystems has been one of the hot issues studied by scholars. The maximum sustainable yield policy obtained by studying the optimal harvesting of biological populations is an important ecological management tool to protect the survival of populations and to maximize economic benefits [6,7]. Faustmann's formula is a method used in forest economics to determine the optimal rotation age for a forest stand. While Faustmann's formula is a powerful tool in forest economics, it has limitations. One of the main challenges is accurately predicting future timber prices, costs, and growth rates over long periods, which can be highly uncertain [8]. The use of linear planning methods can use land, forest resources, equipment, labor, capital, etc., effectively, which is achieved by integrating numerous production and operational activities and related complex factors and various needs into the model integration, and these methods can accurately reflect the vertical and horizontal connection between the input and output of various activities in the process of change. This is difficult to achieve by other conventional methods, as it can not only reflect and feedback adjustment after a limited selection, so that the selected decision to complete is very convenient. Now, in the enterprise management of forestry production, many practical problems can be used in linear planning for optimal management [9,10].

Forests are important natural resources, which not only provide the necessary economic support for human production and life but also play a role in regulating the climate, water conservation, air purification, and biodiversity conservation [11,12]. In recent years, the increasing demand of the timber market and the intensification of commercial exploitation have led to the over-harvesting of forest resources, and the balance of timber and forest product supply has been greatly damaged. In order to ensure the sustainable development of forest resources, a series of logging policies have been established in various regions, and it is therefore necessary to develop reasonable timber harvesting strategies to obtain higher ecological benefits. However, because of such restrictions, it may not be economically viable to provide sufficient income for local residents and timber harvesters. Non-timber products such as fruits, seeds, leaves, bark, gum, etc., can also generate significant economic and ecological benefits and can even generate more economic income than timber harvesting or agricultural production. Therefore, the study of the ecological impacts of the utilization of non-timber forest products is also very important for the sustainable use of forest resources and biodiversity conservation [13,14]. Most previous studies have been devoted to timber harvesting, while non-timber harvesting has been studied less frequently and in a discontinuous manner. For example, in 2011, Isabel B et al. [15] modeled the ecological impacts of harvesting non-timber products using stage structure matrix models based on projection matrices. Although these models can quantify the effects of different life stages on plant population dynamics, they do not explicitly represent harvest intensity, which poses a challenge to quantify the effects of the harvest intensity on each stage of transition. In addition, matrix models have more parameters than classical logistic growth models and may be difficult to relate to well-established harvesting theories based on logistic growth models.

In 2016, Gaoue et al. [16] developed a joint harvest model for timber and non-timber products based on a logistic timber growth equation with proportional harvest, which is the first continuous theoretical model for non-timber harvest. The model includes harvesting of timber and non-timber products and additional synergistic effects of harvesting on the growth rate of plant populations.

$$\begin{cases} \frac{dx}{dt} = rx(1 - \frac{x}{K}) - h_L x \\ \tau\frac{dr}{dt} = r_e - r - \alpha h_N - \beta h_L, \end{cases} \quad (1)$$

It is also shown that the sustainability of timber and non-timber harvests depends on the effect of harvesting on species' growth rates for each type of population, and that there are two states in this differential equation: x denotes the population density, r represents the endogenous growth rate of the plant, and r_e is the maximum growth rate in the absence of harvest. The population x has logistic growth, and K is the environmental holding capacity. h_L is the timber harvest intensity, h_N is the non-timber harvest intensity, τ is the average population longevity, α is the population decay rate due to non-timber harvest, and β is the population decay rate due to timber harvest.

The harvest term of the first differential equation in this model uses proportional harvesting, but in practical ecological problems, the human harvest does not increase infinitely with the increase in harvest effort and biological resources. Therefore, more and more scholars have started to study predation systems with nonlinear harvest rates [17–19].

Therefore, this paper investigates the problem of joint harvesting of timber and non-timber products with nonlinear harvest items based on the current exploitation status of the relevant background of timber and non-timber products in forests, so as to derive the optimal harvesting strategy that is conducive to the conservation and recovery of populations.

2. Model Building

Agnew [20] considered the competition between fishing boats as an example of fishery harvesting, and the nonlinear harvest term was improved by taking into account the competition among fishing boats and the processing time of the captured fishery, and for a specific model that conforms to the logistic growth law, a nonlinear harvest function term of the following form was given after a simplified analysis.

$$H(x,E) = \frac{xE}{1 + a_1 E + a_2 x}, \tag{1a}$$

where E is the harvesting effort of timber products, a_1 is used to measure the multiple user groups with competing interests, and a_2 represents the proportionality constant of the handling time.

The harvesting and processing of timber products is more complicated and requires more processing time, while generally, for timber, permits need to be established and there are fixed contractors, so there is not much competition. Therefore, in this paper, we only consider the timber handling time without considering the competition among multiple user groups with competing interests and simplify the nonlinear harvesting term as follows:

$$H(x,E) = \frac{E_1 x}{1 + ax}, \tag{1b}$$

where x denotes the population density, E_1 is the harvesting effort of timber products, which represents the amount of harvesting over time, and a is the handling time of timber products, such as the transit time, etc. Non-timber products are easier to handle and are represented in the model as proportional harvest, i.e., the amount of harvesting effort for non-timber products E_2.Therefore, we introduced the nonlinear harvesting function into the model established by Gaoue et al. and established a harvesting model for timber and non-timber products with a nonlinear harvesting function:

$$\begin{cases} \frac{dx}{dt} = rx(1 - \frac{x}{K}) - \frac{E_1 x}{1+ax}, \\ \tau\frac{dr}{dt} = r_e - r - \alpha E_2 - \beta\frac{E_1}{1+ax}. \end{cases} \tag{1c}$$

3. Qualitative Analysis

3.1. Existence of Equilibrium Point

Theorem 1. *Equation (1c) has a trivial equilibrium point* $x_0 = 0$*, and when the condition* $r_e > \alpha E_2 + (1+\beta)E_1$ *is satisfied, the equation has a unique positive equilibrium point* x^*.

Proof. Considering the harvest of timber and non-timber, the dynamics of the long-term range is in quasi-steady state; therefore,

$$r = r_e - \alpha E_2 - \beta\frac{E_1}{1 + ax}, \tag{2a}$$

We use this to reduce Equation (2) into the following single equation:

$$\frac{dx}{dt} = (r_e - \alpha E_2 - \beta \frac{E_1}{1+ax})x(1-\frac{x}{K}) - \frac{E_1 x}{1+ax}. \tag{2b}$$

By discussing Equation (3), we have:

(1) The equation always has a trivial equilibrium point $x_0 = 0$.
(2) Otherwise, there is

$$(r_e - \alpha E_2 - \beta \frac{E_1}{1+ax})(1-\frac{x}{K}) - \frac{E_1}{1+ax} = 0, \tag{2c}$$

From the basic theoretical knowledge of quadratic equations with one variable, the discriminant of the root is

$$\Delta = ((ka-1)(r_e - \alpha E_2) + \beta E_1)^2 + 4ka(r_e - \alpha E_2)(r_e - \alpha E_2 - (1+\beta)E_1) \tag{2d}$$

□

If $\Delta > 0$, the equation has two unequal real roots, and we know that $r_e > \alpha E_2 + (1+\beta)E_1$.

Because the quadratic coefficients of the equation $-a(r_e - \alpha E_2) < 0$, the parabola opens down.

When $r_e > \alpha E_2 + (1+\beta)E_1$,

according to Veda's theorem, $\frac{k(r_e - \alpha E_2 - (1+\beta)E_1}{-a(r_e - \alpha E_2)} < 0$. The equation has two different roots, in which case Equation (3) has a unique positive equilibrium point; thus,

$$\begin{aligned} x^* &= \frac{\sqrt{((ka-1)(r_e-\alpha E_2)+\beta E_1)^2 + 4ka(r_e-\alpha E_2)(r_e-\alpha E_2-(1+\beta)E_1)}}{2a(r_e-\alpha E_2)} \\ &+ \frac{((ka-1)(r_e-\alpha E_2)+\beta E_1)}{2a(r_e-\alpha E_2)}. \end{aligned} \tag{2e}$$

3.2. Stability of Equilibrium Point

Theorem 2. *Equation (1c) has a locally asymptotically stable equilibrium point x_0 if $r_e < \alpha E_2 + (1+\beta)E_1$; Equation (1c) has a unique locally asymptotically stable positive equilibrium point x^* if $r_e > \alpha E_2 + (1+\beta)E_1$ is satisfied.*

Proof. (1) The Jacobian matrix at equilibrium x_0 is given by

$$J(x) = [r_e - \alpha E_2 - (1+\beta)E_1], \tag{2f}$$

and it can be obtained that the eigenvalues

$$\lambda = r_e - \alpha E_2 - (1+\beta)E_1 \tag{2g}$$

Thus, where $r_e < \alpha E_2 + (1+\beta)E_1$, the equilibrium is locally asymptotically stable.

The Jacobian matrix x^* at the equilibrium is given by

$$J(x^*) = \left[\frac{x^*}{K}(\frac{KaE_1(1+\beta) + \beta E_1}{(1+ax)^2} + \alpha E_2 - r_e)\right], \tag{2h}$$

and the eigenvalues is

$$\lambda = \frac{x^*}{K}(\frac{KaE_1(1+\beta) + \beta E_1}{(1+ax)^2} + \alpha E_2 - r_e) \tag{2i}$$

where $\frac{x^*}{K} > 0$. We can obtain that

$$r_e > \frac{KaE_1(1+\beta)+\beta E_1}{(1+ax^*)^2} + \alpha E_2, \tag{2j}$$

and the condition can be strengthened by taking the maximum value at $x = 0$,

$$r_e > KaE_1(1+\beta) + \beta E_1 + \alpha E_2 \tag{2k}$$

□

When discussing the existence of the solution, there is a unique positive equilibrium point x^* of the equation if $r_e > \alpha E_2 + (1+\beta)E_1$. At this time, if the positive equilibrium is stable, the condition $r_e > KaE_1(1+\beta) + \beta E_1 + \alpha E_2$ will also be satisfied, and the above analysis holds.

In summary, when the condition $r_e < \alpha E_2 + (1+\beta)E_1$ is satisfied, Equation (1c) has a locally asymptotically stable trivial equilibrium point x_0. Harvesting timber and non-timber in this case leads to a high decay rate of the plant population, which will eventually lead to extinction if the plant population keeps growing at such a growth rate; when condition $r_e > \alpha E_2 + (1+\beta)E_1$ is satisfied, the equation has a unique positive equilibrium point x^*, and x^* is locally asymptotically stable. The plant growth rate is sustainable when combined timber and non-timber harvesting is carried out in this case.

4. Optimal Harvesting Strategy

In this section, we consider the issue of harvesting timber and non-timber products. The economic revenue benefits are maximized while minimizing the harvesting costs of timber and non-timber products, while ensuring the sustainability of system populations. Economic benefits are considered in the objective generalization to establish the optimal control problem.

$$\begin{aligned}\max_{E_1,E_2\in U} J(E_1,E_2) = \; & A_T x(t) + \int_0^T e^{-\delta t}\Big(Ax(t) + B_1\frac{E_1(t)}{1+ax(t)}x(t) \\ & + B_2E_2(t)x(t) - C_1\Big(\frac{E_1(t)}{1+ax(t)}\Big)^2 - C_2E_2^2(t)\Big)dt\end{aligned}$$

$$\text{s.t.}\begin{cases}\dfrac{dx(t)}{dt} = r(t)x(t)\Big(1-\dfrac{x(t)}{K}\Big) - \dfrac{E_1(t)}{1+ax(t)}x(t). \\ \tau\dfrac{dr(t)}{dt} = r_e - r(t) - \alpha\dfrac{E_1(t)}{1+ax(t)} - \beta E_2(t). \\ 0 \le E_1(t) \le 0.7, 0 \le E_2(t) \le 1,\end{cases} \tag{3a}$$

where J is the objective function of the optimal control problem, and it is desired to find an optimal control pair (E_1^*, E_2^*) so that the objective function is maximized. In addition, the coefficient B_1, B_2 denotes the price of the two types of harvesting, and $B_1\frac{E_1(t)x(t)}{1+ax(t)} + B_2E_2(t)x(t)$ is the corresponding income; $e^{-\delta t}$ denotes the discount term, and a basic problem in the development of renewable resources is to determine the optimal balance between the current harvest and the future harvest. From the perspective of economics, a "time discount" can be used to solve the problem of inter-period economic benefits. Existing studies also show that the change in discount rate will affect the optimal solution of the harvest [21]; $C_1\big(\frac{E_1(t)}{1+ax(t)}\big)^2 + C_2E_2^2(t)$ is the cost term, and in reference [15], Gaoue et al. used the nonlinear cost term of harvesting and the quadratic form of control. In order to facilitate the comparison of the difference between the harvesting strategies corresponding to nonlinear harvesting and proportional harvesting, the quadratic form of control is also used for the cost term in this paper.

The weighting factor A balances the importance of stock conservation, and $A_T x(t)$ indicates the conservation value of the stock at the end of the harvest. The total economic return is

$$\max_{E_1,E_2 \in U} P(E_1,E_2) = \int_0^T e^{-\delta t}(B_1 \frac{E_1(t)}{1+ax(t)} x(t) + B_2 E_2(t)x(t) - C_1(\frac{E_1(t)}{1+ax(t)})^2 - C_2 E_2^2(t))dt, \tag{3b}$$

The control set of the Lebesque measurable function boundary of the equation is

$$u = \left\{(E_1,E_2) \in (L^\infty(0,T))^2 : 0 \le E_1 \le M_1, 0 \le E_2 \le M_2, 0 \le t \le T\right\}, \tag{3c}$$

where M_1, M_2 is an upper bound on the control, for which the control set and the target generalization have appropriate tightness and convexity assumptions to guarantee the existence of optimal control pairs and corresponding states. The Hamiltonian function constructed here is

$$\begin{aligned} H = \; & \int_0^T e^{-\delta t}(Ax(t) + B_1(t)\frac{E_1(t)x(t)}{1+ax(t)} + B_2 E_2(t)x(t) - C_1(\frac{E_1(t)}{1+ax(t)})^2 - C_2 E_2^2(t)) \\ & + \lambda_x(r(t)x(t)(1-\frac{x}{K}) - \frac{E_1(t)}{1+ax(t)}) + \frac{\lambda_r}{\tau}(r_e - r(t) - (\alpha E_2(t) + \beta \frac{E_1(t)}{1+ax(t)})dt. \end{aligned} \tag{3d}$$

The concomitant function is derived from Pontryagin's principle of maximum value as

$$\begin{aligned} \lambda'_x = -\frac{\partial H}{\partial x} & = -e^{-\delta t}(A + \frac{B_1 E_1(t)}{(1+ax(t))^2} + B_2 E_2(t) + \frac{2aC_1 E_1(t)}{(1+ax(t))^3}) \\ & -\lambda_x(r(t) - \frac{2x(t)r(t)}{K} - \frac{E_1}{(1+ax(t))^2}) + \frac{\lambda_r \beta E_1(t) a}{\tau(1+ax(t))^2}, \\ \lambda'_r = -\frac{\partial H}{\partial r} & = -\lambda_x x(t)(1-\frac{x(t)}{K}) + \frac{\lambda_r}{\tau}. \end{aligned} \tag{3e}$$

The transversality conditions are

$$\lambda_x(T) = A_T, \lambda_r(T) = 0. \tag{3f}$$

Also, from $\frac{\partial H_2}{\partial E_1} = 0$, $\frac{\partial H_2}{\partial E_2} = 0$, it can be derived that

$$\begin{cases} e^{-\delta t}(\frac{B_1 x(t)}{1+ax(t)} - \frac{2C_1 E_1(t)}{1+ax(t)}) - \frac{\lambda_x x(t)}{1+ax(t)} + \frac{\lambda_r \beta}{\tau(1+ax(t))} = 0, \\ e^{-\delta t}(B_2 x(t) - 2C_2 E_2(t) - \frac{\lambda_r \alpha}{\tau} = 0. \end{cases} \tag{3g}$$

We have the following:

$$\begin{cases} E_1^* = \frac{B_1 x(t)(1+ax(t) - e^{\delta t}(1+ax(t)(\lambda_x x(t) - \lambda_r \beta)}{2C_1}, \\ E_2^* = \frac{B_2 x(t) - \alpha \frac{\lambda_r}{\tau} e^{\delta t}}{2C_2}. \end{cases} \tag{3h}$$

For the timber harvesting problem with a nonlinear harvesting term, the objective function can be maximized when the optimal control pair (E_1^*, E_2^*) takes the value of J, so that the economic and ecological benefits are optimized.

5. Numerical Simulation

In this section, the optimal harvesting strategy is simulated numerically, and the numerical results of the optimal harvesting strategy with a nonlinear harvesting term are compared with proportional harvesting, and parameter sensitivity analysis is performed. The values of the parameters are shown in Table 1.

Table 1. Notation for the model and optimal control and value.

	Values	Definition	References
x_0	80	Initial population density at $t = 0$(each−1)	[22]
K	100	Carrying capacity for the plant (each−1)	[22]
r_e	0.03, 0.25	Maximum growth rate without harvest (years−1)	[23,24]
τ	1, 5, 10, 20	Average lifespan of the plant in years (years−1)	Estimated
α	0.4	Growth decay rate for non-timber harvest	[25]
β	0.23	Growth decay rate due to timber harvest	[26]
A	0, 0.1	Weight for the value of conservation	[22]
A_T	0, 0.1	Weight for the value of conservation at the end of harvest	[22]
δ	0.05	Discount rate	[22]
B_1	0.3	Benefit from timber harvest (1 × 10−2 dollar)	[22]
B_2	0.15	Benefit from non-timber harvest (1 × 10−2 dollar)	[22]
C_1	15	Cost coefficient of timber harvesting (dollar−1)	[22]
C_2	15	Cost coefficient of non-timber harvest (dollar−1)	[22]
a	0.01, 0.1	processing time for timber harvesting (year−1)	Estimated
M_1	0.7	Upper bound for timber harvest rate	[22]
M_2	1	Upper bound for non-timber harvest rate	[22]

5.1. The Effect of Proportional Harvesting and Nonlinear Harvesting on the Optimal Harvesting Strategy

1. Some parameters of proportional harvesting and nonlinear harvesting are taken as $T = 5, \tau = 5, r_e = 0.25, a = 0.1, A = 0.1, A_T = 0.1, \delta = 0.05$. See Table 1 for other parameters.

In the actual harvest problem, there are many influencing factors, and it cannot be a simple linear harvest, so this paper adopts the nonlinear harvest to build the model and uses the optimal control theory to study the optimal capture problem. Figure 1 shows the harvesting strategy with proportional harvesting, and it can be seen that the timber harvesting starts around the fourth year after the non-timber harvesting starts, and at the end of harvesting, the timber population decreases by about 10%, and the objective function of the optimal control problem has a maximum value of $J_{\max} = 60.779, p_{\max} = 19.783$. Figure 2 shows the nonlinear harvesting strategy, and it can be seen that when nonlinear harvesting is used, the timber harvesting starts around year 3.7, and at the end of harvesting, the population size is the maximum value of the objective function of the optimal control problem is $J_{\max} = 60.2475, p_{\max} = 16.8275$. Compared with proportional harvesting, the economic benefit is reduced by 14.87%, but the economic benefit plus ecological benefit is only reduced by 0.8%. This shows that compared with the existing results of proportional harvest, the nonlinear harvest method has greatly improved the ecological benefits, which is more conducive to the recovery of the population.

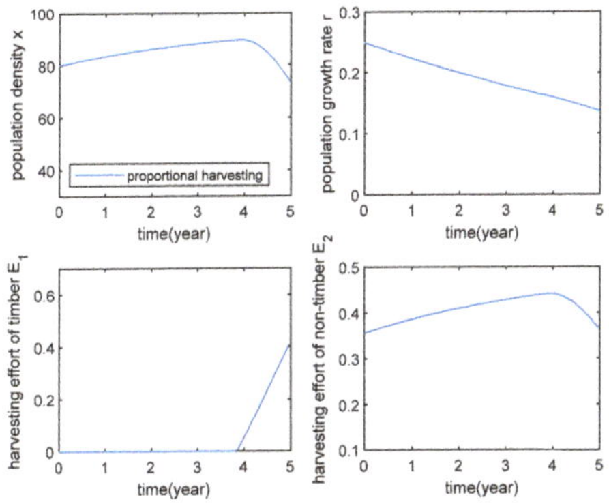

Figure 1. Optimal solution with proportional harvesting.

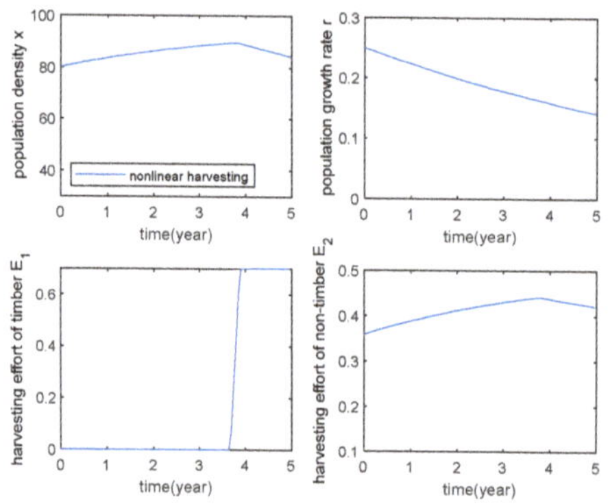

Figure 2. Optimal solution with nonlinear harvesting.

5.2. *Sensitivity Analysis of Parameters*

Sensitivity analysis is a test of the sensitivity to changes in the parameters of the model results and can help evaluate the stability and reliability of the model. In this section, the sensitivity of the objective function with respect to each parameter is calculated using the partial rank correlation coefficient (PRCC) method for the optimal control problem.

Figure 3 shows the parameter sensitivity analysis of J, and it can be seen that the importance of population conservation at the end of harvest A_T has a greater impact on the objective function; at the same time, the timber treatment time a also has an impact on the objective function, indicating that it is necessary for us to consider the timber treatment time; the price and cost of non-timber B_2, C_2 also have a greater impact on the sensitivity of J, so a combined harvest of timber and non−timber can yield increased benefits.

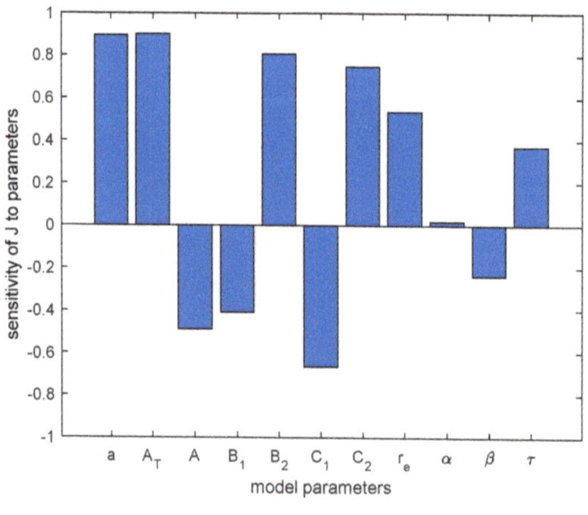

Figure 3. Sensitivity analysis of the objective value J.

5.3. *Effect of Different Parameters on the Optimal Harvesting Strategy*

Based on the conclusion in Section 5.2., this section specifically examines the effects of the timber treatment time a, population growth rate r_e, species lifespan τ, importance of species conservation during harvest A, and species conservation at the end of harvest A_T, which affects the optimal harvesting strategy. The price of timber B_1, the cost of timber harvesting C_1, the price of non-timber B_2, and the cost of non-timber harvesting C_2 are influenced by the market and are not specifically analyzed here.

1. To determine the effect of the timber processing time on the optimal control strategy, some parameters are taken as $T = 5, \tau = 5, r_e = 0.25, A = 0.1, A_T = 0.1$. See Table 1 for other parameters.

The objective functions of the optimal harvesting strategies for different timber treatment times are $J_{\max} = 60.2475, p_{\max} = 16.8275$ $J_{\max} = 60.6665, p_{\max} = 19.7374$ As shown in Figure 4 when the nonlinear harvest is used, the lower the processing time for the timber is, the higher the economic benefit is, the lower the ecological benefit is, and the smaller the population is. Therefore, if you want to harvest with high economic benefits, try to choose species with short processing times, and if you want to have high ecological benefits, try to choose species with long processing times.

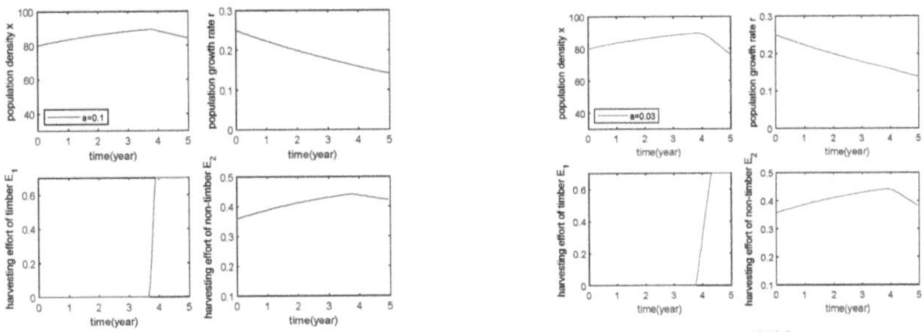

(a) a=0.1 (b) a=0.03.

Figure 4. Effect of optimal harvest for different timber treatment times.

2. To determine the effect of the plant growth rate on the optimal control strategy, some parameters are taken as $T = 5, \tau = 20, a = 0.1, A = 0.1, A_T = 0.1$. See Table 1 for other parameters.

The objective functions for slow-growing and fast-growing trees are as follows: $J_{\max} = 54.9543, p_{\max} = 14.8346$, $J_{\max} = 60.918 p_{\max} = 17.1486$. As shown in Figure 5 the plants with a fast growth rate can obtain more economic and ecological benefits. Slow-growing plants can start harvesting timber earlier and do not reduce the biological population, or they decrease less, while enabling harvesting of more non−timber products. Therefore, selecting species with fast plant growth as far as possible can obtain higher economic and ecological benefits.

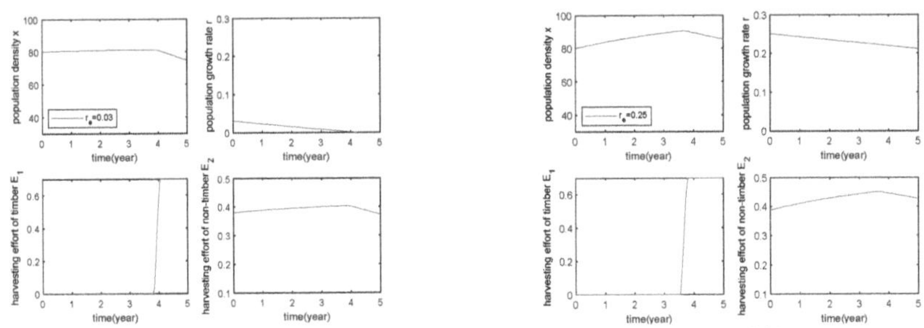

(a) $r_e = 0.03$ (b) $r_e = 0.25$

Figure 5. Effect of optimal harvest for fast-growing species and slow-growing species.

3. To determine the effect of different species' lifespan on the optimal control strategy, some parameters are taken as $T = 5, r_e = 0.25, a = 0.1, A = 0.1, A_T = 0.1$. See Table 1 for other parameters.

The species objective function for the short and long harvest lifespans are $J_{\max} = 60.2457, p_{\max} = 16.8275$; $J_{\max} = 60.9181, p_{\max} = 17.1486$; at the same time, it can be analyzed through Figure 6 the length of life has little effect on the optimal harvest strategy. Species with different lifespans also approximate populations at the end of the harvest. However, the population growth rate at the last moment of harvest is much lower than the long-lifespan species, indicating that timber harvest has a greater impact on short-lived timber.

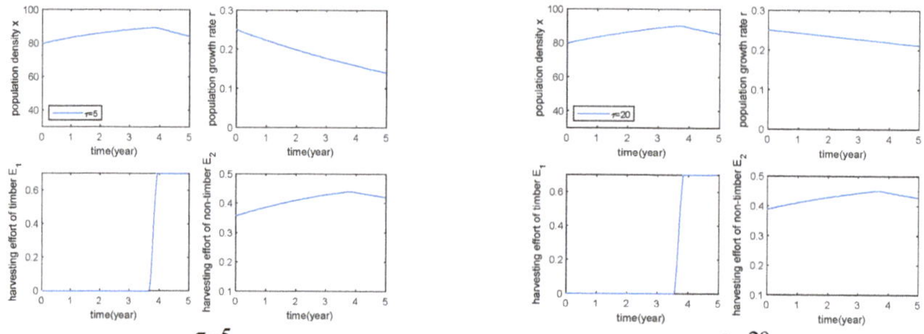

(a) τ=5 (b) τ=20

Figure 6. Effect of optimal harvest for short- and long-lived species.

4. To determine the importance of species conservation and the influence of the importance of species conservation at the end of harvest on the optimal control strategy, some parameters are taken as $T = 5, \tau = 5, r_e = 0.25, a = 0.01$. See Table 1 for other parameters.

By comparing (b) with (c) in Figure 7, it is concluded that species with lower importance for species conservation are harvested from the beginning and maintain the harvest behavior until the end of the harvest, when the population decreases more. By comparing (c) with (d), it can be concluded that species with higher conservation importance begin wood harvesting several years later, and that fewer populations decrease at the end of the harvest. Therefore, species with low conservation importance impact the harvest.

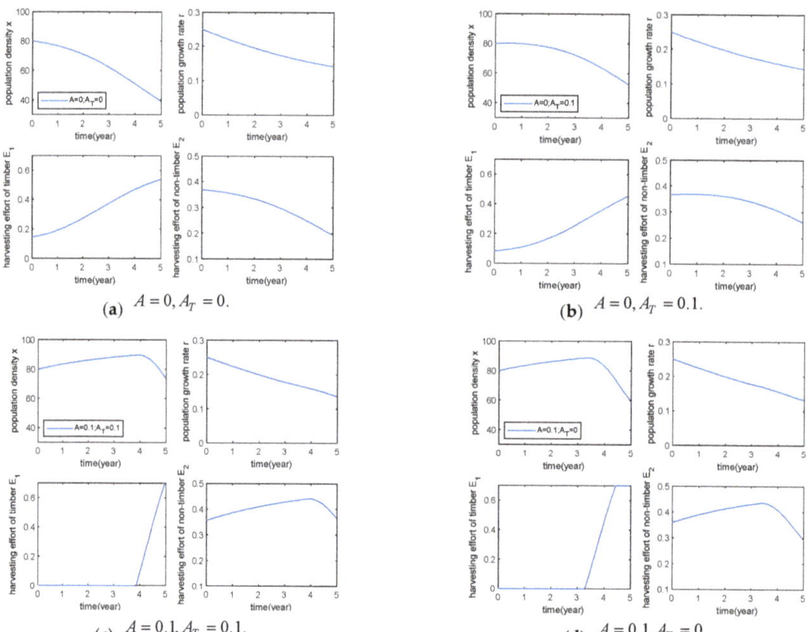

(a) $A = 0, A_T = 0.$ (b) $A = 0, A_T = 0.1.$ (c) $A = 0.1, A_T = 0.1.$ (d) $A = 0.1, A_T = 0.$

Figure 7. Effect of optimal harvest for conservation weight coefficient A and conservation weight coefficient at the end of the harvest A_T.

6. Conclusions

Most of the current harvest studies are based on proportional harvesting. In this paper, we assess timber and non−timber products in nonlinear harvest projects and present the optimal harvest strategy. Compared with the existing proportional harvest study results, the optimal harvest strategy given under this nonlinear harvest model can lead to higher ecological benefits and be more conducive to the sustainable development of the population. The combination of the nonlinear cutting period of timber and the nonlinear cutting strategy can ensure higher ecological benefits. The numerical simulation results provide theoretical suggestions for the harvest strategy and provide a theoretical basis for the sustainable development of forestry's ecological economy.

We studied the dynamic behavior of the model. It was concluded that when combined harvesting was carried out, there was a unique locally asymptotically stable positive equilibrium point in Equation (1c) when the condition $r_e > \alpha E_2 + (1+\beta)E_1$ was satisfied, and the plant growth rate was sustainable at that time for both timber and non−timber harvesting. When $r_e < \alpha E_2 + (1+\beta)E_1$, there was only one trivial equilibrium point in Equation (1c), and harvesting timber and non−timber resulted in a large decay rate of the plant population, which eventually led to extinction if the plant population kept growing at such a growth rate.

For the optimal control problem of combined timber and non−timber harvesting with nonlinear harvesting, expression (3h) of the optimal control strategy was obtained using the Hamilitonian function and Pontryagin's optimality principle, and numerical simulations were carried out using MATLAB. Compared with the existing proportional harvest results, the optimal harvesting strategy with a nonlinear harvesting term can lead to higher ecological benefits and more sustainable development of the population.

Through the parameter sensitivity analysis, it is concluded that the price and cost of timber and non−timber, B_2 and C_2, have a great impact on the harvest benefit, so more economic and ecological benefits can be obtained from the combined harvest of timber and non−timber. Considering the specific effects of parameters on the harvest strategy, the analysis concluded that higher economic and ecological benefits can be obtained for species with fast growth rates and low importance to species conservation. However, the timber's livespan τ had little effect on the optimal harvesting strategy. The numerical simulation provided theoretical suggestions for the harvest strategy.

Author Contributions: Conceptualization L.H. and S.Z.; writing—original draft preparation Y.Z., L.H. and S.Z.; Conceptualization, L.H., S.Z. and Y.Z.: software, Y.Z.; data curation, Y.Z. validation L.H., S.Z. and Y.Z. All authors have read and agreed to the published version of the manuscript.

Funding: This work was supported by the National Natural Science Foundation of China (Program No. 11126239, No.11301036, No. 1140011471) and by Jilin provincial education department "13th Five-Year planning" (No. JJKH20200645KJ, No. JJKH20220662KJ).

Data Availability Statement: The data used to support the findings of this study are available from the corresponding author upon request.

Conflicts of Interest: The authors have no relevant financial or non−financial interests to disclose.

References

1. Liu, X.X. *Dynamics Analysis and Harvesting Strategy of Predation System*; Jilin University: Changchun, China, 2019.
2. Chen, X.F. Harvesting of a Prey-predator fisher based on leslie-gaower model. *J. Math. Study* **2010**, *3*, 256–263.
3. Cheng, H.D.; Yin, Z.Y.; Liu, H.X. Analysis of the dynamic of stage-structured pest control model. *Math. Appl.* **2012**, *25*, 816–823.
4. Sudhakar, Y.; Vivek, K. A prey-predator model and control of a nematodes pest using control in banana: Mathematical modeling and qualitative analysis. *Int. J. Biomath.* **2022**, *15*, 2150089.
5. Argyros, I.K.; Shakhno, S.; Regmi, S.; Yarmola, H.; Argyros, M.I. Symmetric-Type Multi-Step Difference Methods for Solving Nonlinear Equations. *Symmetry.* **2024**, *16*, 330. [CrossRef]
6. Lv, Y.; Yuan, R.; Pei, Y. Dynamics in two nonsmooth predator-prey models with threshold Harvesting. *Nonlinear Dyn.* **2013**, *74*, 107–132. [CrossRef]

7. Mesterton-Gibbons, M. On the optimal policy for combining harvesting of predator and prey. *Nat. Resour. Model.* **1988**, *3*, 63–90. [CrossRef]
8. Ding, W.L.; Jiang, S.S.; Liu, C.H.; Kang, H.L.; Deng, X.W.; Ding, S.L.; Xiao, Y.S.; Wen, X.D. Determination of the optimum rotation period of Chenshan red-heart Chinese fir plantation. *For. Sci. South. China* **2023**, *51*, 34–40.
9. Ni, J.F. The application of linear programming in forestry production. *Anhui For.* **2004**, *4*, 25.
10. Liu, X.Y. On the application of linear planning in forestry projects. *Hebei For. Sci. Technol.* **2016**, *5*, 84–85.
11. Lu, A.J. Research on forest pest control in forest protection. *New Farmers* **2024**, *8*, 84–86.
12. Zhao, G. Sustainable development strategy of forest resources based on forest resource management. *New Farmers* **2024**, *7*, 64–66.
13. Yang, J.; Luan, X.F. Ecological impacts of non−timber forest product use. *Chin. J. Appl. Ecol.* **2011**, *22*, 800–809.
14. Zhang, X.Y.; Xu, D.Y.; Wu, Y.H. Research on Value chain Model Construction and Brand value-added of Forest products. *Chin. Bus. Theory.* **2020**, *2*, 59–60+63. [CrossRef]
15. Schmidt, I.B.; Mandle, L.; Ticktin, T.; Gaoue, O.G. What do matrix population model sreveal about the sustainability of non−timber forest product harvest? *J. Appl. Ecol.* **2011**, *48*, 815–826. [CrossRef]
16. Gaoue, O.G.; Ngonghala, C.N.; Jiang, J.; Lelu, M. Towards a mechanistic understanding of the synergistic effects of harvesting timber and non−timber forest products. *Methods Ecol. Evol.* **2016**, *7*, 398–406. [CrossRef]
17. Yu, X.; Chen, F.; Lai, L. Dynamic behaviors of may type cooperative system with Michaelis-menten type harvesting. *Ann. Appl. Math.* **2019**, *35*, 374–391.
18. Heggerud, C.M.; Lan, K.Q. Local stability analysis of ratio-dependent predator–prey models with predator harvesting rates. *Appl. Math. Comput.* **2015**, *270*, 349–357. [CrossRef]
19. Zhang, D.; Sun, G.; Xu, M.; Chen, J.; Zhou, W. Spatial Dynamic Predator-Prey System with Time Delay and Nonlinear Harvesting Effect. *J. Jilin Univ.* **2018**, *56*, 515–522.
20. Agnew, T.T. Optimal exploitation of a fishery employ inganon−linear harvesting function. *Ecol. Model.* **1979**, *6*, 47–57. [CrossRef]
21. Preisler, H.; Ager, A.; Hayes, J.L. Probabilistic risk models for multipl disturbances: An example of forest insects and wildfires. *Gen. Tech. Rep. Pac. Northwest Res. Stn.* **2010**, *802*, 371–379.
22. Gaoue, O.G.; Jiang, J.; Ding, W.; Agusto, F.B.; Lenhart, S. Optimal harvesting strategies for timber and non−timber forest products in tropical ecosystems. *Theor. Ecol.* **2016**, *9*, 287–297. [CrossRef]
23. Armsworth, P.R.; Block, B.A.; Eagle, J.; Roughgarden, J.E. The role of discounting and dynamics in determining the economic efficiency of time-area closures for managing fishery bycatch. *Theor. Ecol.* **2011**, *4*, 513–526. [CrossRef]
24. Ticktin, T.; Nantel, P.; Ramirez, F.; Johns, T. Effects of variation on harvest limits for nontimber forest species in Mexico. *Conserv. Biol.* **2002**, *16*, 691–705. [CrossRef]
25. Gaoue, O.G.; Ticktin, T. Fulani knowledge of the ecological impacts of Khaya senegalensis (Meliaceae) foliage harvest in Benin and its implications for sustainable harvest. *Econ. Bot.* **2009**, *63*, 256–270. [CrossRef]
26. Lande, R.; Engen, S.; Saether, B.E. Optimal harvesting, economic discounting and extinction risk in fluctuating populations. *Nature* **1994**, *372*, 88–90. [CrossRef]

symmetry

MDPI

Article

Bogdanov–Takens Bifurcation of Kermack–McKendrick Model with Nonlinear Contact Rates Caused by Multiple Exposures

Jun Li [1,*] and Mingju Ma [2,*]

1 School of Mathmatics and Statistics, Xidian University, Xi'an 710071, China
2 School of Science, Xi'an Polytechnic University, Xi'an 710048, China
* Correspondence: lijun@xidian.edu.cn (J.L.); mingjuma@163.com (M.M.)

Abstract: In this paper, we consider the influence of a nonlinear contact rate caused by multiple contacts in classical SIR model. In this paper, we unversal unfolding a nilpotent cusp singularity in such systems through normal form theory, we reveal that the system undergoes a Bogdanov-Takens bifurcation with codimension 2. During the bifurcation process, numerous lower codimension bifurcations may emerge simultaneously, such as saddle-node and Hopf bifurcations with codimension 1. Finally, employing the Matcont and Phase Plane software, we construct bifurcation diagrams and topological phase portraits. Additionally, we emphasize the role of symmetry in our analysis. By considering the inherent symmetries in the system, we provide a more comprehensive understanding of the dynamical behavior. Our findings suggest that if this occurrence rate is applied to the SIR model, it would yield different dynamical phenomena compared to those obtained by reducing a 3-dimensional dynamical model to a planar system by neglecting the disease mortality rate, which results in a stable nilpotent cusp singularity with codimension 2. We found that in SIR models with the same occurrence rate, both stable and unstable Bogdanov-Takens bifurcations occur, meaning both stable and unstable limit cycles appear in this system.

Keywords: limit cycle; Hopf bifurcation; cusp; nilpotent singularity

MSC: 34C05; 34C07; 34C23

1. Introduction

Kermack–McKendrick models of SIR type are always used to describe infectious diseases where the immunity of infected individuals can persist,

$$\begin{aligned}\frac{dS}{dt} &= A - \beta SI - dS,\\ \frac{dI}{dt} &= \beta SI - (d+\mu+\delta)I,\\ \frac{dR}{dt} &= \mu I - dR,\end{aligned}$$

such as measles, smallpox, and polio, et al. In the model, the population is divided into three categories: susceptible (S), infected (I), and removed (R). A and d are the birth rate and natural death rate of people in the area, μ is the removal rate, δ denotes the disease-related death rate, β denotes the effective contact rate between susceptible and infected person, which is the average probability of infection per infected person per contact with a susceptible person, and βS is the the number of susceptible people who are infected by an infected person. The bilinear incidence rate βSI is considered a mass action incidence, and it is considered to be correct in the early stages of an outbreak of diseases or a huge number of the population. During the recent COVID-19 pandemic, this incidence rate was widely adopted [1]. However, this is insufficient for many epidemics.

For example, the effective contact rate sometimes depends on the proportion of infected persons. To overcome the deficiencies, many nonlinear occurrence rates are used in the epidemic model [2–5]. However, these nonlinear incidence rates often imply more complex dynamical behaviors, such as Hopf bifurcation and nilpotent singularity bifurcations, et al. [6–9]. Moreover, in multi-timescale scenarios, infectious disease models can exhibit new bifurcation phenomena, such as canard explosions and relaxation oscillations, as discussed in works like [10,11], among others. Multiple exposures will increase the possibility of infection, saturation exposure, etc. These factors will significantly change the contact rate. Through experiment and analysis, P. van den Driessche et al. [12] proposed a nonlinear incidence rate that has multiple exposure effects, as follows:

$$\beta SI(1+\nu I). \tag{1}$$

This paper [13] generalizes this incidence rate as

$$\beta SI(1+f(I,v)I). \tag{2}$$

This paper finds that SIV models with this incidence may have a bi-stable phenomenon. By calculating the first Lyapunov coefficient, it is proved that Hopf bifurcation can occur in the system. However, the more degenerate bifurcation of singularities is not covered. Subsequently, the incidence rate (2) is applied to an SIR model with both nonlinear incidence and nonlinear clearance in [14]. It is proved that the system can generate Bautin bifurcation and Bogdanov–Takens bifurcation.

Susceptible individuals become infected due to multiple exposures to certain infected individuals.This incidence rate is used to describe the infection rate of multiple exposures. Compared with experimental results, this incidence rate can better simulate the incidence data of mumps. This incidence rate is frequently used in infectious disease models. Recently, in many COVID-19 models, this multi-exposure transmission rate is often employed to describe the infection of symptomatic and asymptomatic infectious. Ref. [15] provides the basic reproduction number under this transmission rate in a COVID-19 model. Meanwhile, Ref. [16] demonstrates that models of this type can exhibit bistability and even periodic phenomena in an SIRS model. Additionally, Ref. [17] establishes an infectious disease model in a two-patch environment with this incidence rate, analyzing various complex bifurcations in the system; especially, cusps with codimension 2 and codimension 3 are also found in this model. Other information about nilpotent singularity in the infectious disease model can be found in [18,19] et al.

The dynamic properties of the SIR model are explicit in the study of classical epidemic models. By applying the regenerative matrix method [20], it is easy to obtain the basic reproductive number $R_0 = \frac{A\beta_1}{d(d+\mu+\delta)}$. When $R_0 < 1$, the system only has disease-free equilibrium, which is globally stable;when $R_0 > 1$, there is a globally stable positive equilibrium, whereas the disease-free equilibrium becomes unstable. However, if we adopt the incidence rate (1) in the SIR model, will the system generate other interesting dynamic phenomena? To address this, we proceed to investigate the following model in the subsequent sections of this paper:

$$\begin{aligned}
\frac{dS}{dt} &= A - dS - (\beta_1 + \beta_0 I)SI, \\
\frac{dI}{dt} &= (\beta_1 + \beta_0 I)SI - (d+\mu+\delta)I, \\
\frac{dR}{dt} &= \mu I - dR.
\end{aligned} \tag{3}$$

Note that the first two equations of the above system are independent, so we consider the following derived system:

$$\begin{aligned}\frac{dS}{dt} &= A - dS - (\beta_1 + \beta_0 I)SI,\\ \frac{dI}{dt} &= (\beta_1 + \beta_0 I)SI - (d + \mu + \delta)I,\end{aligned} \tag{4}$$

where $\rho = d + \mu + \delta$. In this paper, we will analyze its dynamic properties completely.

This paper is organized as follows: in the next section, we obtain the existence of the equilibria of the system and analyze the type of equilibria. We have obtained the existence of disease-free and epidemic equilibrium. In the third part, we analyze the bifurcation of the system, including the saddle-node bifurcation, Hopf bifurcation, and Bogdanov–Takens bifurcations. In addition, the germs of the system are universally unfolded, and the global phase diagrams on each parameter interval are obtained. Finally, we conducted numerical simulations of this system and discussed related biological significance.

2. Existence and Types of Equilibria

It is easy to obtain that there is a positive invariant set of system (4): $D = \{(S, I) \in [0, +\infty) \times [0, +\infty) | S + I < \frac{A}{d})\}$. In view of the biological significance of the model, we will discuss the dynamic properties of the model in the set in the following proofs. This means that if $S(0) > 0$, $I(0) \geq 0$, then the solution $(S(t), I(t))$ of model (4) is positive for all $t \geq 0$, and all non-negative solutions of model (4) are ultimately uniformly bounded in forward time.

Firstly, to find the equilibria, we let system (4) have zero rights.A disease-free equilibrium $E_0 = (\frac{A}{d}, 0)$ always exists. Furthermore, the other equilibrium satisfies

$$A - dS - \rho I = 0, (\beta_1 + \beta_0 I)S - \rho = 0.$$

By direct calculation, the coordinates of the non-negative equilibria should satisfy

$$S^* = \frac{\rho}{\beta_0 I + \beta_1},$$

and the coordinates I are to be the positive roots of the quadratic equation

$$\rho\beta_0 I^2 + (\rho\beta_1 - A\beta_0)I + (d\rho - A\beta_1) = 0.$$

If the discriminant of the equation above is positive, the equation may have two roots

$$I_1^* = \frac{A\beta_0 - \rho\beta_1 - \sqrt{\Delta}}{2\rho\beta_0}, I_2^* = \frac{A\beta_0 - \rho\beta_1 + \sqrt{\Delta}}{2\rho\beta_0},$$

where

$$\Delta = 4\rho\beta_0(A\beta_1 - d\rho) + (A\beta_0 - \rho\beta_1)^2,$$

which imply that the system can have two different positive equilibria $E_1^* = (S_1^*, I_1^*)$ and $E_2^* = (S_2^*, I_2^*)$. Although $\Delta = 0$, i.e., $A = \frac{\rho\left(2\sqrt{\beta_0 d} - \beta_1\right)}{\beta_0}$ and $\beta_1 < \sqrt{\beta_0 d}$, these two equilibria collide into a unique positive equilibrium with multiplicity 2, $E^* = (\frac{\rho}{\sqrt{\beta_0 d}}, \frac{\sqrt{\beta_0 d} - \beta_1}{\beta_0})$.

Theorem 1. *For system (4),*

(1) If $A < \frac{\rho\left(2\sqrt{\beta_0 d} - \beta_1\right)}{\beta_0}$*, only disease-free equilibrium* E_0 *exists.*

(2) If $A = \frac{\rho\left(2\sqrt{\beta_0 d} - \beta_1\right)}{\beta_0}$*, and*

(i) $\beta_1 < \sqrt{\beta_0 d}$*, epidemic equilibrium* E^* *and disease-free equilibrium* E_0 *exist.*

(ii) $\beta_1 \geq \sqrt{\beta_0 d}$*, only* E_0 *exists.*
(3) If $A > \frac{\rho\left(2\sqrt{\beta_0 d}-\beta_1\right)}{\beta_0}$*, and*
(i) $\beta_0 \leq \frac{A^2 d}{\rho^2}, \beta_1 < \frac{d\rho}{A}$ *or* $\beta_1 < \frac{A\beta_0}{\rho}, \beta_0 > \frac{A^2 d}{\rho^2}$*, system (4) has two epidemic equilibria* E_1^**,* E_2^* *and and disease-free equilibrium* E_0*.*
(ii) $\beta_1 > \frac{d\rho}{A}$*, there is an epidemic equilibrium* E_2^* *and a disease-free equilibrium* E_0*.*
(iii) $\frac{A\beta_0}{\rho} < \beta_1 < \frac{d\rho}{A}, \beta_0 > \frac{A^2 d}{\rho^2}$*, only epidemic equilibrium* E_0 *exists.*

Types of Equilibria

In this section, and throughout the subsequent discussions, we will employ the Central Limit Theorem and the Reduction Principle, presented in lemma form. For further details, please refer to the citation [21].

Consider a continuous-time dynamical system defined by

$$\frac{dx}{dt} = f(x), x \in R^n, \tag{5}$$

where $f \in C^\infty$ and $f(0) = 0$. $\lambda_1, \lambda_2 ....\lambda_n$ are the eigenvalues of the Jacobian matrix A at the equilibrium point $x_0 = 0$. If the eigenvalues with zero real part, the equilibrium is not hyperbolic. Suppose there are n_+ eigenvalues with Re $\lambda > 0$, n_0 eigenvalues with Re $\lambda = 0$, and n_- eigenvalues with Re $\lambda < 0$. T^c is the linear eigenspace of A corresponding to the collection of the n_0 eigenvalues on the imaginary axis, and ϕ^t denotes the flow associated with Equation (5). Given the assumptions outlined above, the following lemma is valid.

Lemma 1. *There is a locally defined smooth* n_0 *dimensional invariant manifold* $W^c_{loc}(0)$ *of (5) that is tangent to* T^c *at* $x = 0$*. Moreover, there is a neighborhood* U *of* $x_0 = 0$*, such that if* $\phi^t x \in U$ *for all* $t \geq 0 (t \leq 0)$*, then* $\phi^t x \to W^c_{loc}(0)$ *for* $t \to +\infty (t \to -\infty)$*.*

$W^c_{loc}(0)$ is called the center manifold. Applying the lemma above, we can derive the following conclusion.

Theorem 2. *For system (4), the disease-free equilibrium* $E_0(\frac{A}{d}, 0)$
(1) if $\beta_1 > \frac{d\rho}{A}$ *is a saddle;*
(2) if $\beta_1 < \frac{d\rho}{A}$ *is a stable node;*
(3) if $\beta_1 = \frac{d\rho}{A}$ *is a saddle-node. Moreover,*
(i) the codimension is 1 if $\beta_0 = \frac{d\rho^2}{A^2}$*,*
(ii) the codimension is 2 if $\beta_0 = \frac{d\rho^2}{A^2}$*.*

Proof. With the change of variables $(S, I) \to (x, y)$ by $x = S - A/d, y = I$. The eigenvalues of Jacobian at E_0 are $-d$, $A\beta_1/d - \rho$. Hence, these are the first two conclusions of Theorem 2. If $\beta_1 = \frac{d\rho}{A}$, the system (4) can be rewritten as

$$\begin{aligned}
\frac{dx}{dt} &= -dx + \frac{\rho(\rho - d)}{A}xy + \frac{(d-\rho)(d\rho^2 - \beta_0 A^2)}{d^2 A}y^2 + (\frac{\rho}{d} - 1)\beta_0 xy^2 \\
&\quad + \frac{(d-\rho)\rho\beta_0}{d^2}y^3 := X(x, y), \\
\frac{dy}{dt} &= \frac{d\rho}{A}xy + (\frac{A\beta_0}{d} - \frac{\rho^2}{A})y^2 + \beta_0 xy^2 - \frac{\rho\beta_0}{d}y^3 := Y(x, y).
\end{aligned} \tag{6}$$

By the Lemma 1, there is a unique function $x = x(y)$, such that $x(0) = 0$ and $X(x, x(y)) = 0$. In fact, the solution can be given as

$$x(y) = \frac{(d-\rho)\left(A^2\beta_0 - d\rho^2\right)}{Ad^2}y^2 + \frac{\rho(d-\rho)\left(A^2\beta_0(\rho-2d) + d\rho^2(d-\rho)\right)}{A^2d^3}y^3 + \mathcal{O}(|y|^4).$$

Substituting this expression into Equation (6), we can obtain

$$\frac{dy}{dt} = (\frac{A\beta_0}{d} - \frac{\rho^2}{A})y^2 + \frac{\rho\left(\frac{d\rho^2(d-\rho)}{A^2} + \beta_0(\rho-2d)\right)}{d^2}y^3 + \mathcal{O}(|y|^4).$$

From [22], E_0 is a saddle-node of codimension 1 if $\beta_0 \neq \frac{d\rho^2}{A^2}$. If $\beta_0 = \frac{d\rho^2}{A^2}$, the system has been changed into

$$\frac{dy}{dt} = -\frac{\rho^3}{A^2}y^3 + \mathcal{O}(|y|^4),$$

hence, the codimension is 2. □

Remark 1. *The existence of a saddle-node E^* reflects the critical conditions for disease occurrence. When the infection rate β_1 is relatively small, the disease-free equilibrium is stable, indicating that the disease will not become prevalent. However, if β_1 increases, under certain parameter conditions, the disease will spiral out of control, leading to its sustained existence.*

Theorem 3. *For system (4), if $A = \frac{\rho\left(2\sqrt{\beta_0 d} - \beta_1\right)}{\beta_0}$, $\beta_1 < \sqrt{\beta_0 d}$, the unique epidemic equilibrium E^* is a saddle-node.*

Proof. At E^*, by $X = S - S^*, Y = I - I^*$, we translate this equilibrium to zero and linearize the system (4), and obtain the following system:

$$\begin{aligned}
\frac{dx}{dt} &= d\left(\frac{\beta_1}{\sqrt{\beta_0 d}} - 2\right)x + \rho\left(\frac{\beta_1}{\sqrt{\beta_0 d}} - 2\right)y + (\beta_1 - 2\sqrt{\beta_0 d})xy \\
&\quad - \frac{\rho\sqrt{\beta_0 d}}{d}y^2 + O(|x,y|^3), \\
\frac{dy}{dt} &= \left(d - \frac{\beta_1 d}{\sqrt{\beta_0 d}}\right)x + \left(\rho - \frac{\beta_1\rho}{\sqrt{\beta_0 d}}\right)y + \left(2\sqrt{\beta_0 d} - \beta_1\right)xy \\
&\quad + \frac{\rho\sqrt{\beta_0 d}}{d}y^2 + O(|x,y|^3).
\end{aligned}$$

Next, we make the transformation $x_1 = d\left(\frac{\beta_1}{\sqrt{\beta_0 d}} - 2\right) + \rho\left(\frac{\beta_1}{\sqrt{\beta_0 d}} - 2\right)y, y_1 = y$; then, the system can be changed into

$$\begin{aligned}
\frac{dx_1}{dt} &= a_{1,0}x_1 + a_{1,1}x_1y_1 + a_{0,2}y_1^2 + O(|x_1,y_1|^3), \\
\frac{dy_1}{dt} &= b_{1,1}x_1y_1 + b_{0,2}y_1^2 + O(|x_1,y_1|^3),
\end{aligned} \tag{7}$$

where

$$\begin{aligned}
a_{1,0} &= \frac{\beta_1(d-\rho)}{\sqrt{\beta_0 d}} - 2d + \rho, a_{1,1} = \frac{\left(\beta_1 - 2\sqrt{\beta_0 d}\right)(d-\rho)}{d}, \\
a_{0,2} &= -\frac{\rho\left(-\beta_1^3 + 4(\beta_0 d)^{3/2} + 5\beta_1^2\sqrt{\beta_0 d} - 8\beta_0\beta_1 d\right)(d-\rho)}{d(2\beta_0 d - \beta_1\sqrt{\beta_0 d})}, \\
b_{1,1} &= \sqrt{\beta_0 d}, b_{0,2} = \rho\left(\sqrt{\beta_0 d} - \beta_1\right).
\end{aligned}$$

If $\beta_1 \neq \frac{\sqrt{\beta_0 d}(2d-\rho)}{d-\rho}$, then $a_{1,0} \neq 0$. Applying the center manifold theorem to system Lemma 1, the system has a center manifold

$$x_1 = -\frac{a_{0,2}}{a_{1,0}} y_1^2 + \frac{a_{0,2}a_{1,1} - a_{0,3}a_{1,0}}{a_{1,0}^2} y_1^3 + O(y_1^4).$$

We can obtain the equation on the center manifold,

$$\frac{dy}{dt} = \rho\left(\sqrt{\beta_0 d} - \beta_1\right)y^2 + \mathcal{O}(|y|^3).$$

Hence, if $\beta_1 < \sqrt{\beta_0 d}$, the equilibrium is saddle-node with codimension 1. □

As for E_1^* and E_2^*, we have the following conclusion:

Theorem 4. *For system (4), if simple endemic equilibrium E_1^* exists, it is a hyperbolic saddle. If E_2^* exists, it is an anti-saddle.*

Proof. Denoting any endemic equilibrium as $\widetilde{E}(\widetilde{S}, \widetilde{I})$, and noting $\widetilde{S}(\beta_0\widetilde{I} + \beta_1) = \rho$, then the Jacobian matrix of (4) is given by

$$\begin{pmatrix} -d - \widetilde{I}(\beta_1 + \beta_0\widetilde{I}) & -\widetilde{S}(2\widetilde{I}\beta_0 + \beta_1) \\ \widetilde{I}(\beta_1 + \beta_0\widetilde{I}) & \beta_0\widetilde{S}\widetilde{I} \end{pmatrix},$$

the eigenvalues of this matrix are roots of $\lambda^2 + C_1\lambda + C_0 = 0$, where

$$C_1 = d + \widetilde{I}(\beta_1 + \beta_0\widetilde{I} + \beta_0\widetilde{S}), C_0 = \widetilde{S}\widetilde{I}\left(\widetilde{I}^2\beta_0^2 + \beta_1^2 - \beta_0(d - 2\widetilde{I}\beta_1)\right).$$

Notice $\widetilde{S} = \frac{\rho}{\beta_1 + \beta_0\widetilde{I}}$, hence,

$$C_0(\widetilde{I}) = \rho\widetilde{I}\left(\beta_1 + \beta_0\widetilde{I} - \frac{d\beta_0}{\beta_1 + \beta_0\widetilde{I}}\right).$$

On the other hand, discriminant $\Delta > 0$ is equivalent to $\beta_1 > 2\sqrt{d\beta_0} - \frac{A\beta_0}{\rho}$. Through this inequality, we can easily prove

$$\beta_1 + \beta_0\widetilde{I}_1^* - \frac{d\beta_0}{\beta_1 + \beta_0\widetilde{I}_1^*} < 0,$$
$$\beta_1 + \beta_0\widetilde{I}_2^* - \frac{d\beta_0}{\beta_1 + \beta_0\widetilde{I}_2^*} > 0,$$

i.e., $C_0(\widetilde{I}_1^*) < 0, C_0(\widetilde{I}_2^*) > 0$. That is to say, E_1^* is a hyperbolic saddle and E_2^* is an anti-saddle. Especially, if $C_1 = 0$, E_2^* is a weak focus or center; if $C_1 > 0$, E_2^* it is attracting a node or focus. If $C_1 < 0$, E_2^*, it is repelling a node or focus. □

If we denote $S_0^* = \frac{\rho}{\sqrt{\beta_0 d}}, I_0^* = \frac{d^2}{\sqrt{\beta_0 d}(\rho - d)}$, then the system has a nilpotent singularity. For further information on this topic, readers are referred to the literature [23]. For system (4), we have the following:

Theorem 5. *Suppose* $A = \frac{d\rho^2}{\sqrt{\beta_0 d(\rho-d)}}$, $\beta_1 = \frac{\sqrt{\beta_0 d}(\rho-2d)}{\rho-d}$, $\rho > 2d$ *and* $\rho \neq 3d$ *system (4) has a unique positive equilibrium* $E_0^*(S_0^*, I_0^*)$, *which is a codimension 2 cusp-type nilpotent singularity, and the system at* E_0^* *is topologically equivalent to system*

$$\begin{aligned} \frac{dx}{d\tau} &= y, \\ \frac{dy}{d\tau} &= x^2 \pm xy + O(|x,y|^3), \end{aligned} \tag{8}$$

where if $2d < \rho < 3d$, *then the "* $\pm$ *" above takes a positive sign, but if* $\rho > 3d$, *then the "* $\pm$ *" above takes a negative sign. Hence,* E_0^* *is a codimension 2 cusp-type nilpotent singularity.*

Proof. If $A = \frac{d\rho^2}{\sqrt{\beta_0 d(\rho-d)}}$, $\beta_1 = \frac{\sqrt{\beta_0 d}(2d-\rho)}{d-\rho}$, $\rho > 2d$, the existence of E_0^* can be proved easily, so we omit here, and only prove this equilibrium is a degenerate nilpotent singularity, and the system at E_0^* is topologically equivalent to system (8). After translating the equilibrium to origin and performing Taylor expansion, we obtain

$$\begin{aligned} \frac{dx_1}{dt} &= \sum_{i+j=1}^{2} \tilde{a}_{i,j} x_1^i y_1^j + \mathcal{O}(|x_1, y_1|^3), \\ \frac{dy_1}{dt} &= \sum_{i+j=1}^{2} \tilde{b}_{i,j} x_1^i y_1^j + \mathcal{O}(|x_1, y_1|^3), \end{aligned} \tag{9}$$

where

$$\begin{aligned} \tilde{a}_{1,0} &= \frac{d\rho}{d-\rho}, \tilde{a}_{0,1} = \frac{\rho^2}{d-\rho}, \tilde{a}_{1,1} = \frac{\rho\sqrt{\beta_0 d}}{d-\rho}, \tilde{a}_{0,2} = -\frac{\rho\sqrt{\beta_0 d}}{d}, \\ \tilde{b}_{1,0} &= -\frac{d^2}{d-\rho}, \tilde{b}_{0,1} = \frac{d\rho}{\rho-d}, \tilde{b}_{1,1} = -\frac{\rho\sqrt{\beta_0 d}}{d-\rho}, \tilde{b}_{0,2} = \frac{\rho\sqrt{\beta_0 d}}{d}. \end{aligned}$$

Let $x_2 = x_1$ and $y_2 = \frac{d\rho}{d-\rho}x_1 + + \frac{\rho^2}{d-\rho}y_1$, then system (9) can be changed into

$$\begin{aligned} \frac{dx_2}{dt} &= y_2 + \sum_{i+j=2} \tilde{c}_{i,j} x_2^i y_2^j + \mathcal{O}(|x_2, y_2|^3), \\ \frac{dy_2}{dt} &= \sum_{i+j=2} \tilde{d}_{i,j} x_2^i y_2^j + \mathcal{O}(|x_2, y_2|^3), \end{aligned} \tag{10}$$

where

$$\begin{aligned} \tilde{c}_{2,0} &= -\frac{d^2\sqrt{\beta_0 d}}{d\rho-\rho^2}, \tilde{a}_{1,1} = \frac{\sqrt{\beta_0 d}(2d-\rho)}{\rho^2}, \tilde{c}_{0,2} = -\frac{\sqrt{\beta_0 d}(d-\rho)^2}{d\rho^3}, \\ \tilde{d}_{2,0} &= -\frac{d^2\sqrt{\beta_0 d}}{d-\rho}, \tilde{d}_{1,1} = \frac{\sqrt{\beta_0 d}(2d-\rho)}{\rho}, \tilde{d}_{0,2} = -\frac{\sqrt{\beta_0 d}(d-\rho)^2}{d\rho^2}. \end{aligned}$$

Make near-identity transformation

$$x_3 = x_2, y_3 = y_2 + \sum_{i+j=2} \tilde{c}_{i,j} x_2^i y_2^j + \mathcal{O}(|x_2, y_2|^3),$$

in system (10) to eliminate the non-resonant terms. Then, we obtain

$$\begin{aligned} \frac{dx_3}{dt} &= y_3, \\ \frac{dy_3}{dt} &= \sum_{i+j=1}^{2} \tilde{e}_{i,j} x_3^i y_3^j + O(|x_3, y_3|^3), \end{aligned} \tag{11}$$

where

$$\begin{aligned} \tilde{e}_{2,0} &= \frac{d^2\sqrt{\beta_0 d}}{\rho - d} > 0, \\ \tilde{e}_{1,1} &= \frac{\sqrt{\beta_0 d}(\rho - 3d)}{d - \rho} \neq 0, \\ \tilde{e}_{0,2} &= \frac{\sqrt{\beta_0 d}(d^2 + d\rho - \rho^2)}{d\rho^2}. \end{aligned}$$

At the last step, by scale transformation

$$x_3 = \frac{\tilde{e}_{2,0}}{\tilde{e}_{1,1}^2} x_4, y_3 = \frac{\tilde{e}_{2,0}^2}{\tilde{e}_{1,1}^3} y_4, t = \frac{\tilde{e}_{1,1}}{\tilde{e}_{2,0}} \tau,$$

the system is C^∞ equivalent to system (8). Thus, we prove that there exist smooth coordinate changes which take system (4) into the system above. From [22,24–26], the germ in the system will produce a nilpotent singularity bifurcation of codimension 2. This completes the proof of Theorem 5. □

Remark 2. *Theorem 5 discusses the case when* $\rho > 2d$ *and* $\rho \neq 3d$, *but if* $\rho = 3d$, *then the situation is very complicated; the system may have a degenerate shoot of higher codimension, which will be discussed in the following works.*

Remark 3. *The nilpotent singularity serves as the organizational core of the model, and its existence reflects the complexity of the model.*

3. Bifurcation

To investigate the dynamics implied in system (4), we first consider the bifurcation direction and codimension of the Hopf bifurcation.

3.1. Hopf Bifurcation

Recall $S_1^* = \frac{A - \rho I_1^*}{d}$ and $A(E_1^*) = -d - I_2^*(\beta_1 + \beta_0 I_1^* + \beta_0 S_1^*) = -\frac{A}{S_1^*} + \rho - \beta_1 S_1^*$, and we have the following:

Theorem 6. *A generic Hopf bifurcation could occur if* $A(E_1^*(\beta_0)) = 0$.

Proof. We only need to verify the transversal condition. The real part of the eigenvalue of system (4) is $-A/2$. In the following, we will prove $\partial A/\partial \beta_0 \neq 0$.

$$\begin{aligned} \frac{\partial A(\beta_0)}{\partial \beta_0} &= -\frac{\partial S_1^*}{\partial \beta_0}(\beta_1 + \frac{A}{S_1^{*2}}) \\ &= \frac{\rho(\beta_1 + \frac{A}{S_1^{*2}})}{2d\beta_0^2\sqrt{A^2\beta_0^2 + \rho^2\beta_1^2 + 2\rho\beta_0(A\beta_1 - 2d\rho)}} f(\beta_0), \end{aligned}$$

here $f(\beta_0) = \beta_0(A\beta_1 - 2d\rho) + \beta_1\left(\rho\beta_1 - \sqrt{A^2\beta_0^2 + \rho^2\beta_1^2 + 2\rho\beta_0(A\beta_1 - 2d\rho)}\right)$, and $f(\beta_0) = 0$ holds if and only if $\beta_0 = 0$, contradicting the range of β_0. Thus, Theorem 6 holds. □

3.2. *Cusp-Type Nilpotent Bifurcation with Codimension 2*

If $A^* = \frac{d\rho^2}{\sqrt{\beta_0 d}(\rho - d)}, \beta_1^* = \frac{\sqrt{\beta_0 d}(2d-\rho)}{d-\rho}, \rho > 2d$ and $\rho \neq 3d$, E_0^* is a cuspital point from Theorem 5. In this section, we will unfold the singularity. First, we chose β_1 and d as bifurcation parameters and let $(A, \beta_1) = (A^*, \beta_1^*)$, satisfying the conditions in Theorem 5. To prove that these parameters can unfold the singularity, we perturb the parameters and eliminate β_1 and d. Let $A = A^* + \epsilon_1, \beta_1 = \beta_1^* + \epsilon_2$. Next, we will study the bifurcation of the perturbed system

$$\begin{aligned} \frac{dS}{dt} &= A + \epsilon_1 - dS - (\beta_1^* + \epsilon_2 + \beta_0 I)SI, \\ \frac{dI}{dt} &= (\beta_1^* + \epsilon_2 + \beta_0 I)SI - \rho I. \end{aligned} \tag{12}$$

By

$$x_1 = S - S_0^*, y_1 = I - I_0^*,$$

we have

$$\begin{aligned} \frac{dx_1}{dt} &= \sum_{i+j=0}^{2} \hat{a}_{i,j} x_1^i y_1^j + O(|x_1, y_1|^3), \\ \frac{dy_1}{dt} &= \sum_{i+j=0}^{2} \hat{b}_{i,j} x_1^i y_1^j + O(|x_1, y_1|^3), \end{aligned} \tag{13}$$

where

$$\begin{aligned}
\hat{a}_{0,0} &= \epsilon_1 + \frac{d\rho\epsilon_2}{\beta_0(d-\rho)} + O(|\epsilon_1, \epsilon_2|^2), \hat{a}_{1,0} = \frac{d\rho}{d-\rho} + \frac{d^2\epsilon_2}{\sqrt{\beta_0 d}(d-\rho)} + O(|\epsilon_1, \epsilon_2|^2), \\
\hat{a}_{0,1} &= \frac{\rho^2}{d-\rho} - \frac{\rho\epsilon_2}{\sqrt{\beta_0 d}} + O(|\epsilon_1, \epsilon_2|^2), \hat{a}_{2,0} = 0, \\
\hat{a}_{1,1} &= \frac{\rho\sqrt{\beta_0 d}}{d-\rho} - \epsilon_2 + O(|\epsilon_1, \epsilon_2|^2), \quad \hat{a}_{0,2} = -\frac{\rho\sqrt{\beta_0 d}}{d}, \\
\hat{b}_{0,0} &= \frac{d\rho\epsilon_2}{\beta_0(\rho-d)} + O(|\epsilon_1, \epsilon_2|^2), \\
b_{1,0} &= \frac{d^2}{\rho-d} + \frac{d^2\epsilon_2}{\sqrt{\beta_0 d}(\rho-d)} + O(|\epsilon_1, \epsilon_2|^2), \\
\hat{b}_{0,1} &= -\frac{d\rho}{d-\rho} + \frac{\rho\epsilon_2}{\sqrt{\beta_0 d}} + O(|\epsilon_1, \epsilon_2|^2), \\
\hat{b}_{1,1} &= -\frac{\rho\sqrt{\beta_0 d}}{d-\rho} + \epsilon_2 + O(|\epsilon_1, \epsilon_2|^2), \hat{b}_{0,2} = \frac{\rho\sqrt{\beta_0 d}}{d}.
\end{aligned}$$

By the transformation

$$x_1 = x_2 - \frac{\hat{a}_{0,0}}{\hat{a}_{1,0}}, y_1 = y_2.$$

System (13) is C^∞ equivalent to

$$\begin{aligned}\frac{dx_2}{dt} &= \sum_{i+j=1}^{2} \hat{c}_{i,j}x_2^i y_2^j + O(|x_2,y_2|^3),\\ \frac{dy_2}{dt} &= \sum_{i+j=0}^{2} \hat{d}_{i,j}x_2^i y_2^j + O(|x_2,y_2|^3),\end{aligned} \tag{14}$$

where

$$\hat{c}_{1,0} = \hat{a}_{1,0}, \hat{c}_{0,1} = \hat{a}_{0,1} - \frac{\hat{a}_{0,0}\hat{a}_{1,1}}{\hat{a}_{1,0}}, \hat{c}_{1,1} = \hat{a}_{1,1}, \hat{c}_{0,2} = \hat{a}_{0,2},$$
$$\hat{d}_{0,0} = \hat{b}_{0,0} - \frac{\hat{a}_{0,0}\hat{b}_{1,0}}{\hat{a}_{1,0}}, \hat{d}_{1,0} = \hat{b}_{1,0}, \hat{d}_{0,1} = \hat{b}_{0,1} - \frac{\hat{a}_{0,0}\hat{b}_{1,1}}{\hat{a}_{1,0}}, \hat{d}_{1,1} = \hat{b}_{1,1}, \hat{d}_{0,2} = \hat{b}_{0,2}.$$

Next, we perform the following transmission,

$$x_3 = x_2, y_3 = \hat{c}_{1,0}x_2 + \hat{c}_{0,1}y_2,$$

then the system can be changed into

$$\begin{aligned}\frac{dx_3}{dt} &= y_3 + \sum_{i+j=2} \hat{e}_{i,j}x_3^i y_3^j + O(|x_3,y_3|^3),\\ \frac{dx_3}{dt} &= \sum_{i+j=0}^{2} \hat{f}_{i,j}x_3^i y_3^j + O(|x_3,y_3|^3),\end{aligned} \tag{15}$$

where

$$\hat{e}_{2,0} = \frac{\hat{c}_{0,2}\hat{c}_{1,0}^2}{\hat{c}_{0,1}^2} - \frac{\hat{c}_{1,0}\hat{c}_{1,1}}{\hat{c}_{0,1}}, \hat{e}_{1,1} = \frac{\hat{c}_{1,1}}{\hat{c}_{0,1}} - \frac{2\hat{c}_{0,2}\hat{c}_{1,0}}{\hat{c}_{0,1}^2}, \hat{e}_{0,2} = \frac{\hat{c}_{0,2}}{\hat{c}_{0,1}^2},$$
$$\hat{f}_{0,0} = \hat{c}_{0,1}\hat{d}_{0,0}, \hat{f}_{1,0} = \hat{c}_{0,1}\hat{d}_{1,0} - \hat{c}_{1,0}\hat{d}_{0,1}, \hat{f}_{0,1} = \hat{c}_{1,0} + \hat{d}_{0,1},$$
$$\hat{f}_{2,0} = \frac{\hat{c}_{0,2}\hat{c}_{1,0}^3 - \hat{c}_{0,1}\hat{c}_{1,0}\left(\hat{c}_{1,0}\left(\hat{c}_{1,1} - \hat{d}_{0,2}\right) + \hat{c}_{0,1}\hat{d}_{1,1}\right)}{\hat{c}_{0,1}^2},$$
$$\hat{f}_{1,1} = \frac{\hat{c}_{0,1}\left(\hat{c}_{1,0}\left(\hat{c}_{1,1} - 2\hat{d}_{0,2}\right) + \hat{c}_{0,1}\hat{d}_{1,1}\right) - 2\hat{c}_{0,2}\hat{c}_{1,0}^2}{\hat{c}_{0,1}^2}, \hat{f}_{0,2} = \frac{\hat{c}_{0,1}\hat{d}_{0,2} + \hat{c}_{0,2}\hat{c}_{1,0}}{\hat{c}_{0,1}^2}.$$

Next, letting

$$x_4 = x_3, y_4 = y_3 + \sum_{i+j=2} \hat{e}_{i,j}x_3^i y_3^j + O(|x_3,y_3|^3),$$

then system (15) becomes

$$\begin{aligned}\frac{dx_4}{dt} &= y_4,\\ \frac{dy_4}{dt} &= \sum_{i+j=0}^{2} \hat{g}_{i,j}x_4^i y_4^j + O(|x_4,y_4|^3),\end{aligned} \tag{16}$$

where

$$\hat{g}_{0,0} = \hat{f}_{0,0}, \hat{g}_{1,0} = \hat{e}_{1,1}\hat{f}_{0,0} + \hat{f}_{1,0}, \hat{g}_{0,1} = 2\hat{e}_{0,2}\hat{f}_{0,0} + \hat{f}_{0,1},$$
$$\hat{g}_{2,0} = -2\hat{e}_{0,2}\hat{e}_{2,0}\hat{f}_{0,0} - \hat{e}_{2,0}\hat{f}_{0,1} + \hat{e}_{1,1}\hat{f}_{1,0} + \hat{f}_{2,0},$$
$$\hat{g}_{1,1} = \hat{e}_{0,2}\left(2\hat{f}_{1,0} - 2\hat{e}_{1,1}\hat{f}_{0,0}\right) + 2\hat{e}_{2,0} + \hat{f}_{1,1},$$
$$\hat{g}_{0,2} = -2\hat{e}_{0,2}^2\hat{f}_{0,0} + \hat{e}_{0,2}\hat{f}_{0,1} + \hat{e}_{1,1} + \hat{f}_{0,2}.$$

Make the following transformation

$$x_5 = x_4, y_5 = \frac{y_4}{\sqrt{\hat{g}_{2,0}}}, \tau = \int_0^t \sqrt{\hat{g}_{2,0}}ds,$$

then system (16) can be rewritten as

$$\begin{aligned} \frac{dx_5}{dt} &= y_5, \\ \frac{dy_5}{dt} &= h_{0,0} + h_{1,0}x_5 + x_5^2 + y_5\left(h_{0,1} + h_{1,1}x_5 + \mathcal{O}(x_5^2)\right) + y_5^2 O(|x_5, y_5|), \end{aligned} \tag{17}$$

where

$$h_{0,0} = \frac{\hat{g}_{0,0}}{\hat{g}_{2,0}}, h_{1,0} = \frac{\hat{g}_{1,0}}{\hat{g}_{2,0}}, h_{0,1} = \frac{\hat{g}_{0,1}}{\hat{g}_{2,0}}, h_{1,1} = \frac{\hat{g}_{1,1}}{\hat{g}_{2,0}}.$$

At the last step, let $u = x_5 + \frac{h_{1,0}}{2}, v = h_{1,1}y_5, t = h_{1,1}\tau$, and system (17) can be changed into

$$\begin{aligned} \frac{du}{d\tau} &= v, \\ \frac{dv}{d\tau} &= \nu_1(\epsilon_1, \epsilon_2) + \nu_2(\epsilon_1, \epsilon_2)v + x^2 + xy + O\left(|u, v|^3, \epsilon_1, \epsilon_2\right), \end{aligned} \tag{18}$$

where

$$\begin{aligned} \nu_1 &= h_{0,0} - \frac{h_{1,0}^2}{4} \\ &= -\frac{\rho}{d\sqrt{\beta_0 d}}\epsilon_1 - \frac{\rho^2\sqrt{\beta_0 d}}{\beta_0^2 d^2}\epsilon_2 + O(|\epsilon_1, \epsilon_2|^2), \\ \nu_2 &= \frac{h_{0,1}}{h_{1,1}} - \frac{h_{1,0}}{2} \\ &= \frac{4d^4 - 2d^3\rho - d\rho^3 + \rho^4}{2d^2\rho^2(3d - \rho)}\epsilon_1 + \frac{4d^4 - 4d^3\rho + 4d^2\rho^2 - 3d\rho^3 + \rho^4}{2\beta_0 d^2\rho(3d - \rho)}\epsilon_2 + O(|\epsilon_1, \epsilon_2|^2). \end{aligned}$$

and if $2d < \rho < 3d$,

$$\frac{D(\nu_1, \nu_2)}{D(\epsilon_1, \epsilon_2)}|_{(\epsilon_1, \epsilon_2) = (0,0)} = \frac{\beta_0\rho(d - \rho)^2}{(\beta_0 d)^{5/2}(3d - \rho)} \neq 0. \tag{19}$$

Hence, we have the following conclusion.

Theorem 7. *For $\epsilon = (\epsilon_1, \epsilon_2)$, which is sufficiently small, system (12) is a universal unfolding of the cusp singularity of codimension 2.*

Remark 4. *The existence of unstable periodic solutions provides a threshold condition. If the initial values lie within the limit cycle, the number of infected individuals stabilizes at a constant after a period of oscillation. However, if the initial values lie outside the limit cycle, the number of infected individuals tends to die out after oscillation.*

3.3. *Bifurcation Diagram and the Phase Diagrams*

In this section, we will conduct numerical simulations based on the previous analysis. Firstly, we employ the MatCont7P4 program to generate bifurcation diagrams. Taking $A = 0.864$, $d = 0.2$, and $\mu = 0.2$, $\delta = 0.15$, then $\rho = d + \mu + \delta = 0.55 < 3d$. We keep these parameters constant and only vary the values of β_0 and β_1, thus obtaining the bifurcation diagram Figure 1a. In this figure, the blue curve represents the saddle-node bifurcation curve, whereas the red curve represents the Hopf bifurcation curve. BT denotes the Bogdanov–Takens point with codimension 2. These three curves divide the parameter plane $\beta_1 - \beta_0$ into three parts. In Figure 2, we use the Phase Plane software to provide the global phase portraits in these three parts. Combining Figures 1a and 2, we can clearly observe the variation process of the phase portraits with the changes in parameters β_0 and β_1.

Next, we consider the case where $\rho > 3d$, taking $A = 0.98$, $d = 0.2$, $\mu = 0.3$, and $\delta = 0.2$. Then, $\rho = 0.7 > 3d$. In this case, the Hopf bifurcation curve and the saddle-node bifurcation curve divide the entire region into five parts (see Figure 3). Unlike Figure 1a, the Hopf bifurcation curve exhibits self-intersections. This complicates the dynamical properties of the system. In fact, through the phase portraits, we discover that multiple limit cycles may emerge outside the positive singularity point E_2^* in regions III and V, and the stability of these two limit cycles may be opposite. To thoroughly understand the relative positions and stability of these two limit cycles, it may be necessary to compute higher-order focal quantities, which is inherently very challenging. We will discuss this in future work.

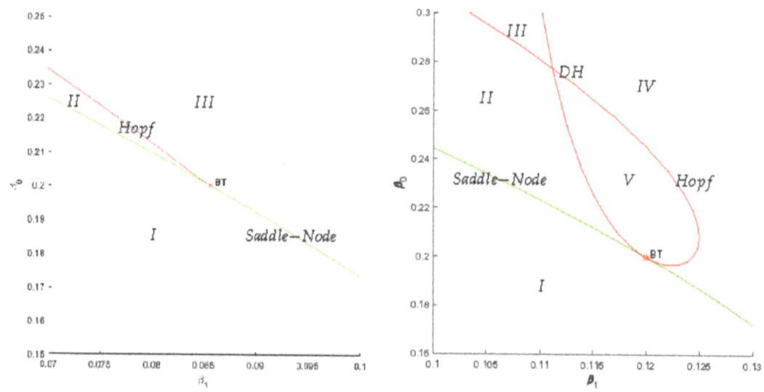

(a) $2d < \rho < 3d$ **(b)** $\rho > 3d$

Figure 1. Bifurcation diagram of system (4). "Hopf" represents the Hopf bifurcation curve, "Saddle-Node" refers to the saddle-node bifurcation curve, "DH" represents the degenerate Hopf bifurcation point, and "BT" represents the location of the Bogdanov–Takens bifurcation.

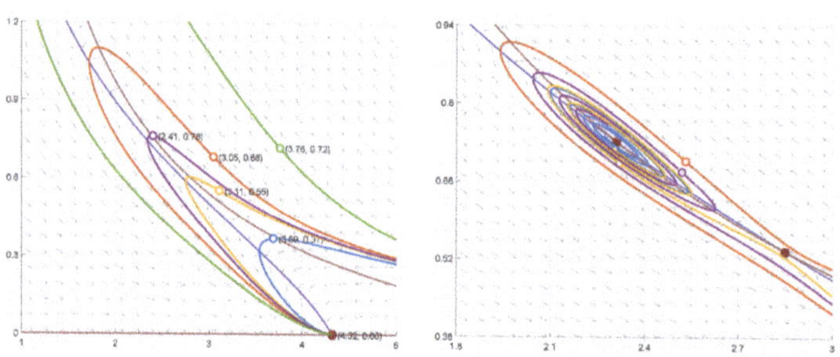

(a) **(b)**

Figure 2. *Cont.*

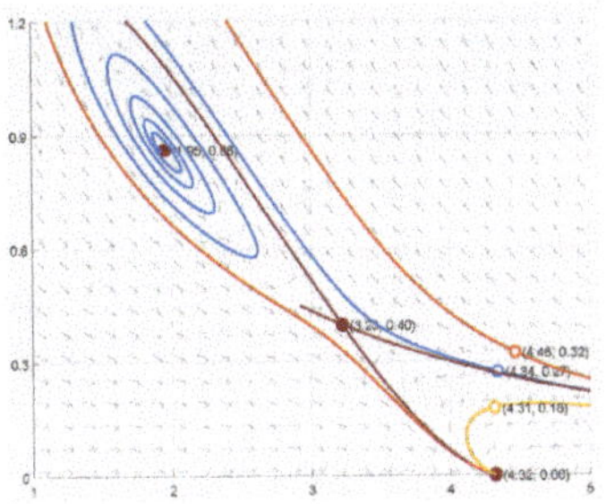

(c)

Figure 2. Global phase diagram of system (4) in Figure 1a when $2d < \rho < 3d$. (**a**) In region I, the system has only one disease-free equilibrium E_0, which is globally stable; (**b**) in region II, there are two positive equilibrium points E_1^* and E_2^* in the system, and near E_2^* there exists an unstable limit cycle; (**c**) in region III, there are two positive equilibrium points E_1^* and E_2^* in the system. E_2^* is a stable focus.

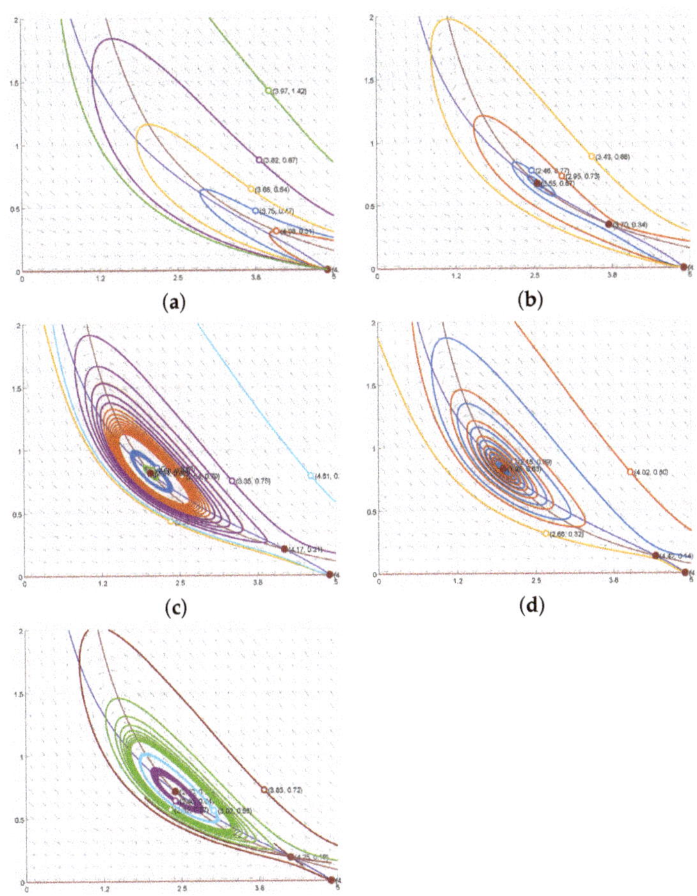

(e)

Figure 3. Global phase diagram of system (4) in Figure 1b when $\rho > 3d$. (**a**) In region I, the system has only one disease-free equilibrium E0, which is globally stable; (**b**) in region II, there are two positive equilibrium points E_1^* and E_2^* in the system, and E_2^* is a stable focus or node, whereas E_1^* is a saddle; (**c**) in region III, the system may exhibit two limit cycles; (**d**) in region IV, E_2^* is a stable focus or node, and E_1^* is a saddle; (**e**) in region V, the system may exhibit two limit cycles.

Remark 5. *In Figure 3c,e, although there are two concentric limit cycles around E_2^*, the stability of the larger and smaller cycles may be opposite. We did not provide a formal proof for this in the paper, but we observed this phenomenon through numerical simulations.*

4. Discussion

This paper presents an analysis of the dynamics of an epidemic model featuring a nonlinear incidence rate, originally proposed by Van den Driessche and Watmough [12], and subsequently studied by Jin [7]. Jin's findings indicate that in the SIRS model, after neglecting the disease-induced mortality rate, the three-dimensional model can be reduced to a planar polynomial system. Utilizing qualitative theory, it was discovered that the system may harbor a stable cusp-type singularity, leading to the emergence of stable Bogdanov–Takens bifurcations accompanied by stable limit cycles. Here, we extend the same incidence rate to the SIR model. Consequently, the stable nodes in the system become unstable, resulting in the emergence of unstable limit cycles through bifurcation. Dynamically, if the limit cycle is stable, trajectories near it tend towards the cycle. Conversely, if the limit cycle is unstable, the system exhibits a peculiar bistable structure, with the limit cycle itself acting as a boundary. Trajectories starting within the limit cycle converge towards a positive equilibrium point, whereas those outside tend towards a boundary equilibrium point, indicating disease extinction.

In practical applications, our results underscore that the most effective disease control strategy involves regulating β_1, representing the probability of contact between susceptible and infected individuals. This highlights the paramount importance of controlling the effective contact rates between these two groups when managing infectious diseases. Additionally, we observe that elevated multiple contact rates lead to unstable periodic solutions in the system. Consequently, the system's dynamics become less governed by the basic reproduction number R_0 and entail a more intricate mechanism. Importantly, the disease's progression depends not only on system parameters but also on initial conditions. Trajectories initiated within the limit cycle stabilize at a constant level of infected individuals, whereas those outside lead to disease eradication. This underscores the necessity of controlling the populations of susceptible and infected individuals.

It is worth noting that whereas this paper identifies a Bogdanov–Takens bifurcation with codimension 2, further analysis of higher codimension bifurcations and the dynamic impact of immune factors and social distancing measures remain avenues for future research in our model.

Author Contributions: Formal analysis, M.M.; investigation, M.M.; writing–original draft preparation, J.L.; writing–review and editing, M.M.; funding acquisition, J.L. and M.M. All authors have read and agreed to the published version of the manuscript.

Funding: This research was funded by the Research Development Fund of Xidian University (No. 80103206145), and the Ph.D. Fellowship of Xi'an Polytechnic University (No. 107020344). The Natural Science Basic Research Plan in Shaanxi Province of China (No. 20139028401).

Data Availability Statement: Data are contained within the article.

Conflicts of Interest: The authors declare no conflict of interest.

References

1. Msmali, A.; Zico, M.; Mechai, I.; Ahmadini, A. Modeling and simulation: A study on predicting the outbreak of COVID-19 in Saudi Arabia. *Discret. Dyn. Nat. Soc.* **2021**, *2021*, 5522928 .
2. Liu, W.M.; Levin, S.A.; Iwasa, Y. Influence of nonlinear incidence rates upon the behavior of SIRS epidemiological models. *J. Math. Biol.* **1986**, *23*, 187–204.

3. Ruan, S.; Wang, W. Dynamical behavior of an epidemic model with a nonlinear incidence rate. *J. Differ. Equ.* **2003**, *188*, 135–163.
4. Tang, Y.; Huang, D.; Ruan, S.; Zhang, W. Coexistence of limit cycles and homoclinic loops in a SIRS model with a nonlinear incidence rate. *SIAM J. Appl. Math.* **2008**, *69*, 621–639.
5. Li, G.; Wang, W. Bifurcation analysis of an epidemic model with nonlinear incidence. *Appl. Math. Comput.* **2009**, *214*, 411–423.
6. Lu, M.; Huang, J.; Ruan, S.; Yu, P. Bifurcation analysis of an SIRS epidemic model with a generalized nonmonotone and saturated incidence rate. *J. Differ. Equ.* **2019**, *267*, 1859–1898.
7. Jin, Y.; Wang, W.; Xiao, S. An SIRS model with a nonlinear incidence rate. *Chaos Solitons Fractals* **2007**, *34*, 1482–1497.
8. Lu, M.; Xiang, C.; Huang, J. Bogdanov-Takens bifurcation in a SIRS epidemic model with a generalized nonmonotone incidence rate. *Discret. Contin. Dyn. Syst.-S* **2020**, *13*, 3125–3138.
9. Huang, C.; Jiang, Z.; Huang, X.; Zhou, X. Bifurcation analysis of an SIS epidemic model with a generalized non-monotonic and saturated incidence rate. *Int. J. Biomath.* **2024**, *17*, 2350033.
10. Li, C.; Li, J.; Ma, Z.; Zhu, H. Canard phenomenon for an SIS epidemic model with nonlinear incidence. *J. Math. Anal. Appl.* **2014**, *420*, 987–1004.
11. Li, J.; Li, S.; Wang, X. Canard, homoclinic loop, and relaxation oscillations in a Lotka–Volterra system with Allee effect in predator population. *Chaos Interdiscip. J. Nonlinear Sci.* **2023**, *33*, 073130.
12. van den Driessche, P.; Watmough, J. A simple SIS epidemic model with a backward bifurcation. *J. Math. Biol.* **2000**, *40*, 525–540.
13. Alexander, M.E.; Moghadas, S.M. Bifurcation analysis of an SIRS epidemic model with generalized incidence. *SIAM J. Appl. Math.* **2005**, *65*, 1794–1816.
14. Moghadas, S.M.; Alexander, M.E. Bifurcations of an epidemic model with non-linear incidence and infection-dependent removal rate. *Math. Med. Biol. J. IMA* **2006**, *23*, 231–254.
15. Ali, Z.; Rabiei, F.; Rashidi, M.M.; Khodadadi, T. A fractional-order mathematical model for COVID-19 outbreak with the effect of symptomatic and asymptomatic transmissions. *Eur. Phys. J. Plus* **2022**, *137*, 395.
16. Wang, D.; Zhao, Y.; Luo, J.; Leng, H. Simplicial SIRS epidemic models with nonlinear incidence rates. *Chaos Interdiscip. J. Nonlinear Sci.* **2021**, *31*, 053112.
17. Lu, M.; Gao, D.; Huang, J.; Wang, H. Relative prevalence-based dispersal in an epidemic patch model. *J. Math. Biol.* **2023**, *86*, 52.
18. Shan, C.; Yi, Y.; Zhu, H. Nilpotent singularities and dynamics in an SIR type of compartmental model with hospital resources. *J. Differ. Equ.* **2016**, *260*, 4339–4365.
19. Cui, W.; Zhao, Y. Saddle-node bifurcation and Bogdanov-Takens bifurcation of a SIRS epidemic model with nonlinear incidence rate. *J. Differ. Equ.* **2024**, *384*, 252–278.
20. Van den Driessche, P.; Watmough, J. Reproduction numbers and sub-threshold endemic equilibria for compartmental models of disease transmission. *Math. Biosci.* **2002**, *180*, 29–48.
21. Kuznetsov, Y.A.; Kuznetsov, I.A.; Kuznetsov, Y. *Elements of Applied Bifurcation Theory*; Springer: Berlin/Heidelberg, Germany, 1998; Volume 112.
22. Zhang, Z. *Qualitative Theory of Differential Equations*; American Mathematical Soc.: Providence, RI, USA, 1992; Volume 101.
23. Chow, S.N.; Li, C.; Wang, D. *Normal Forms and Bifurcation of Planar Vector Fields*; Cambridge University Press: Cambridge, UK, 1994.
24. Dumortier, F.; Fiddelaers, P.; Li, C. Generic unfolding of the nilpotent saddle of codimension four. In *Global Analysis of Dynamical Systems*; CRC Press: Boca Raton, FL, USA, 2001; pp. 137–172.
25. Dumortier, F.; Roussarie, R.; Sotomayor, J. Generic 3-parameter families of vector fields on the plane, unfolding a singularity with nilpotent linear part. The cusp case of codimension 3. *Ergod. Theory Dyn. Syst.* **1987**, *7*, 375–413.
26. Dumortier, F.; Roussarie, R.; Sotomayor, J.; Zoladek, H. *Bifurcations of Planar Vector Fields: Nilpotent Singularities and Abelian Integrals*; Springer: Berlin/Heidelberg, Germany, 2006.

symmetry MDPI

Article

Stability and Hopf Bifurcation of a Delayed Predator–Prey Model with a Stage Structure for Generalist Predators and a Holling Type-II Functional Response

Zi-Wei Liang and Xin-You Meng *

School of Science, Lanzhou University of Technology, Lanzhou 730050, China; zwliang1998@163.com
* Correspondence: xymeng@lut.edu.cn

Abstract: In this paper, we carry out some research on a predator–prey system with maturation delay, a stage structure for generalist predators and a Holling type-II functional response, which has already been proposed. First, for the delayed model, we obtain the conditions for the occurrence of stability switches of the positive equilibrium and possible Hopf bifurcation values owing to the growth of the value of the delay by applying the geometric criterion. It should be pointed out that when we suppose that the characteristic equation has a pair of imaginary roots $\lambda = \pm i\omega(\omega > 0)$, we just need to consider $i\omega(\omega > 0)$ due to the symmetry, which alleviates the computation requirements. Next, we investigate the nature of Hopf bifurcation. Finally, we conduct numerical simulations to verify the correctness of our findings.

Keywords: maturation delay; geometric criterion; stability switch; Hopf bifurcation; predator–prey

1. Introduction

Interspecies relationships include competition, predation, parasitism and mutualism, where predation describes the interplay between the predator and prey. It is crucial to explore the interaction between them and then formulate an appropriate mathematical model to accurately capture the dynamics of the predator–prey model. The classic predator–prey model was first put forward by Lotka [1] and Volterra [2]. Since then, a lot of scholars have incorporated multifarious factors into the classic model to expound intricate biological processes in a more realistic way [3–6].

Since all biological processes take time to complete, one tends to take into account time delays in the modeling efforts [7–10]. This will produce delay differential equation models in most instances. Some of these models result from age structure models or elaborate formulations, which means that time lags often arise in the survival rates of the populations, such as $e^{-d\tau}$ [11]. Clearly, these models possess delay-dependent parameters, while most of delay differential equation models only have parameters independent of time delays [12–16].

In ecological research, stability analysis is a key task. Common stability analysis includes finite-time stability, exponential stability, local asymptotic stability and global asymptotic stability [17]. In this paper, we focus on analyzing the local asymptotic stability of the positive equilibrium. Studying the stability of the delayed system has aroused wide concern in mathematical biology since the time lag plays a surprisingly vital role in affecting dynamics of the model. It may make the model stable or unstable, relying on the length of the time delay [18]. Cooke and Grossman [12] first demonstrated that constructing a system with stability switches was possible. By combining graphical information with analytical work, Beretta and Kuang [18] proposed a geometric criterion to effectively study the stability switches of the model with only one discrete delay. Furthermore, the parameters of this model are relevant to the delay. The corresponding characteristic equation for the above model can be written as

$$D(\lambda,\tau) := P_0(\lambda,\tau) + P_1(\lambda,\tau)e^{-\lambda\tau} = 0, \tag{1}$$

where $P_0(\lambda,\tau)$, $P_1(\lambda,\tau)$ are polynomials in λ. Recently, the prominent geometric method set forth by Beretta and Kuang [18] has been applied by a lot of scholars [16,19,20]. Subsequently, Beretta and Tang [21] extended the geometric stability switch criterion introduced in [18] to be appropriate for the more general characteristic equation

$$D(\lambda,\tau) := P_0(\lambda,\tau) + P_1(\lambda,\tau)e^{-\lambda\tau} + P_2(\lambda,\tau)e^{-2\lambda\tau} = 0, \tag{2}$$

where $P_0(\lambda,\tau)$, $P_1(\lambda,\tau)$, and $P_2(\lambda,\tau)$ are polynomials in λ.

For the scenario that parameters of the model fail to be related to the delay, Gu et al. [22] put forward the crossing curves method for general systems with double delays. They studied the change of system stability for the following characteristic equation as delays vary.

$$D(\lambda,\tau,\tau_1) := P_0(\lambda) + P_1(\lambda)e^{-\lambda\tau} + P_2(\lambda)e^{-\lambda\tau_1} = 0, \tag{3}$$

where $P_l(\lambda), l = 0,1,2$ are polynomials in λ. The application of this crossing curves method can be found in [23].

The geometric method developed by Gu et al. [22] was extended by An et al. [24] to explore the stability switches of a system with two discrete delays and delay-dependent parameters relevant only to one of the time delays. Clearly, the stability of such a model is absolutely decided by the roots of its characteristic equation

$$D(\lambda,\tau,\tau_1) := P_0(\lambda,\tau) + P_1(\lambda,\tau)e^{-\lambda\tau} + P_2(\lambda,\tau)e^{-\lambda\tau_1} = 0, \tag{4}$$

where $P_l(\lambda,\tau), l = 0,1,2$ are polynomials in λ whose coefficients, say $p_{kl}(\tau)$, are bounded functions $p_{kl} : I \longrightarrow \mathbb{R}$ of class C^1. Some applications of this geometric method are available in [11,25,26].

Recently, based on the models in [27–32] and the hypothesis that the predator is generalist, that is, it can achieve an alternative food apart from the prey, Roy et al. [33] formulated the following predator–prey model with the generalist predator:

$$\begin{cases} \dfrac{\mathrm{d}X}{\mathrm{d}T} = X(r_1 - b_1X) - \dfrac{c_1XY}{1+aX}, \\ \dfrac{\mathrm{d}Y}{\mathrm{d}T} = Y(r_2 - b_2Y) + \dfrac{cc_1XY}{1+aX}, \end{cases} \tag{5}$$

where $X(T)$ and $Y(T)$ represent the densities of prey and generalist predator populations at time T, respectively. r_1 and r_2 are the growth rates of prey and predator populations, respectively. b_1 and b_2 denote the intra-specific competition among prey and predator populations, respectively. c_1 refers to the capture rate, a is the time of handling each captured prey, c represents the efficiency that predators convert consumed prey into new predators. In order to simplify the calculations, they rescaled model (5) by $x = \frac{b_1X}{r_1}$, $y = \frac{b_2Y}{r_2}$, $t = Tr_1$ and then obtained the following model:

$$\begin{cases} \dfrac{\mathrm{d}x}{\mathrm{d}t} = x(1-x) - \dfrac{\beta xy}{1+\alpha x}, \\ \dfrac{\mathrm{d}y}{\mathrm{d}t} = y\tilde{\rho}(1-y) + \dfrac{\gamma xy}{1+\alpha x}, \end{cases} \tag{6}$$

where $\beta = \frac{c_1r_2}{b_2r_1}$, $\alpha = \frac{ar_1}{b_1}$, $\tilde{\rho} = \frac{r_2}{r_1}$ and $\gamma = \frac{cc_1}{b_1}$. All above parameters in model (6) are supposed to be positive. Moreover, inspired by the modeling method in [27,34,35], they modified model (6) by considering a stage structure for generalist predators. They classified the predator population into two stages: the immature stage and the mature stage. It is well known that immature predators require some time to mature. In the maturation process, there exists a natural death of immature predators. After accomplishing the maturation process, they deviate from the immature class and join the mature class. Thus, it can be seen that a maturation delay is common in a predator–prey model with a stage structure. That is to say, there is a close connection between the maturation delay and the model with stage structure. So the research of the model with a stage structure should focus on the maturation delay. Based on the above analysis and the hypothesis that immature predators are incapable of reproducing or capturing prey because they are weaker than mature predators, model (6) can be converted into

$$\begin{cases} \frac{dx}{dt} = x(1-x) - \frac{\beta x y_a}{1+\alpha x}, \\ \frac{dy_j}{dt} = \frac{\gamma x y_a}{1+\alpha x} - \frac{\gamma e^{-\delta_j \tau} x(t-\tau) y_a(t-\tau)}{1+\alpha x(t-\tau)} - \delta_j y_j, \\ \frac{dy_a}{dt} = y_a \tilde{\rho}(1-y_a) + \frac{\gamma e^{-\delta_j \tau} x(t-\tau) y_a(t-\tau)}{1+\alpha x(t-\tau)}, \end{cases} \tag{7}$$

with $(x(\theta), y(\theta)) \in C_+ \equiv C\left[[-\tau, 0], \mathbb{R}^2_{\geq 0}\right]$ and $x(0) > 0, y_j(0) > 0, y_a(0) > 0$. In the above model, y_j and y_a represent the densities of immature and mature predator populations, respectively. δ_j denotes the death rate of immature predator populations. τ is the maturation delay and $e^{-\delta_j \tau}$ refers to the probability that a juvenile predator grows up to become an adult predator successfully. The biological significances of the remaining parameters are the same as those in model (6). For all we know, no one puts forward such a model apart from Roy et al. [33]. And it is more reasonable and more grounded in reality to investigate a model with a generalist predator and a maturation delay. Because $x(t)$ and $y_a(t)$ absolutely determined $y_j(t)$, they just considered the following delayed model for further investigation.

$$\begin{cases} \frac{dx}{dt} = x(1-x) - \frac{\beta x y}{1+\alpha x}, \\ \frac{dy}{dt} = y \tilde{\rho}(1-y) + \frac{\gamma e^{-\delta_j \tau} x(t-\tau) y(t-\tau)}{1+\alpha x(t-\tau)}. \end{cases} \tag{8}$$

For the delayed model (8), they studied the positivity and boundedness of solutions, the stability of all equilibriums and local bifurcations. The conclusions they have reached are colorful. However, they demonstrated that under certain conditions, model (8) would not occur with a stability switch (see Proposition 6.1 in [33]), which means that Hopf bifurcations would not occur either. The main target of this paper is to extend the work carried out by Roy et al. [33] to further study the occurrence of stability switches and Hopf bifurcation near the positive equilibrium for model (8) by dint of the geometric stability switch criterion introduced in [18]. We hypothesize that incorporating a maturation delay in a predator–prey model with a stage structure for generalist predators and a Holling type-II functional response will influence the dynamic behavior of the system, potentially leading to stability switches and Hopf bifurcations. The subsequent sections will be devoted to exploring how the maturation delay affects the dynamics of model (8).

The organization of the remainder of the paper is as follows. In Section 2, we apply a geometric criterion to present the conditions for the occurrence of stability switches and Hopf bifurcations induced by the maturation delay. Section 3 focuses on the exploration of the nature of Hopf bifurcation by solving its normal form. To confirm our theoretical findings, numerical simulations are proceeded in Section 4. Finally, we summarize this paper with a conclusion section.

2. A Geometric Criterion for Hopf Bifurcation Values

In this section, we study the occurrence of possible stability switches and Hopf bifurcation values induced by the increase in time lag. According to Subsection 5.1 in [33], we can directly obtain the following details about the existence of positive equilibriums.

Lemma 1. *The following statements are correct for the model* (8).

(i) *If $\beta < 1$, there exists at least one interior equilibrium $E^*(x^*, y^*)$ for the delayed model* (8).

(ii) *If $\beta > 1$, there is at least one positive equilibrium $E^*(x^*, y^*)$ with the following sufficient condition holding:*

$$\tau \geq \frac{1}{\delta_j} \ln \frac{4(\alpha-1)\beta\gamma}{\tilde{\rho}(\alpha+1)[(\alpha+1)^2 - 4\alpha\beta]} := \tau_{\min}.$$

It is direct from Subsection 5.2 in [33] that the characteristic equation of the model (8) at E^* is

$$\lambda^2 - (a_1 + b_3)\lambda + a_1 b_3 + (a_1 b_2 - a_2 b_1 - b_2 \lambda)e^{-\lambda\tau} = 0, \tag{9}$$

where

$$\begin{aligned} a_1 &= 1 - 2x^* - \frac{\beta y^*}{(1+\alpha x^*)^2}, \quad a_2 = -\frac{\beta x^*}{1+\alpha x^*}, \\ b_1 &= \frac{\gamma e^{-\delta_j \tau} y^*}{(1+\alpha x^*)^2}, \quad b_2 = -\tilde{\rho}(1 - y^*), \quad b_3 = \tilde{\rho}(1 - 2y^*). \end{aligned} \tag{10}$$

When $\tau = 0$, we can further receive the following lemma about the local stability of E^* by the use of Routh–Hurwitz criteria.

Lemma 2. *When $\tau = 0$, if the condition (H_1): $a_1 + b_2 + b_3 < 0$, $a_1 b_3 + a_1 b_2 - a_2 b_1 > 0$ holds, then the interior equilibrium E^* is locally asymptotically stable.*

In what follows, when $\tau \neq 0$, we plan to explore the stability switches and Hopf bifurcations of model (8) resulting from the maturation delay τ by applying the geometric criterion introduced in [18].

Equation (9) can be rewritten as

$$D(\lambda, \tau) := P_0(\lambda, \tau) + P_1(\lambda, \tau)e^{-\lambda\tau} = 0, \tag{11}$$

where $P_0(\lambda, \tau) = \lambda^2 - (a_1 + b_3)\lambda + a_1 b_3$ and $P_1(\lambda, \tau) = a_1 b_2 - a_2 b_1 - b_2 \lambda$.

Obviously, $P_0(\lambda, \tau)$ and $P_1(\lambda, \tau)$ are analytic functions in λ and differentiable in τ. To utilize the geometric criterion, we also need to verify the following conclusions (see [18]):

(i) $P_0(0, \tau) + P_1(0, \tau) \neq 0$ for any τ;

(ii) If $\lambda = i\omega$, $\omega \in \mathbb{R}$, then $P_0(i\omega, \tau) + P_1(i\omega, \tau) \neq 0$ for any τ;

(iii) $\limsup\limits_{\lambda\to\infty, \mathrm{Re}\lambda \geq 0} \left(\left| \frac{P_1(\lambda,\tau)}{P_0(\lambda,\tau)} \right| \right) < 1$ for any τ;

(iv) $F(\omega, \tau) := |P_0(i\omega, \tau)|^2 - |P_1(i\omega, \tau)|^2$ for each τ has at most a finite number of real zeros;

(v) Any positive root $\omega(\tau)$ of $F(\omega, \tau) = 0$ is continuous and differentiable in τ whenever it exists.

Next, we will corroborate the above results in turn. In addition, it is posited that the hypothesis (H_1) in Lemma 2 is true, that is to say, $a_1 + b_2 + b_3 < 0$, $a_1 b_3 + a_1 b_2 - a_2 b_1 > 0$.

(i) $P_0(0, \tau) + P_1(0, \tau) = a_1 b_3 + a_1 b_2 - a_2 b_1 > 0$ for any τ;

(ii) $P_0(i\omega, \tau) + P_1(i\omega, \tau) = -\omega^2 + (a_1 b_3 + a_1 b_2 - a_2 b_1) - i(a_1 + b_2 + b_3)\omega \neq 0$ for any τ on account of $a_1 + b_2 + b_3 < 0$;

(iii) For any τ, $\limsup\limits_{\lambda\to\infty, \mathrm{Re}\lambda \geq 0} \left(\left| \frac{P_1(\lambda,\tau)}{P_0(\lambda,\tau)} \right| \right) = \limsup\limits_{\lambda\to\infty, \mathrm{Re}\lambda \geq 0} \left(\left| \frac{a_1 b_2 - a_2 b_1 - b_2\lambda}{\lambda^2 - (a_1+b_3)\lambda + a_1 b_3} \right| \right) = 0 < 1$;

(iv) Due to

$$F(\omega,\tau) = |P_0(i\omega,\tau)|^2 - |P_1(i\omega,\tau)|^2 = \omega^4 + (a_1^2 + b_3^2 - b_2^2)\omega^2 + a_1^2 b_3^2 - (a_1 b_2 - a_2 b_1)^2,$$

it is clearly true that $F(\omega,\tau)$ admits at most a finite number of real zeros for each τ;

(v) This conclusion can be verified by the use of the implicit theorem directly.

Assume that $\lambda = \pm i\omega(\omega > 0)$ are a pair of imaginary roots of Equation (11). Because $\overline{P_0(-i\omega,\tau)} = P_0(i\omega,\tau)$ and $\overline{P_1(-i\omega,\tau)} = P_1(i\omega,\tau)$, in line with the symmetry, we just need to take into account $\lambda = i\omega(\omega > 0)$. Plug $i\omega$ into Equation (11) and then separate real and imaginary parts, we obtain

$$\begin{cases} -b_2\omega\sin(\omega\tau) + (a_1b_2 - a_2b_1)\cos(\omega\tau) = \omega^2 - a_1b_3, \\ (a_1b_2 - a_2b_1)\sin(\omega\tau) + b_2\omega\cos(\omega\tau) = -(a_1 + b_3)\omega, \end{cases} \tag{12}$$

which gives

$$\begin{cases} \sin(\omega\tau) = \dfrac{-(\omega^2 - a_1b_3)b_2\omega - (a_1 + b_3)(a_1b_2 - a_2b_1)\omega}{(a_1b_2 - a_2b_1)^2 + b_2^2\omega^2}, \\ \cos(\omega\tau) = \dfrac{(\omega^2 - a_1b_3)(a_1b_2 - a_2b_1) - (a_1 + b_3)b_2\omega^2}{(a_1b_2 - a_2b_1)^2 + b_2^2\omega^2}. \end{cases} \tag{13}$$

On the other side of the coin, if Equation (11) admits a root $\lambda = i\omega(\omega > 0)$, then it follows that

$$\frac{P_0(i\omega,\tau)}{P_1(i\omega,\tau)} = -\cos(\omega\tau) + i\sin(\omega\tau).$$

Hence, we can rewrite (13) as

$$\sin(\omega\tau) = \mathrm{Im}\left(\frac{P_0(i\omega,\tau)}{P_1(i\omega,\tau)}\right), \quad \cos(\omega\tau) = -\mathrm{Re}\left(\frac{P_0(i\omega,\tau)}{P_1(i\omega,\tau)}\right),$$

which means that

$$\left|\frac{P_0(i\omega,\tau)}{P_1(i\omega,\tau)}\right|^2 = 1.$$

Consequently, if $\omega(\tau)$ satisfies (13), then it must satisfy the following equation:

$$\begin{aligned} F(\omega,\tau) &= |P_0(i\omega,\tau)|^2 - |P_1(i\omega,\tau)|^2 \\ &= \omega^4 + (a_1^2 + b_3^2 - b_2^2)\omega^2 + a_1^2b_3^2 - (a_1b_2 - a_2b_1)^2 = 0. \end{aligned} \tag{14}$$

Define $I \subseteq \mathbb{R}_{+0}$ as the set of τ such that $\omega(\tau)$ is a positive root of Equation (14). If I is empty, then there does not exist any stability switch and Hopf bifurcation value, which has been discussed and proven in [33]. However, they did not consider the case that I is nonempty any more. To fill up this gap, we extend the analysis in [33] by supposing that I is nonempty. In addition, we can sum up the following proposition.

Proposition 1. *If conditions* (H_1) *and* (H_2): $a_1b_3 - a_1b_2 + a_2b_1 < 0$ *hold, then Equation* (14) *has a unique positive root* $\omega_+(\tau)$, $\tau \in I$, *which means that I is nonempty.*

Proof. By a series of calculations, we can obtain the roots of Equation (14) given by

$$\omega_+^2 = \frac{1}{2}\left\{\Delta^{\frac{1}{2}} - (a_1^2 + b_3^2 - b_2^2)\right\}, \quad \omega_-^2 = \frac{1}{2}\left\{-\Delta^{\frac{1}{2}} - (a_1^2 + b_3^2 - b_2^2)\right\}, \tag{15}$$

where

$$\Delta = (a_1^2 + b_3^2 - b_2^2)^2 - 4\left[a_1^2b_3^2 - (a_1b_2 - a_2b_1)^2\right].$$

It is direct from (10) and $y^* > 1$ that $a_1^2 + b_3^2 - b_2^2 > 0$. Therefore, $\omega_-^2 < 0$. Due to $a_1^2 b_3^2 - (a_1 b_2 - a_2 b_1)^2 = (a_1 b_3 + a_1 b_2 - a_2 b_1)(a_1 b_3 - a_1 b_2 + a_2 b_1)$, we can further obtain $\omega_+^2 > 0$ with conditions (H_1) and (H_2) holding. The proof is thus completed. □

For any $\tau \in I$, the angle $\theta(\tau) \in [0, 2\pi]$ can be defined as the solution of

$$\begin{cases} \sin\theta(\tau) = \dfrac{-(\omega_+^2 - a_1 b_3) b_2 \omega_+ - (a_1 + b_3)(a_1 b_2 - a_2 b_1)\omega_+}{(a_1 b_2 - a_2 b_1)^2 + b_2^2 \omega_+^2}, \\ \cos\theta(\tau) = \dfrac{(w_+^2 - a_1 b_3)(a_1 b_2 - a_2 b_1) - (a_1 + b_3) b_2 \omega_+^2}{(a_1 b_2 - a_2 b_1)^2 + b_2^2 \omega_+^2}. \end{cases} \tag{16}$$

Hence, for any $\tau \in I$, we have $\omega_+(\tau)\tau = \theta(\tau) + 2n\pi$, $n \in \mathbb{N}_0$. Then, we can construct the maps $\tau_n : I \longrightarrow \mathbb{R}_{+0}$, which is given by

$$\tau_n(\tau) := \frac{\theta(\tau) + 2n\pi}{\omega_+(\tau)}, \quad n \in \mathbb{N}_0, \quad \tau \in I,$$

where $\omega_+(\tau) > 0$ is a root of Equation (14). We further define the functions $I \longrightarrow \mathbb{R}$:

$$S_n(\tau) := \tau - \tau_n(\tau), \quad \tau \in I, \quad n \in \mathbb{N}_0, \tag{17}$$

which are continuous and differentiable in τ. Then, we can obtain the following geometric criterion to certify the transversality condition and describe the direction of λ crossing the imaginary axis.

Theorem 1. *Assume that (H_2) holds and that $S_n(\tau)$ admits one positive root $\tau^* \in I$ for some $n \in \mathbb{N}_0$, then at $\tau = \tau^*$, Equation (11) has a pair of simple conjugate pure imaginary roots $\lambda_+(\tau^*) = i\omega_+(\tau^*)$, $\lambda_-(\tau^*) = -i\omega_+(\tau^*)$, which crosses the imaginary axis from left to right when $\delta(\tau^*) > 0$ and crosses the imaginary axis from right to left when $\delta(\tau^*) < 0$, where $\delta(\tau^*)$ is the transversality condition denoted by*

$$\delta(\tau^*) = sign\left\{\frac{\mathrm{dRe}\lambda}{\mathrm{d}\tau}\bigg|_{\lambda = i\omega_+(\tau^*)}\right\} = sign\left\{\frac{\mathrm{d}S_n(\tau)}{\mathrm{d}\tau}\bigg|_{\tau = \tau^*}\right\}. \tag{18}$$

Proof. Compared to the proof of Theorem 2.2 in [18], we just need to further prove the transversality condition (18). From Theorem 2.2 in [18], we obtain that

$$\delta(\tau^*) = sign\left\{\frac{\mathrm{dRe}\lambda}{\mathrm{d}\tau}\bigg|_{\lambda = i\omega_+(\tau^*)}\right\} = sign\{F'_\omega(\omega_+(\tau^*), \tau^*)\} sign\left\{\frac{\mathrm{d}S_n(\tau)}{\mathrm{d}\tau}\bigg|_{\tau = \tau^*}\right\}. \tag{19}$$

It is direct from Equation (14) that

$$F'_\omega(\omega_+(\tau^*), \tau^*) = 4\omega_+^3 + 2\omega_+(a_1^2 + b_3^2 - b_2^2) = 2\omega_+(2\omega_+^2 + a_1^2 + b_3^2 - b_2^2).$$

On the other hand, from (15), we can obtain $\omega_+^2 = \frac{1}{2}\left\{\Delta^{\frac{1}{2}} - (a_1^2 + b_3^2 - b_2^2)\right\}$, which implies that $2\omega_+^2 + a_1^2 + b_3^2 - b_2^2 = \Delta^{\frac{1}{2}}$. Therefore, $F'_\omega(\omega_+(\tau^*), \tau^*) = 2\omega_+(\tau^*)\Delta^{\frac{1}{2}} > 0$, which is equivalent to $sign\{F'_\omega(\omega_+(\tau^*), \tau^*)\} = 1$. The proof is completed. □

Clearly, $S_n(\tau) > S_{n+1}(\tau)$ for all $n \in \mathbb{N}_0$, $\tau \in I$. Hence, if $S_0(\tau) < 0$ on I, then $S_n(\tau)(n \in \mathbb{N}_0)$ admits no zeros on I. To sum up, we show the following theorem with respect to the stability switches of E^* and the occurrence of Hopf bifurcations.

Theorem 2. *Take into account model (8) with conditions (H_1) and (H_2) being satisfied.*

(i) *If $S_0(\tau)$ admits no positive real root $\tau \in I$, then when $\beta < 1$, E^* is locally asymptotically stable for any $\tau > 0$ and when $\beta > 1$, E^* is locally asymptotically stable for $\tau \geq \tau_{\min}$.*

(ii) *Assume that for some $n \in \mathbb{N}_0$, $S_n(\tau)$ admits the unique positive real root $\tau_n \in I$ and satisfies $\mathrm{d}S_n(\tau_n)/\mathrm{d}\tau > 0$. If $\beta < 1$, then E^* is locally asymptotically stable for $\tau \in (0, \tau_0)$ and unstable for $\tau \in (\tau_0, \infty)$. Moreover, the model* (8) *undergoes a Hopf bifurcation at E^* when $\tau = \tau_n$, $n \in \mathbb{N}_0$. If $\beta > 1$, then E^* is locally asymptotically stable for $\tau \in (0, \tau_0) \cap [\tau_{\min}, \infty)$ and unstable for $\tau \in (\tau_0, \infty) \cap [\tau_{\min}, \infty)$.*

(iii) *Assume that for some $n \in \mathbb{N}_0$, $S_n(\tau)$ has two positive real roots $\tau_n^1, \tau_n^2 \in I$ and satisfies $\mathrm{d}S_n(\tau_n^1)/\mathrm{d}\tau > 0$, $\mathrm{d}S_n(\tau_n^2)/\mathrm{d}\tau < 0$. Clearly, $\tau_0^1 < \tau_1^1 < \tau_2^1 < \cdots < \tau_2^2 < \tau_1^2 < \tau_0^2$. If $\beta < 1$, then E^* is locally asymptotically stable for $\tau \in (0, \tau_0^1) \cup (\tau_0^2, \infty)$ and unstable for $\tau \in (\tau_0^1, \tau_0^2)$. In addition, a Hopf bifurcation occurs at E^* when $\tau = \tau_n^1, \tau_n^2$, $n \in \mathbb{N}_0$. If $\beta > 1$, then E^* is locally asymptotically stable for $\tau \in ((0, \tau_0^1) \cup (\tau_0^2, \infty)) \cap [\tau_{\min}, \infty)$ and unstable for $\tau \in (\tau_0^1, \tau_0^2) \cap [\tau_{\min}, \infty)$.*

(iv) *Assume that for some $n \in \mathbb{N}_0$, $S_n(\tau)$ has k positive real roots $\tau_n^k \in I$ and that ω_n^k is the corresponding root of* (12)*, $n \in \mathbb{N}_0$, $k \in \mathbb{N}$. Similar to the above process, we can probe into the stability switches and Hopf bifurcation of E^* by judging the value of β and the sign of $\mathrm{d}S_n(\tau_n^k)/\mathrm{d}\tau$.*

3. Direction of Hopf Bifurcation and Stability of Bifurcated Periodic Solutions

In this section, we intend to apply the center manifold theorem and normal form method put forward by Hassard et al. [36] to discuss the direction of Hopf bifurcation and the stability of bifurcated periodic solutions of model (8) at $\tau = \tau_n^k$.

Let $\tau = \tau_n^k + \mu$, $\mu \in \mathbb{R}$. Therefore, the model (8) experiences a Hopf bifurcation when $\mu = 0$. Let $x_1(t) = x(\tau t) - x^*$, $y_1(t) = y(\tau t) - y^*$ and replace $x_1(t), y_1(t)$ with $x(t), y(t)$, respectively. Then model (8) can be converted to the functional differential equation in the phase space $\mathcal{C} = C([-1, 0], \mathbb{R}^2)$ as

$$\dot{U}(t) = L_\mu(U_t) + f(\mu, U_t), \tag{20}$$

where $U(t) = [x(t), y(t)]^T \in \mathbb{R}^2$, $U_t(\theta) = U(t + \theta) \in \mathcal{C}$, $L_\mu : \mathcal{C} \to \mathbb{R}^2$ and $f : \mathbb{R} \times \mathcal{C} \to \mathbb{R}^2$ are given as follows.

$$L_\mu(\phi) = \left(\tau_n^k + \mu\right)[B_1\phi(0) + B_2\phi(-1)] \quad \text{and} \quad f(\mu, \phi) = (\tau_n^k + \mu)(f_1, f_2)^T,$$

where $\phi(\theta) = (\phi_1(\theta), \phi_2(\theta))^T \in \mathcal{C}$,

$$\begin{aligned}
B_1 &= \begin{pmatrix} a_1 & a_2 \\ 0 & b_3 \end{pmatrix}_{\tau = \tau_n^k}, \\
B_2 &= \begin{pmatrix} 0 & 0 \\ b_1 & b_2 \end{pmatrix}_{\tau = \tau_n^k}, \\
f_1 &= k_{11}\phi_1^2(0) + k_{12}\phi_1(0)\phi_2(0), \\
f_2 &= k_{21}\phi_2^2(0) + k_{22}\phi_1^2(-1) + k_{23}\phi_1(-1)\phi_2(-1),
\end{aligned}$$

with

$$k_{11} = \frac{\alpha\beta y^*}{(1 + \alpha x^*)^3} - 1, \quad k_{12} = -\frac{\beta}{(1 + \alpha x^*)^2},$$

$$k_{21} = -\tilde{\rho}, \quad k_{22} = -\frac{\alpha\gamma y^* e^{-\delta_j \tau_n^k}}{(1 + \alpha x^*)^3}, \quad k_{23} = \frac{\gamma e^{-\delta_j \tau_n^k}}{(1 + \alpha x^*)^2}.$$

By utilizing the Riesz representation theorem, it is quite easy to know that there is a 2×2 matrix function $\eta(\theta, \mu)$ filled with bounded variation ($\theta \in [-1, 0]$), such that

$$L_\mu(\phi) = \int_{-1}^{0} d\eta(\theta, \mu)\phi(\theta), \quad \phi \in C\left([-1, 0], \mathbb{R}^2\right).$$

As a matter of fact, we can select

$$\eta(\theta,\mu) = \left(\tau_n^k + \mu\right) B_1 \delta(\theta) - \left(\tau_n^k + \mu\right) B_2 \delta(\theta + 1),$$

where δ represents the Dirac-delta function. For $\phi \in C^1([-1,0],\mathbb{R}^2)$, we define

$$A(\mu)\phi(\theta) = \begin{cases} \dfrac{d\phi(\theta)}{d\theta}, & \theta \in [-1,0), \\ \displaystyle\int_{-1}^{0} d\eta(\mu,s)\phi(s), & \theta = 0, \end{cases}$$

and

$$R(\mu)\phi(\theta) = \begin{cases} 0, & \theta \in [-1,0), \\ f(\mu,\phi), & \theta = 0. \end{cases}$$

Then Equation (20) is equal to

$$\dot{U}_t = A(\mu)U_t + R(\mu)U_t. \tag{21}$$

For $\psi \in C^1\left([0,1],(\mathbb{R}^2)^*\right)$, the adjoint operator A^* of $A(0)$ can be denoted by

$$A^*\psi(s) = \begin{cases} -\dfrac{d\psi(s)}{ds}, & s \in (0,1], \\ \displaystyle\int_{-1}^{0} d\eta^T(t,0)\psi(-t), & s = 0. \end{cases} \tag{22}$$

For $\phi \in C^1([-1,0],\mathbb{R}^2)$, $\psi \in C^1\left([0,1],(\mathbb{R}^2)^*\right)$, a bilinear form is given by

$$\langle \psi(s), \phi(\theta) \rangle = \bar{\psi}(0)\phi(0) - \int_{-1}^{0}\int_{\xi=0}^{\theta} \bar{\psi}(\xi - \theta) d\eta(\theta)\phi(\xi) d\xi, \tag{23}$$

where $\eta(\theta) = \eta(\theta,0)$.

Through the argument in the previous section, we see that $\pm i\omega_n^k \tau_n^k$ are the eigenvalues of $A(0)$. Hence, they are also the eigenvalues of A^*. Moreover, we hold the assumption that $q(\theta) = (1,\rho)^T e^{i\theta\omega_n^k\tau_n^k}$ and $q^*(s) = D(1,\rho^*)^T e^{is\omega_n^k\tau_n^k}$ are the eigenvectors of $A(0)$ and A^*, which correspond to eigenvalues $i\omega_n^k\tau_n^k$ and $-i\omega_n^k\tau_n^k$, respectively.

A careful calculation gives

$$\rho = \frac{i\omega_n^k - a_1}{a_2} \quad \text{and} \quad \rho^* = -\frac{a_1 + i\omega_n^k}{b_1 e^{i\omega_n^k\tau_n^k}}.$$

Direct from Equation (23), we obtain

$$\begin{aligned} \langle q^*(s), q(\theta) \rangle &= \overline{q^*}^T(0)q(0) - \int_{-1}^{0}\int_{\xi=0}^{\theta} \overline{q^*}^T(\xi - \theta) d\eta(\theta) q(\xi) d\xi \\ &= \bar{D}(1,\overline{\rho^*})\begin{pmatrix} 1 \\ \rho \end{pmatrix} - \int_{-1}^{0}\int_{\xi=0}^{\theta} \bar{D}(1,\overline{\rho^*}) e^{-i\omega_n^k\tau_n^k(\xi-\theta)} d\eta(\theta) \begin{pmatrix} 1 \\ \rho \end{pmatrix} e^{i\omega_n^k\tau_n^k\xi} d\xi \\ &= \bar{D}\left[1 + \overline{\rho^*}\rho - \int_{-1}^{0}\int_{\xi=0}^{\theta} (1,\overline{\rho^*}) e^{i\theta\omega_n^k\tau_n^k} d\eta(\theta) \begin{pmatrix} 1 \\ \rho \end{pmatrix} d\xi\right] \\ &= \bar{D}\left[1 + \overline{\rho^*}\rho + \tau_n^k e^{-i\omega_n^k\tau_n^k}(1,\overline{\rho^*}) B_2 \begin{pmatrix} 1 \\ \rho \end{pmatrix}\right] \\ &= \bar{D}\left[1 + \overline{\rho^*}\rho + \tau_n^k e^{-i\omega_n^k\tau_n^k}(b_1\overline{\rho^*} + b_2\rho\overline{\rho^*})\right]. \end{aligned}$$

As a result, we define

$$\bar{D} = \left[1 + \overline{\rho^*}\rho + \tau_n^k e^{-i\omega_n^k\tau_n^k}(b_1\overline{\rho^*} + b_2\rho\overline{\rho^*})\right]^{-1}$$

such that $\langle q^*(s), q(\theta)\rangle = 1$.

Furthermore, we can easily obtain $\langle q^*(s), \bar{q}(\theta)\rangle = 0$ due to $\langle q^*, A(0)\bar{q}\rangle = \langle A^*(0)q^*, \bar{q}\rangle$.

In what follows, we intend to apply the same nations as those in [36]. We plan to work out the coordinates to describe the center manifold C_0 at $\mu = 0$. When $\mu = 0$, the solution of Equation (21) is denoted by U_t. Define

$$z(t) = \langle q^*, U_t\rangle, \quad W(t,\theta) = U_t(\theta) - zq(\theta) - \bar{z}\bar{q}(\theta) = U_t(\theta) - 2\mathrm{Re}\{z(t)q(\theta)\}. \tag{24}$$

On the center manifold C_0, it follows that

$$W(t,\theta) = W(z(t), \bar{z}(t), \theta) \triangleq W_{20}(\theta)\frac{z^2}{2} + W_{11}(\theta)z\bar{z} + W_{02}(\theta)\frac{\bar{z}^2}{2} + W_{30}(\theta)\frac{z^3}{6} + \cdots, \tag{25}$$

where z and $\bar{z}$ refer to local coordinates for C_0 in the direction of q^* and $\overline{q^*}$. If U_t is real, it is obvious to recognize that W is real. In consequence, we only consider real solutions.

For the solution of Equation (21) $U_t \in C_0$, because of $\mu = 0$, we obtain

$$\begin{aligned}
\dot{z}(t) &= \langle q^*, \dot{U}_t\rangle = \langle q^*, A(0)U_t + R(0)U_t\rangle \\
&= \langle A^*(0)q^*, U_t\rangle + \overline{q^*}(0)f(0, U_t) \\
&\triangleq i\omega_n^k\tau_n^k z + \overline{q^*}(0)f_0(z, \bar{z}).
\end{aligned}$$

The equation above can be rewritten as

$$\dot{z}(t) = i\omega_n^k\tau_n^k z + g(z, \bar{z}),$$

with

$$g(z,\bar{z}) = \overline{q^*}(0)f_0(z,\bar{z}) = g_{20}\frac{z^2}{2} + g_{11}z\bar{z} + g_{02}\frac{\bar{z}^2}{2} + g_{21}\frac{z^2\bar{z}}{2} + \cdots. \tag{26}$$

Being aware that $U_t(\theta) = (x_t(\theta), y_t(\theta))^T = W(t,\theta) + zq(\theta) + \bar{z}\bar{q}(\theta)$, $q(\theta) = (1,\rho)^T e^{i\theta\omega_n^k\tau_n^k}$ and Equation (25), we have

$$\begin{aligned}
x_t(\theta) &= ze^{i\theta\omega_n^k\tau_n^k} + \bar{z}e^{-i\theta\omega_n^k\tau_n^k} + W_{20}^{(1)}(\theta)\frac{z^2}{2} + W_{11}^{(1)}(\theta)z\bar{z} + W_{02}^{(1)}(\theta)\frac{\bar{z}^2}{2} + O(|(z,\bar{z})|^3), \\
y_t(\theta) &= \rho ze^{i\theta\omega_n^k\tau_n^k} + \bar{\rho}\bar{z}e^{-i\theta\omega_n^k\tau_n^k} + W_{20}^{(2)}(\theta)\frac{z^2}{2} + W_{11}^{(2)}(\theta)z\bar{z} + W_{02}^{(2)}(\theta)\frac{\bar{z}^2}{2} + O(|(z,\bar{z})|^3).
\end{aligned}$$

Consequently, from Equation (26), we obtain

$$\begin{aligned}
g(z,\bar{z}) =& \overline{q^*}(0)f_0(z,\bar{z}) = \bar{D}(1,\overline{\rho^*})\tau_n^k\begin{pmatrix} k_{11}x_t^2(0) + k_{12}x_t(0)y_t(0) \\ k_{21}y_t^2(0) + k_{22}x_t^2(-1) + k_{23}x_t(-1)y_t(-1) \end{pmatrix} \\
=& \bar{D}\tau_n^k\Big[k_{11}\Big(z + \bar{z} + W_{20}^{(1)}(0)\frac{z^2}{2} + W_{11}^{(1)}(0)z\bar{z} + W_{02}^{(1)}(0)\frac{\bar{z}^2}{2} + O(|(z,\bar{z})|^3)\Big)^2 \\
&+ k_{12}\Big(z + \bar{z} + W_{20}^{(1)}(0)\frac{z^2}{2} + W_{11}^{(1)}(0)z\bar{z} + W_{02}^{(1)}(0)\frac{\bar{z}^2}{2} + O(|(z,\bar{z})|^3)\Big) \\
&\times\Big(\rho z + \bar{\rho}\bar{z} + W_{20}^{(2)}(0)\frac{z^2}{2} + W_{11}^{(2)}(0)z\bar{z} + W_{02}^{(2)}(0)\frac{\bar{z}^2}{2} + O(|(z,\bar{z})|^3)\Big)\Big] \\
&+ \bar{D}\tau_n^k\overline{\rho^*}\Big[k_{21}\Big(\rho z + \bar{\rho}\bar{z} + W_{20}^{(2)}(0)\frac{z^2}{2} + W_{11}^{(2)}(0)z\bar{z} \\
&+ W_{02}^{(2)}(0)\frac{\bar{z}^2}{2} + O(|(z,\bar{z})|^3)\Big)^2
\end{aligned}$$

$$
\begin{aligned}
&+k_{22}\Big(ze^{-i\omega_n^k\tau_n^k}+\bar{z}e^{i\omega_n^k\tau_n^k}+W_{20}^{(1)}(-1)\frac{z^2}{2}+W_{11}^{(1)}(-1)z\bar{z}\\
&+W_{02}^{(1)}(-1)\frac{\bar{z}^2}{2}+O(|(z,\bar{z})|^3)\Big)^2\\
&+k_{23}\Big(ze^{-i\omega_n^k\tau_n^k}+\bar{z}e^{i\omega_n^k\tau_n^k}+W_{20}^{(1)}(-1)\frac{z^2}{2}+W_{11}^{(1)}(-1)z\bar{z}\\
&+W_{02}^{(1)}(-1)\frac{\bar{z}^2}{2}+O(|(z,\bar{z})|^3)\Big)\times\Big(\rho ze^{-i\omega_n^k\tau_n^k}+\bar{\rho}\bar{z}e^{i\omega_n^k\tau_n^k}\\
&+W_{20}^{(2)}(-1)\frac{z^2}{2}+W_{11}^{(2)}(-1)z\bar{z}+W_{02}^{(2)}(-1)\frac{\bar{z}^2}{2}+O(|(z,\bar{z})|^3)\Big)\Big].
\end{aligned}
$$

Comparing the above formula with Equation (26), we can obtain

$$
\begin{aligned}
g_{20}&=2\bar{D}\tau_n^k(k_{11}+\rho k_{12})+2\bar{D}\tau_n^k\overline{\rho^*}(\rho^2k_{21}+e^{-2i\omega_n^k\tau_n^k}k_{22}+\rho e^{-2i\omega_n^k\tau_n^k}k_{23}),\\
g_{11}&=\bar{D}\tau_n^k[2k_{11}+(\bar{\rho}+\rho)k_{12}]+\bar{D}\tau_n^k\overline{\rho^*}[2\rho\bar{\rho}k_{21}+2k_{22}+(\bar{\rho}+\rho)k_{23}],\\
g_{02}&=2\bar{D}\tau_n^k(k_{11}+\bar{\rho}k_{12})+2\bar{D}\tau_n^k\overline{\rho^*}(\bar{\rho}^2k_{21}+e^{2i\omega_n^k\tau_n^k}k_{22}+\bar{\rho}e^{2i\omega_n^k\tau_n^k}k_{23}),\\
g_{21}&=\bar{D}\tau_n^k\Big[\Big(4W_{11}^{(1)}(0)+2W_{20}^{(1)}(0)\Big)k_{11}+\Big(2W_{11}^{(2)}(0)+W_{20}^{(2)}(0)+\bar{\rho}W_{20}^{(1)}(0)+2\rho W_{11}^{(1)}(0)\Big)k_{12}\Big]\\
&\quad+\bar{D}\tau_n^k\overline{\rho^*}\Big[\Big(4\rho W_{11}^{(2)}(0)+2\bar{\rho}W_{20}^{(2)}(0)\Big)k_{21}+\Big(4W_{11}^{(1)}(-1)e^{-i\omega_n^k\tau_n^k}+2W_{20}^{(1)}(-1)e^{i\omega_n^k\tau_n^k}\Big)k_{22}\\
&\quad+\Big(2W_{11}^{(2)}(-1)e^{-i\omega_n^k\tau_n^k}+W_{20}^{(2)}(-1)e^{i\omega_n^k\tau_n^k}+\bar{\rho}W_{20}^{(1)}(-1)e^{i\omega_n^k\tau_n^k}+2\rho W_{11}^{(1)}(-1)e^{-i\omega_n^k\tau_n^k}\Big)k_{23}\Big].
\end{aligned}
$$

We further require to derive the expression of $W_{20}(\theta)$ and $W_{11}(\theta)$ on account of their appearance in g_{21}.

From Equations (21) and (24), we gain

$$
\begin{aligned}
\dot{W}&=\dot{U}_t-\dot{z}q-\dot{\bar{z}}\bar{q}\\
&=\begin{cases}AW-2\mathrm{Re}\{\overline{q^*}(0)f_0q(\theta)\}, & \theta\in[-1,0),\\ AW-2\mathrm{Re}\{\overline{q^*}(0)f_0q(\theta)\}+f_0, & \theta=0,\end{cases}\\
&\triangleq AW+H(z,\bar{z},\theta),
\end{aligned}
\tag{27}
$$

where

$$
H(z,\bar{z},\theta)=H_{20}(\theta)\frac{z^2}{2}+H_{11}(\theta)z\bar{z}+H_{02}(\theta)\frac{\bar{z}^2}{2}+\cdots. \tag{28}
$$

Notice that $\dot{W}=W_z\dot{z}+W_{\bar{z}}\dot{\bar{z}}=AW+H(z,\bar{z},\theta)$, that is to say

$$
\begin{aligned}
&[W_{20}(\theta)z+W_{11}(\theta)\bar{z}]\Big[i\omega_n^k\tau_n^kz+g(z,\bar{z})\Big]+[W_{11}(\theta)z+W_{02}(\theta)\bar{z}]\Big[-i\omega_n^k\tau_n^k\bar{z}+\bar{g}(z,\bar{z})\Big]+\cdots\\
&=AW_{20}(\theta)\frac{z^2}{2}+AW_{11}(\theta)z\bar{z}+AW_{02}(\theta)\frac{\bar{z}^2}{2}+\cdots+H_{20}(\theta)\frac{z^2}{2}+H_{11}(\theta)z\bar{z}+H_{02}(\theta)\frac{\bar{z}^2}{2}+\cdots.
\end{aligned}
$$

Paying attention to the corresponding coefficients, we can obtain

$$
\begin{aligned}
(A-2i\omega_n^k\tau_n^k)W_{20}(\theta)&=-H_{20}(\theta),\\
AW_{11}(\theta)&=-H_{11}(\theta),\\
(A+2i\omega_n^k\tau_n^k)W_{20}(\theta)&=-H_{02}(\theta),\\
&\cdots
\end{aligned}
\tag{29}
$$

From (27), we observe that for $\theta\in[-1,0)$,

$$
H(z,\bar{z},\theta)=-\overline{q^*}(0)f_0q(\theta)-q^*(0)\bar{f}_0\bar{q}(\theta)=-g(z,\bar{z})q(\theta)-\bar{g}(z,\bar{z})\bar{q}(\theta). \tag{30}
$$

Comparing the coefficients of the above equation with those in Equation (28), we have

$$H_{20}(\theta) = -g_{20}q(\theta) - \bar{g}_{02}\bar{q}(\theta), \quad H_{11}(\theta) = -g_{11}q(\theta) - \bar{g}_{11}\bar{q}(\theta). \tag{31}$$

It is direct from (29), (31) and the definition of A that

$$\begin{cases} \dot{W}_{20}(\theta) = 2i\omega_n^k\tau_n^k W_{20}(\theta) + g_{20}q(\theta) + \bar{g}_{02}\bar{q}(\theta), \\ \dot{W}_{11}(\theta) = g_{11}q(\theta) + \bar{g}_{11}\bar{q}(\theta), \end{cases}$$

which indicates that

$$\begin{cases} W_{20}(\theta) = \dfrac{ig_{20}q(0)}{\omega_n^k\tau_n^k}e^{i\theta\omega_n^k\tau_n^k} + \dfrac{i\bar{g}_{02}\bar{q}(0)}{3\omega_n^k\tau_n^k}e^{-i\theta\omega_n^k\tau_n^k} + E_1 e^{2i\theta\omega_n^k\tau_n^k}, \\ W_{11}(\theta) = -\dfrac{ig_{11}q(0)}{\omega_n^k\tau_n^k}e^{i\theta\omega_n^k\tau_n^k} + \dfrac{i\bar{g}_{11}\bar{q}(0)}{\omega_n^k\tau_n^k}e^{-i\theta\omega_n^k\tau_n^k} + E_2, \end{cases} \tag{32}$$

where $E_1 = \left(E_1^{(1)}, E_1^{(2)}\right) \in \mathbb{R}^2$, $E_2 = \left(E_2^{(1)}, E_2^{(2)}\right) \in \mathbb{R}^2$. In addition, they are all constant vectors. Next, we shall be devoted to finding appropriate E_1 and E_2.

It is obvious that when $\theta = 0$, $H(z, \bar{z}, 0) = -2\mathrm{Re}\{\overline{q^*}(0) f_0 q(0)\} + f_0$. So it follows that

$$\begin{cases} H_{20}(0) = -g_{20}q(0) - \bar{g}_{02}\bar{q}(0) + 2\tau_n^k \begin{pmatrix} k_{11} + \rho k_{12} \\ \rho^2 k_{21} + e^{-2i\omega_n^k\tau_n^k}k_{22} + \rho e^{-2i\omega_n^k\tau_n^k}k_{23} \end{pmatrix}, & (33) \\ H_{11}(0) = -g_{11}q(0) - \bar{g}_{11}\bar{q}(0) + \tau_n^k \begin{pmatrix} 2k_{11} + (\bar{\rho} + \rho)k_{12} \\ 2\rho\bar{\rho}k_{21} + 2k_{22} + (\bar{\rho} + \rho)k_{23} \end{pmatrix}. & (34) \end{cases}$$

Moreover, according to the expression of A and (29), we obtain

$$\int_{-1}^{0} d\eta(\theta) W_{20}(\theta) = 2i\omega_n^k\tau_n^k W_{20}(0) - H_{20}(0), \tag{35}$$

and

$$\int_{-1}^{0} d\eta(\theta) W_{11}(\theta) = -H_{11}(0). \tag{36}$$

Now, substituting the first equation of (32) and (33) into (35) and observing that

$$\left(i\omega_n^k\tau_n^k I - \int_{-1}^{0} e^{i\theta\omega_n^k\tau_n^k} d\eta(\theta)\right) q(0) = 0,$$

and

$$\left(-i\omega_n^k\tau_n^k I - \int_{-1}^{0} e^{-i\theta\omega_n^k\tau_n^k} d\eta(\theta)\right) \bar{q}(0) = 0,$$

then we obtain

$$\left(2i\omega_n^k\tau_n^k I - \int_{-1}^{0} e^{2i\theta\omega_n^k\tau_n^k} d\eta(\theta)\right) E_1 = 2\tau_n^k \begin{pmatrix} k_{11} + \rho k_{12} \\ \rho^2 k_{21} + e^{-2i\omega_n^k\tau_n^k}k_{22} + \rho e^{-2i\omega_n^k\tau_n^k}k_{23} \end{pmatrix},$$

which results in

$$\begin{pmatrix} 2i\omega_n^k - a_1 & -a_2 \\ -b_1 e^{-2i\omega_n^k\tau_n^k} & 2i\omega_n^k - b_3 - b_2 e^{-2i\omega_n^k\tau_n^k} \end{pmatrix} E_1 = 2 \begin{pmatrix} k_{11} + \rho k_{12} \\ \rho^2 k_{21} + e^{-2i\omega_n^k\tau_n^k}k_{22} + \rho e^{-2i\omega_n^k\tau_n^k}k_{23} \end{pmatrix},$$

that is

$$E_1 = 2\begin{pmatrix} 2i\omega_n^k - a_1 & -a_2 \\ -b_1 e^{-2i\omega_n^k\tau_n^k} & 2i\omega_n^k - b_3 - b_2 e^{-2i\omega_n^k\tau_n^k} \end{pmatrix}^{-1} \begin{pmatrix} k_{11} + \rho k_{12} \\ \rho^2 k_{21} + e^{-2i\omega_n^k\tau_n^k} k_{22} + \rho e^{-2i\omega_n^k\tau_n^k} k_{23} \end{pmatrix}. \tag{37}$$

Similarly, substituting the second equation of (32) and (34) into (35), we receive

$$E_2 = \begin{pmatrix} -a_1 & -a_2 \\ -b_1 & -b_2 - b_3 \end{pmatrix}^{-1} \begin{pmatrix} 2k_{11} + (\bar{\rho} + \rho)k_{12} \\ 2\rho\bar{\rho}k_{21} + 2k_{22} + (\bar{\rho} + \rho)k_{23} \end{pmatrix}. \tag{38}$$

Thus, we can determine g_{21} from (32), (37) and (38). Furthermore, we are able to calculate such values:

$$\begin{aligned} c_1(0) =& \frac{i}{2\omega_n^k\tau_n^k}\left(g_{20}g_{11} - 2|g_{11}|^2 - \frac{|g_{02}|^2}{3}\right) + \frac{g_{21}}{2}, \\ \mu_2 =& -\frac{\mathrm{Re}\{c_1(0)\}}{\mathrm{Re}\{\lambda'(\tau_n^k)\}}, \\ \beta_2 =& 2\mathrm{Re}\{c_1(0)\}, \\ T_2 =& -\frac{\mathrm{Im}\{c_1(0)\} + \mu_2\mathrm{Im}\left\{\lambda'\left(\tau_n^k\right)\right\}}{\omega_n^k\tau_n^k}, \end{aligned} \tag{39}$$

which describe the nature of bifurcated periodic solutions in the center manifold at the threshold value $\tau = \tau_n^k$. Therewith, we can present the following theorem.

Theorem 3. *The following statements are all correct.*

(i) *The direction of the Hopf bifurcation is determined by the sign of μ_2. If $\mu_2 > 0 (< 0)$, the Hopf bifurcation is supercritical (subcritical).*
(ii) *The stability of the bifurcated periodic solutions is decided by the sign of β_2. If $\beta_2 > 0 (< 0)$, the bifurcated periodic solutions are unstable (stable).*
(iii) *The period of the bifurcated periodic solutions is decided by the sign of T_2. The period increases (decreases) if $T_2 > 0 (< 0)$.*

4. Numerical Simulation

In this section, we provide a comprehensive analysis of how the maturation delay influences ecological dynamics of model (8) by giving some numerical examples. In addition, we will provide some biological interpretations.

In the first place, in accordance with the values of parameters in [33] and conditions given in the theoretical part of our paper, we choose

$$\alpha = 2.78, \beta = 0.6, \bar{\rho} = 0.04, \gamma = 0.7, \delta_j = 0.2, \tag{40}$$

with initial conditions $(0.1, 0.1)$.

When $\tau = 0$, there exists one and only one positive equilibrium $E^*(0.0532, 1.8115)$. Moreover, E^* is locally asymptotically stable based on Lemma 2, just as shown in Figure 1. Biologically, when it takes no time for immature predators to mature, two populations can coexist in a stable state for a long time.

We draw the image of the function $S_n(\tau)(n = 0, 1)$ versus τ with the parameters satisfying (40) by using Matlab, just as illustrated in Figure 2. Figure 2a manifests that $S_0(\tau)$ has two zeros, one is $\tau_0^1 = 0.0556$, the other is $\tau_0^2 = 4.3889$, and $\mathrm{d}S_n(\tau_0^1)/\mathrm{d}\tau > 0$, $\mathrm{d}S_n(\tau_0^2)/\mathrm{d}\tau < 0$. Moreover, we find that $S_1(\tau) < 0$ for all $\tau \in I$ from Figure 2b. Because $S_n(\tau) > S_{n+1}(\tau)$ for all $n \in \mathbb{N}_0$, $\tau \in I$. Hence, $S_n(\tau)(n = 1, 2, \cdots)$ admits no zeros on I.

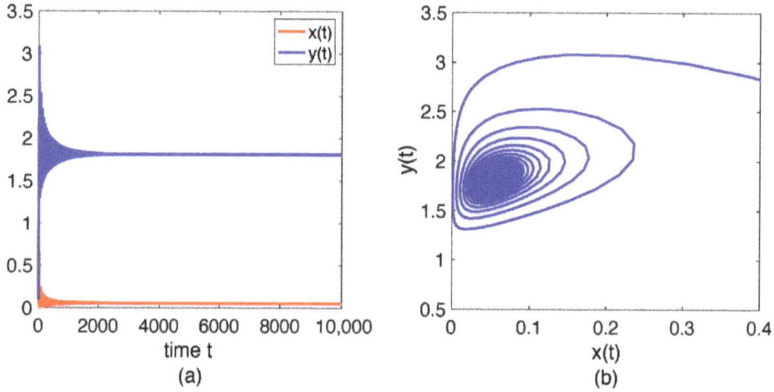

Figure 1. Dynamic behavior of the model (8) with $\tau = 0$, $\alpha = 2.78$, $\beta = 0.6$, $\tilde{\rho} = 0.04$ and $\gamma = 0.7$. In this case, the interior equilibrium E^* is locally asymptotically stable. (**a**) Time series plot, (**b**) phase portrait.

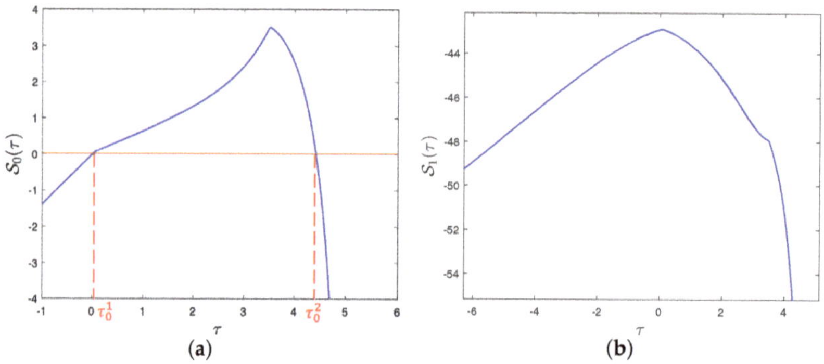

Figure 2. Graphs of $S_n(\tau)$ in terms of maturation delay τ with the values of parameters given in (40). (**a**) $S_0(\tau)$, it has two zeros, named τ_0^1 and τ_0^2, (**b**) $S_1(\tau)$, it has no zeros on I.

It is direct from Figure 2 and Theorem 2 that E^* is locally asymptotically stable for $\tau \in (0, 0.0556) \cup (4.3889, \infty)$ and unstable for $\tau \in (0.0556, 4.3889)$. By considering the maturation delay as the bifurcation parameter, we further plot the bifurcation diagrams of the model (8) to demonstrate the switching process of E^*, just as illustrated in Figure 3. From a biological perspective, if the value of the maturation delay belongs to the interval $(0, 0.0556)$, both populations can survive and tend to a stable state. Once the maturation delay passes through the threshold value $\tau_0^1 = 0.0556$, the positive equilibrium E^* loses it stability and a Hopf bifurcation occurs, which also means that both individuals can still exist but their densities fluctuate periodically with time. When the maturation delay exceeds the threshold value $\tau_0^2 = 4.3889$, the positive equilibrium E^* regains its stability, that is to say, both populations can coexist for a long time. We choose some τ with different values for simulations which are displayed in Figure 4. When $\tau = 0.04$, $4.7 \in (0, 0.0556) \cup (4.3889, \infty)$, E^* is locally asymptotically stable, just as illustrated in Figure 4a,f. When $\tau = 0.09, 0.1, 2, 4.2 \in (0.0556, 4.3889)$, E^* is unstable, just as illustrated in Figure 4b–e. These simulations indicate that stability switches occur as τ moves from 0.04 to 2 to 4.7.

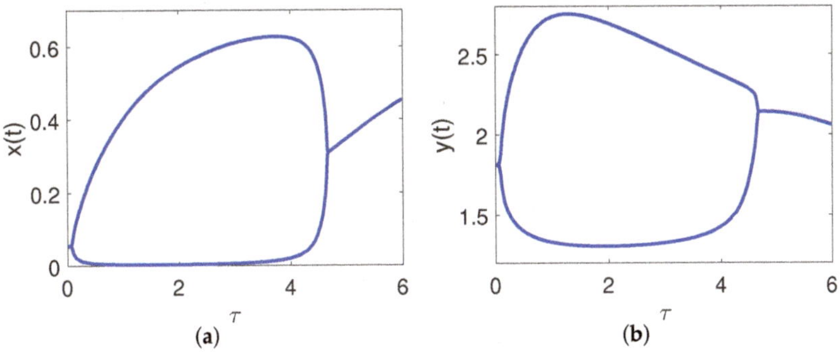

Figure 3. Bifurcation diagrams of the model (8) by considering τ as the bifurcation parameter. (**a**) $x(t)$, (**b**) $y(t)$.

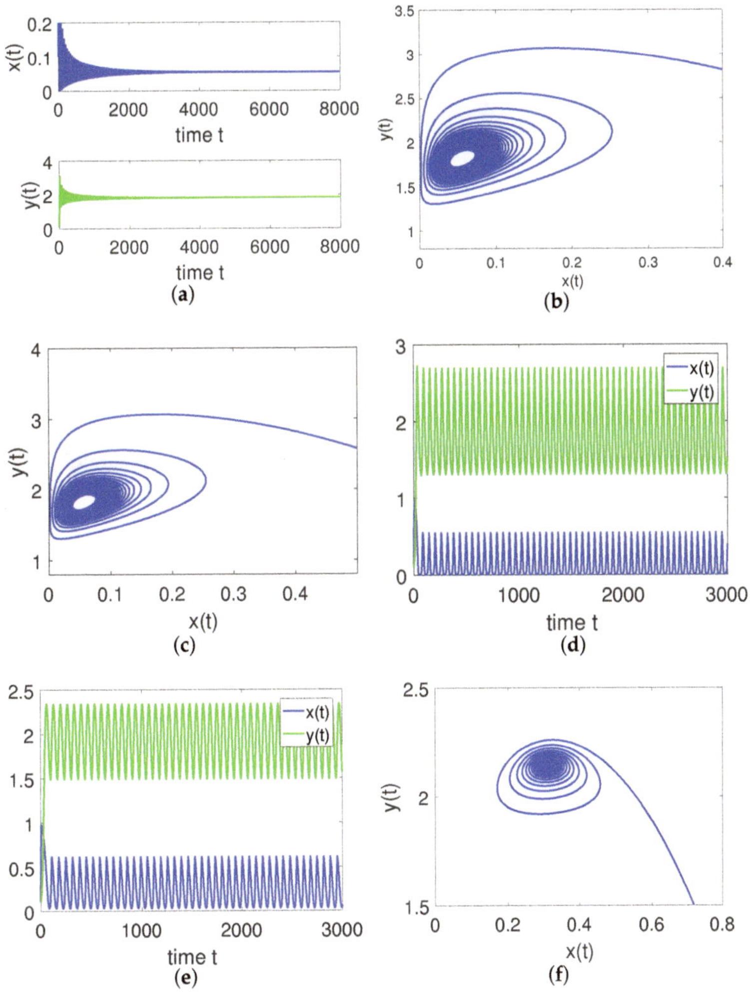

Figure 4. Dynamics of the model (8) with different values of τ. (**a**) $\tau = 0.04$, (**b**) $\tau = 0.09$, (**c**) $\tau = 0.1$, (**d**) $\tau = 2$, (**e**) $\tau = 4.2$, (**f**) $\tau = 4.7$.

5. Conclusions

In this paper, an existing delayed predator–prey model with maturation delay, a stage structure for generalist predators and a Holling type-II functional response was investigated. We first obtained the conditions for the existence of the stability switches of the positive equilibrium and Hopf bifurcations caused by the increase in the value of the maturation delay for model (8) by utilizing the geometric criterion proposed by Beretta and Kuang [18]. After that, we discussed the properties of Hopf bifurcation by dint of the normal form method and center manifold theory. At last, we confirmed our theoretical findings by numerical simulations. Notice that, the authors in [29] considered a predator–prey model with a Holling-II type functional response and a prey refuge and then investigated the Hopf bifurcation of the model by seeing some key parameters as bifurcation parameters, such as the refuge parameter and death rate of the predator. Roy et al. [33] further introduced the maturation delay and generalist predator into the modeling framework and then proposed model (7). Based on model (7), we extended the research carried out in [33]. We further studied the stability-switching properties of the positive equilibrium and Hopf bifurcation by considering the maturation delay as a bifurcation parameter, which was not conducted in [33]. Moreover, the authors in [29,33] all applied the traditional theoretical method to study the bifurcation. Compared to the method in [29,33], we utilized a geometric method, which is novel and practical. The results we obtained in this article are very important in respect of ecology and are essential for enhancing the predictive power of the mathematical model and have significant implications for understanding and managing predator–prey interactions in real-world ecosystems. They indicate that the delay lengths affect the stability of the model. As a result, we can legitimately control the value of the maturation delay to make E^* stable, which is beneficial to the coexistence of populations, beneficial to biodiversity protection.

Some interesting topics also deserve further considerations. For example, one can introduce additional biological delays in model (7), such as gestation delay, because the predator spends time in reproducing after consuming the prey and then try to study the stability switching properties of the positive equilibrium on the two-delay plane. If we consider other types of functional responses, what changes may take place? Moreover, a model incorporating stochastic elements to mimic random environmental fluctuations could be more realistic. Conducting a thorough sensitivity analysis of the key parameters could be conducive to identify which factors most significantly affect the stability of the model. Performing robustness checks would be helpful to ensure that the conclusions are not sensitive to specific starting points or configurations. Hence, considering a model with the above factors and further carrying out some analysis and checks are necessary. All of these are presented here for further research.

Author Contributions: Conceptualization, Z.-W.L. and X.-Y.M.; methodology, Z.-W.L.; software, Z.-W.L. and X.-Y.M.; validation, Z.-W.L. and X.-Y.M.; formal analysis, Z.-W.L.; investigation, Z.-W.L. and X.-Y.M.; writing—original draft, Z.-W.L.; writing—reviewing and editing, Z.-W.L. and X.-Y.M.; visualization, Z.-W.L. and X.-Y.M.; supervision, X.-Y.M. All authors have read and agreed to the published version of the manuscript.

Funding: This research was funded by the National Natural Science Foundation of China (grant numbers 12161054 and 11861044); the Excellent Postgraduate Innovation Star of Gansu Province (grant number 2023CXZX-492); the Doctoral Foundation of Lanzhou University of Technology; and the HongLiu First-Class Disciplines Development Program of Lanzhou University of Technology.

Data Availability Statement: Data are contained within the article.

Acknowledgments: We sincerely appreciate the Editors for their careful guidance and the reviewers for their valuable comments. We thank them for all their efforts in perfecting this paper.

Conflicts of Interest: The authors declare that they have no known competing financial interests or personal relationships that could have appeared to influence the work reported in this paper.

References

1. Lotka, A.J. Elements of physical biology. *Am. J. Public Health* **1926**, *21*, 341–343.
2. Volterra, V. Variations and fluctuations of the number of individuals in animal species living together. *J. Du Conseil* **1928**, *3*, 3–51. [CrossRef]
3. Tang, G.Y.; Tang, S.Y.; Cheke, R.A. Global analysis of a Holling type II predator-prey model with a constant prey refuge. *Nonlinear Dynam.* **2013**, *76*, 635–647. [CrossRef]
4. Khajanchi, S.; Banerjee, S. Role of constant prey refuge on stage structure predator-prey model with ratio dependent functional response. *Appl. Math. Comput.* **2017**, *314*, 193–198. [CrossRef]
5. Zhang, H.S.; Cai, Y.L.; Fu, S.M.; Wang, W.M. Impact of the fear effect in a prey-predator model incorporating a prey refuge. *Appl. Math. Comput.* **2019**, *356*, 328–337. [CrossRef]
6. Huang, Y.; Zhu, Z.L.; Li, Z. Modeling the Allee effect and fear effect in predator-prey system incorporating a prey refuge. *Adv. Differ. Equ.* **2020**, *321*, 321. [CrossRef]
7. Bellman, R.E.; Cooke, K.L. *Differential-Difference Equations*; Academic Press: New York, NY, USA, 1963.
8. Kuang, Y. *Delay Differential Equations with Applications in Population Dynamics*; Academic Press: Boston, MA, USA, 1993.
9. Smith, H. *An Introduction to Delay Differential Equations with Applications to the Life Sciences*; Springer: New York, NY, USA, 2011.
10. Kuang, Y.; Nagy, J.D.; Eikenberry, S.E. *Introduction to Mathematical Oncology*; Chemical Rubber Company Press: Boca Raton, FL, USA, 2016.
11. Li, S.; Yuan, S.L.; Jin, Z.; Wang, H. Bifurcation analysis in a diffusive predator-prey model with spatial memory of prey, Allee effect and maturation delay of predator. *J. Differ. Equ.* **2023**, *357*, 32–63. [CrossRef]
12. Cooke, K.L.; Grossman, Z. Discrete delay, distributed delay and stability switches. *J. Math. Anal. Appl.* **1982**, *86*, 592–627. [CrossRef]
13. Song, Y.L.; Cao, X.; Zhang, T.H. Bistability and delay-induced stability switches in a cancer network with the regulation of microRNA. *Commun. Nonlinear Sci.* **2018**, *54*, 302–319. [CrossRef]
14. Meng, X.Y.; Li, J. Dynamical behavior of a delayed prey-predator-scavenger system with fear effect and linear harvesting. *Int. J. Biomath.* **2021**, *14*, 2150024. [CrossRef]
15. Li, S.; Huang, C.D.; Song, X.Y. Novel method to detect Hopf bifurcation in a delayed fractional-order network model with bidirectional ring structure. *Int. J. Biomath.* **2023**, *16*, 2250117. [CrossRef]
16. Liang, Z.W.; Meng, X.Y. Stability and Hopf bifurcation of a multiple delayed predator–prey system with fear effect, prey refuge and Crowley—Martin function. *Chaos Solitons Fractals* **2023**, *175*, 113955. [CrossRef]
17. Zhang, Z.Q.; Yang, Z. Asymptotic stability for quaternion-valued fuzzy BAM neural networks via integral inequality approach. *Chaos Solitons Fractals* **2023**, *169*, 113227. [CrossRef]
18. Beretta, E.; Kuang, Y. Geometric stability switch criteria in delay differential systems with delay dependent parameters. *SIAM J. Math. Anal.* **2002**, *33*, 1144–1165. [CrossRef]
19. Xu, X.F.; Wei, J.J. Bifurcation analysis of a spruce budworm model with diffusion and physiological structures. *J. Differ. Equ.* **2017**, *262*, 5206–5230. [CrossRef]
20. Meng, X.Y.; Lu, M.M. Stability and bifurcation of a delayed prey-predator eco-epidemiological model with the impact of media. *AIMS Math.* **2023**, *8*, 17038–17066. [CrossRef]
21. Beretta, E.; Tang, Y.B. Extension of a geometric stability switch criterion. *Funkc. Ekvacioj* **2003**, *46*, 337–361. [CrossRef]
22. Gu, K.Q.; Niculescu, S.I.; Chen, J. On stability crossing curves for general systems with two delays. *J. Math. Anal. Appl.* **2005**, *311*, 231–253. [CrossRef]
23. Wang, C.H.; Yuan, S.L.; Wang, H. Spatiotemporal patterns of a diffusive prey-predator model with spatial memory and pregnancy period in an intimidatory environment. *J. Math. Biol.* **2022**, *84*, 12. [CrossRef]
24. An, Q.; Beretta, E.; Kuang, Y.; Wang, C.C.; Wang, H. Geometric stability switch criteria in delay differential equations with two delays and delay dependent parameters. *J. Differ. Equ.* **2019**, *266*, 7073–7100. [CrossRef]
25. Shu, H.Y.; Xu, W.X.; Wang, X.S.; Wu, J.H. Complex dynamics in a delay differential equation with two delays in tick growth with diapause. *J. Differ. Equ.* **2020**, *269*, 10937–10963. [CrossRef]
26. Jiang, Z.C.; Zhao, Y.; Bai, X.L.; Zhang, Z.X. Bifurcation and control of a planktonic ecological system with double delays by delayed feedback control. *J. Frankl. Inst.* **2021**, *358*, 3609–3632. [CrossRef]
27. Gourley, S.A.; Kuang, Y. A stage structured predator-prey model and its dependence on maturation delay and death rate. *J. Math. Biol.* **2004**, *49*, 188–200. [CrossRef] [PubMed]
28. Chen, S.S.; Shi, J.P.; Wei, J.J. The effect of delay on a diffusive predator-prey system with Holling Type-II predator functional response. *Commun. Pure Appl. Math.* **2013**, *12*, 481–501. [CrossRef]
29. Zhou, Y.; Sun, W.; Song, Y.F.; Zheng, Z.G.; Lu, J.H.; Chen, S.H. Hopf bifurcation analysis of a predator–prey model with Holling-II type functional response and a prey refuge. *Nonlinear Dynam.* **2019**, *97*, 1439–1450. [CrossRef]
30. Bai, D.; Yu, J.; Fan, M.; Kang, Y. Dynamics for a non-autonomous predator-prey system with generalist predator. *J. Math. Anal. Appl.* **2020**, *485*, 123820. [CrossRef]
31. Dey, S.; Banerjee, M.; Ghorai, S. Analytical detection of stationary turing pattern in a predator-prey system with generalist predator. *Math. Model. Nat. Phenom.* **2022**, *17*, 33. [CrossRef]

32. Roy, J.; Banerjee, M. Global stability of a predator–prey model with generalist predator. *Appl. Math. Lett.* **2023**, *142*, 108659. [CrossRef]
33. Roy, J.; Dey, S.; Banerjee, M. Maturation delay induced stability enhancement and shift of bifurcation thresholds in a predator–prey model with generalist predator. *Math. Comput. Simul.* **2023**, *211*, 368–393. [CrossRef]
34. Liu, S.; Beretta, E. A stage-structured predator-prey model of Beddington-DeAngelis type. *SIAM J. Appl. Math.* **2006**, *66*, 1101–1129. [CrossRef]
35. Banerjee, M.; Takeuchi, Y. Maturation delay for the predators can enhance stable coexistence for a class of prey-predator models. *J. Theor. Biol.* **2017**, *412*, 154–171. [CrossRef]
36. Hassard, B.D.; Kazarinoff, N.D.; Wan, Y.H. *Theory and Applications of Hopf Bifurcation*; Cambridge University Press: Cambridge, UK, 1981.

symmetry

Article

Dynamics of a Stochastic SVEIR Epidemic Model with Nonlinear Incidence Rate

Xinghao Wang [1], Liang Zhang [1,*] and Xiao-Bing Zhang [2]

[1] College of Science, Northwest A&F University, Yangling 712100, China; diyong99595@163.com
[2] Department of Applied Mathematics, Lanzhou University of Technology, Lanzhou 730050, China; zhangxb@lut.edu.cn
* Correspondence: zhanglsd@126.com or zhangl@nwsuaf.edu.cn

Abstract: This paper delves into the analysis of a stochastic epidemic model known as the susceptible–vaccinated–exposed–infectious–recovered (SVEIR) model, where transmission dynamics are governed by a nonlinear function. In the theoretical analysis section, by suitable stochastic Lyapunov functions, we establish that when the threshold value, denoted as R_0^s, falls below 1, the epidemic is destined for extinction. Conversely, if the reproduction number R_0 of the deterministic model surpasses 1, the model manifests an ergodic endemic stationary distribution. In the numerical simulations and data interpretation section, leveraging a graphical analysis with COVID-19 data, we illustrate that random fluctuations possess the capacity to quell disease outbreaks, underscoring the role of vaccines in curtailing the spread of diseases. This study not only contributes to the understanding of epidemic dynamics but also highlights the pivotal role of stochasticity and vaccination strategies in epidemic control and management. The inherent balance and patterns observed in epidemic spread and control strategies, reflect a symmetrical interplay between stochasticity, vaccination, and disease dynamics.

Keywords: stochastic SVEIR model; stability analysis; stationary distribution

MSC: 92D30; 60H10

1. Introduction

Over the past two decades, mathematical modeling has played a crucial role in both preventing and controlling infectious diseases, including severe acute respiratory syndrome (SARS) [1], human immunodeficiency virus infection/acquired immune deficiency syndrome (HIV/AIDS) [2], and H1N1 (swine flu) [3]. These models describe the evolution of various subpopulations over time within epidemic models. One widely used model is the SEIR (susceptible–exposed–infectious–recovered) model, which divides the population into four compartments: susceptible (S), individuals who are at risk of infection; exposed (E), individuals who have come into contact with infective individuals but show no symptoms; infectious (I), individuals displaying symptoms; and recovered (R), individuals who have recovered from the disease [4]. The SEIR model has various complex variants, including those with different control measures such as various incidence rates, constant and feedback vaccination and treatment controls, as well as models involving multiple interconnected regions or towns [5–10], and others cited within. The rate of incidence is widely recognized as playing a significant role in disease modeling, with factors such as population density and lifestyle influencing the increase and decrease in epidemics [11,12]. Many researchers have employed nonlinear incidence rates in their studies; for more in-depth information, readers are referred to [13–19] and related references. Vaccination is widely acknowledged as one of the most effective means of disease control and prevention [20], playing a pivotal role in the complete eradication of diseases like smallpox and partial control of diseases such as measles [21]. Numerous scholarly works have explored the dynamics of epidemic models with different vaccination schedules [7,13,19,22–26].

In 2018, Gao and Huang [22] conducted a study on the model described below:

$$\begin{cases} \frac{dS}{dt} = A - \frac{\beta SI}{1+aS+bI} - (\delta_0 + \mu)S + \eta V, \\ \frac{dE}{dt} = \frac{\beta SI}{1+aS+bI} - (\delta_0 + \delta_1)E, \\ \frac{dI}{dt} = \delta_1 E - (\delta_0 + \delta_2 + \delta_3)I, \\ \frac{dR}{dt} = \delta_2 I - \delta_0 R, \\ \frac{dV}{dt} = \mu S - (\delta_0 + \eta)V. \end{cases} \tag{1}$$

All the parameters in model (1) are positive. The variables S, E, I, R, and V represent the respective counts of susceptible, exposed, infectious, recovered, and vaccinated individuals at time t. Table 1 provides the biological interpretations of the remaining parameters.

Table 1. Biological interpretations of variables and parameters in model (1).

Parameter	Description
A	The recruitment rate of new individuals
β	The contact rate or the rate of transfer of virus from an infectious individual to the susceptible
δ_0	The natural mortality rate
η	The rate at which the vaccinated individuals lose their immunity and join the susceptible class
μ	The vaccination rate coefficient
δ_1	The rate at which exposed individuals become infectious
δ_2	The recovery rate of the infectious individuals
δ_3	The disease-related death rate of infectious individuals
a	The proportion constant related to susceptible individuals
b	The proportion constant related to infectious individuals

The results in [22] showed that the basic reproduction number of model (1) is

$$R_0 = \frac{\beta\delta_1 S_0}{(1+aS_0)(\delta_0+\delta_1)(\delta_0+\delta_2+\delta_3)}, \text{ where } S_0 = \frac{(\delta_0+\eta)A}{\delta_0^2 + (\mu+\eta)\delta_0}. \tag{2}$$

It is proved that if $R_0 < 1$, the disease-free equilibrium is globally asymptotically stable and if $R_0 > 1$, model (1) has an endemic equilibrium $(S^*, E^*, I^*, R^*, V^*)$ which is globally asymptotically stable.

The inherent randomness of epidemic growth and spread, attributed to the unpredictable nature of person-to-person contacts [27] and the susceptibility of populations to various disturbances [28], suggests that stochastic models may offer a more suitable approach for modeling epidemics in many scenarios [29–42]. Stochastic models are particularly beneficial in capturing the random occurrences of infectious contacts during the latent and infectious periods [43]. Many realistic stochastic epidemic models can be derived from their deterministic counterparts. For instance, Cai [38] developed a general SIRS epidemic model with a ratio-dependent incidence rate and its corresponding stochastic differential equation version. Ball and Neal [44] explored a general stochastic SIR model within a closed finite population, deriving a threshold parameter that determines the possibility of global epidemics. Yang et al. [45] examined the ergodicity and extinction of stochastic SIR and SEIR epidemic models with saturated incidence. Zhang and Zhang [42] investigated the threshold behavior of a deterministic and a stochastic SIQS epidemic model by considering varying total population sizes.

In its investigation of the stochastic epidemic model, our analysis not only sheds light on the dynamics of disease transmission and control but also unravels the symmetrical aspects inherent in epidemic behavior. By exploring the effects of stochasticity and vaccination strategies on disease spread, we can uncover a symmetrical relationship between these factors and the patterns observed in epidemic outcomes.

This paper focuses on a stochastic SVEIR epidemic model with a nonlinear incidence rate.

$$\begin{cases} dS = \left(A - \dfrac{\beta SI}{1+aS+bI} - (\delta_0+\mu)S + \eta V\right)dt + \sigma_1 S dB_1(t), \\ dE = \left(\dfrac{\beta SI}{1+aS+bI} - (\delta_0+\delta_1)E\right)dt + \sigma_2 E dB_2(t), \\ dI = (\delta_1 E - (\delta_0+\delta_2+\delta_3)I)dt + \sigma_3 I dB_3(t), \\ dR = (\delta_2 I - \delta_0 R) + \sigma_4 R dB_4(t), \\ dV = (\mu S - (\delta_0+\eta)V) + \sigma_5 dB_5(t). \end{cases} \quad (3)$$

The parameters in model (1) remain unchanged, with $\sigma_i^2 > 0$ denoting the intensities of white noise. Additionally, $B_i(t)$ $(i = 1, 2, \ldots, 5)$ represents independent standard Brownian motions, initialized at $B_i(0) = 0$.

In the study of epidemic model behavior, analyzing steady states and their stability is crucial [19]. In deterministic models, this analysis involves examining the stability of the disease-free equilibrium (or endemic equilibrium) through the basic reproduction number R_0. However, in the case of the stochastic model (3), there is no endemic equilibrium. Nevertheless, Khasminskii [46] demonstrated that the presence of an ergodic stationary distribution for model (3) can reveal the persistence of the infection.

The primary objective of this paper is to examine the extinction and the existence of an ergodic stationary distribution for model (3). We establish sufficient conditions for both the extinction and the existence of an ergodic stationary distribution.

The paper is organized as follows: Section 2 introduces the necessary preliminaries for subsequent analysis. Section 3 establishes sufficient conditions for both the extinction and the existence of an ergodic stationary distribution in model (3). Section 4 presents numerical simulations based on published data from COVID-19 to support our findings. Lastly, some concluding remarks summarize the results.

2. Preliminaries

Let $(\Omega, \mathscr{F}, \{\mathscr{F}_t\}_{t\geq 0}, P)$ be a complete probability space with a filtration $\{\mathscr{F}_t\}_{t\geq 0}$ satisfying the usual conditions, where it is increasing and right-continuous, and $\{\mathscr{F}_0\}$ contains all P-null sets. Additionally, define $\mathbb{R}_+^d = \{x \in \mathbb{R}^d : x_i > 0, 1 \leq i \leq d\}$.

We consider the d-dimensional stochastic differential equation (SDE) in general:

$$dx(t) = f(t, x(t))dt + g(t, x(t))dB_t, \quad (4)$$

here$f(t, x(t))$ is a function in $\mathbb{R}^d$ defined in $[t_0, \infty] \times \mathbb{R}^d$, $g(t, x(t))$ is a $d \times m$ matrix, and f and g are local Lipschitz functions in x. The term B_t represents an m-dimensional standard Brownian motion defined on the complete probability space $(\Omega, \mathscr{F}, \{\mathscr{F}_t\}_{t\geq 0}, P)$. The notation $C^{2,1}\left(\mathbb{R}^d \times [t_0, \infty]; \mathbb{R}_+\right)$ refers to the family of all non-negative functions $V(x,t)$ defined on $\mathbb{R}^d \times [t_0, \infty]$ such that they are continuously twice differentiable in x and once in t. The differential operator L of Equation (4) is defined [30] as

$$L = \frac{\partial}{\partial t} + \sum_{i=1}^d f_i(t)\frac{\partial}{\partial x_i} + \frac{1}{2}\sum_{i,j=1}^d \left[g^T(x,t)g(x,t)\right]_{ij}\frac{\partial^2}{\partial x_i \partial x_j}.$$

When the operator L operates on a function $V \in C^{2,1}\left(\mathbb{R}^d \times [t_0, \infty]; \mathbb{R}_+\right)$,

$$LV(x,t) = V_t(x,t) + V_x(x,t)f(x,t) + \frac{1}{2}trace\left[g^T(x,t)V_{xx}g(x,t)\right],$$

where $V_t(x,t) = \frac{\partial V}{\partial t}$, $V_x(x,t) = \left(\frac{\partial V}{\partial x_1}, \cdots, \frac{\partial V}{\partial x_d}\right)$, and $V_{xx} = \left(\frac{\partial^2 V}{\partial x_i \partial x_j}\right)_{d\times d}$. By Itô's formula, if $x(t)$ is solution of (4), then $dV(x,t) = LV(x,t)dt + V_x(x,t)g(x,t)dB_t$.

The following lemma pertains to the existence and uniqueness of a global positive solution, which is a prerequisite for investigating the long-term behavior of system (3).

Lemma 1. *Given any initial value $(S(0), E(0), I(0), R(0), V(0)) \in \mathbb{R}^5_+$, there exists a unique solution $X(t) = (S(t), E(t), I(t), R(t), V(t))$ of system (3) on $t \geq 0$ and this solution will almost surely remain within $\mathbb{R}^5_+$.*

Proof. Since the coefficients of the system (3) satisfy the local Lipschitz condition, for any initial value $(S(0), E(0), I(0), R(0), V(0)) \in \mathbb{R}^5_+$ there is a unique local solution in $[0, \tau_e]$, where τ_e denotes the explosion time [30]. To establish global solution existence, it suffices to demonstrate that $\tau_e = \infty$ almost surely (a.s.). To achieve this, let k_0 be sufficiently large such that every component of X_0 lies within the interval $[\frac{1}{k_0}, k_0]$. For each integer $k > k_0$, define the stopping time as follows:

$$\tau_k = inf\left\{t \in [0, \tau_e) : minX(t) \leq \frac{1}{k} \text{ } or \text{ } maxX(t) \geq k\right\}.$$

In this paper, we define $inf\varnothing = \infty$ (where $\varnothing$ denotes the empty set). It is evident that τ_k is increasing as $k \to \infty$. Let $\tau_\infty = \lim_{k\to\infty} \tau_k$, hence $\tau_\infty \leq \tau_e$ almost surely. If we can prove that $\tau_\infty = \infty$ almost surely, then $\tau_e = \infty$ ensuring $X(t) \in \mathbb{R}^5_+$ almost surely. for all $t \geq 0$. Therefore, demonstrating $\tau_\infty = \infty$ almost surely is crucial for completing the proof. If this assertion is contradicted there exit constants $T > 0$ and $\eta \in (0,1)$ such that $P\{\tau_\infty \leq T\} > \eta$. Consequently, there exists an integer $k_1 \geq k_0$ such that $P\{\tau_k \leq T\} > \eta$ for all $k \geq k_1$.

Define a $C^2 - function$ W: $\mathbb{R}^5_+ \to \mathbb{R}^1_+$

$$\begin{aligned} & W(S,E,I,R,V) \\ = \ & (S-1-lnS) + (E-1-lnE) + (I-1-lnI) + (R-1-lnR) + (V-1-lnV). \end{aligned}$$

The non-negativity of this function follows from the inequality $u - 1 - lnu \geq 0$ *for any* $u > 0$.

Using Itô's formula, we have

$$\begin{aligned} dW(S,E,I,R,V) =& LWdt + \sigma_1(S-1)dB_1(t) + \sigma_2(E-1)dB_2(t) + \sigma_3(I-1)dB_3(t) \\ & + \sigma_4(R-1)dB_4(t) + \sigma_5(V-1)dB_5(t), \end{aligned}$$

where

$$\begin{aligned} LW =& \left(1-\frac{1}{S}\right)\left(A - \frac{\beta SI}{1+aS+bI} - (\delta_0+\mu)S + \eta V\right) + \left(1-\frac{1}{E}\right)\left(\frac{\beta SI}{1+aS+bI} - (\delta_0+\delta_1)E\right) \\ & + \left(1-\frac{1}{I}\right)(\delta_1 E - (\delta_0+\delta_2+\delta_3)I) + \left(1-\frac{1}{R}\right)(\delta_2 I - \delta_0 R) + \left(1-\frac{1}{V}\right)(\mu S - (\delta_0+\eta)V) \\ & + \frac{1}{2}(\sigma_1^2+\sigma_2^2+\sigma_3^2+\sigma_4^2+\sigma_5^2) \\ =& A + 5\delta_0 + \delta_1 + \delta_2 + \delta_3 + \eta + \mu + \frac{1}{2}(\sigma_1^2+\sigma_2^2+\sigma_3^2+\sigma_4^2+\sigma_5^2) + \frac{\beta I}{1+aS+bI} \\ & - \frac{\beta SI}{(1+aS+bI)E} - \delta_3 I - \frac{A}{S} - \frac{\eta V}{S} - \frac{\delta_1 E}{I} - \frac{\delta_2 I}{R} - \frac{\mu S}{V} - \delta_0(S+E+I+R+V) \\ \leq& A + 5\delta_0 + \delta_1 + \delta_2 + \delta_3 + \eta + \mu + \frac{1}{2}(\sigma_1^2+\sigma_2^2+\sigma_3^2+\sigma_4^2+\sigma_5^2) + \frac{\beta I}{1+aS+bI}. \end{aligned}$$

If $aS+1 \geq I$, then $\frac{\beta I}{1+aS+bI} = \frac{\beta}{\frac{aS+1}{I}+b} \leq \frac{\beta}{1+b}$. While if $aS+1 < I$, $0 < \frac{aS+1}{I} < 1$, and we can obtain that $\frac{\beta I}{1+aS+bI} < \frac{\beta}{b}$. Therefore, there exists a fixed positive constant F which is independent of $S(t)$, $E(t)$, $I(t)$, $R(t)$, $V(t)$, and t. Thus we obtain

$$\begin{aligned} dW \leq & Fdt + \sigma_1(S-1)dB_1(t) + \sigma_2(E-1)dB_2(t) + \sigma_3(I-1)dB_3(t) \\ & + \sigma_4(R-1)dB_4(t) + \sigma_5(V-1)dB_5(t). \end{aligned}$$

By integrating both sides from 0 to $\tau_k \wedge T$, and taking expectations, we obtain

$$EW \leq W(S(0), E(0), I(0), R(0), V(0)) + FT.$$

For any positive $k \geq k_1$, let us define $\Omega_k = \{\tau_k < T\}$, leading to $P(\Omega_k) > \frac{\eta}{2}$. Note that for every $v \in \Omega_k$, at least one of the values in the set $(S(v), E(v), I(v), R(v), V(v))$ is either $\frac{1}{k}$ or k. Therefore, we have $W \geq \frac{1}{k} - 1 - ln\frac{1}{k}$, or $W \geq k - 1 - lnk$. So we obtain

$$\begin{aligned} W(S(0), E(0), I(0), R(0), V(0)) + FT \geq & E[I_{\Omega_k} W(S(t), E(t), I(t), R(t), V(t))] \\ = & P(\Omega_k) W(S(t), E(t), I(t), R(t), V(t)) \\ > & \frac{\eta}{2}\left[\left(\frac{1}{k} - 1 - ln\frac{1}{k}\right) \wedge (k - 1 - lnk)\right], \end{aligned}$$

where I_{Ω_k} is the indicator function of Ω_k. Setting $k \to \infty$, we have

$$\infty > W(S(0), E(0), I_1(0), I_2(0), R(0)) + FT = \infty.$$

This completes the proof. □

The following lemma can be proven by employing the same arguments presented in lemma 3.1 of [47]; hence, we omit its detailed proof here.

Lemma 2. *Let $(S(t), E(t), I(t), R(t), V(t))$ be any solution of system (3) with any initial value. Assume that $\mu > \frac{\sigma_{max}^2}{2}$, then*

(i) $\lim_{t\to\infty} \frac{S(t)}{t} = \lim_{t\to\infty} \frac{E(t)}{t} = \lim_{t\to\infty} \frac{I(t)}{t} = \lim_{t\to\infty} \frac{R(t)}{t} = \lim_{t\to\infty} \frac{V(t)}{t} = 0$ *a.s. Moreover,*
$\lim_{t\to\infty} \frac{lnS(t)}{t} = \lim_{t\to\infty} \frac{lnE(t)}{t} = \lim_{t\to\infty} \frac{lnI(t)}{t} = \lim_{t\to\infty} \frac{lnR(t)}{t} = \lim_{t\to\infty} \frac{lnV(t)}{t} = 0$ *a.s.*;

(ii) $\lim_{t\to\infty} \frac{1}{t}\int_0^t S(u)dB_1(u) = \lim_{t\to\infty} \frac{1}{t}\int_0^t E(u)dB_2(u) = \lim_{t\to\infty} \frac{1}{t}\int_0^t I(u)dB_3(u)$
$= \lim_{t\to\infty} \frac{1}{t}\int_0^t R(u)dB_4(u) = \lim_{t\to\infty} \frac{1}{t}\int_0^t V(u)dB_5(u) = 0$ *a.s.,*
where $\sigma_{max} = \sigma_1^2 \vee \sigma_2^2 \vee \sigma_3^2 \vee \sigma_4^2 \vee \sigma_5^2$.

Consider a regular time-homogeneous Markov process $X(t)$ in $\mathbb{R}_+^d$, characterized by the following:

$$dX(t) = b(X)dt + \sum_{r=1}^{k} \sigma_r(X)dB_r(t),$$

where the diffusion matrix is given by

$$A(X) = (a_{ij}(x)),\ a_{ij}(x) = \sum_{r=1}^{k} \sigma_r^i(x)\sigma_r^j(x).$$

The lemma below is crucial for proving the existence of a stationary distribution.

Lemma 3 ([46])**.** *The Markov process $X(t)$ possesses a unique ergodic stationary distribution $m(\cdot)$ if there exists a bounded domain $U \in \mathbb{R}^d$ with a smooth boundary such that its closure $\tilde{U} \subset \mathbb{R}^d$ satisfies the following properties:*

(i) *Within the open domain U and its neighborhood, the minimum eigenvalue of the diffusion matrix $A(t)$ remains bounded away from zero.*

(ii) *For any $x \in \mathbb{R}^d \setminus U$, the average time τ for a trajectory originating from x to each the set U is finite. Additionally, $\sup_{x \in K} E^x \tau < \infty$ for every compact $K \subset \mathbb{R}^d$.*

Furthermore, if $f(\cdot)$ is a function integrable with respect to measure m, then

$$P\left(\lim_{T \to \infty} \frac{1}{T} \int_0^T f(X^x(t))dt = \int_{\mathbb{R}^d} f(X^x(t))m(dx)\right) = 1,$$

for every $x \in \mathbb{R}^d$.

Remark 1. *To establish condition (i) it is adequate to demonstrate that F exhibits uniform ellipticity in U. Here, $F(u) = b(x)u_x + \frac{1}{2}trace(A(x)u_{xx})$. This implies the existence of a positive constant M such that $\sum_{i,j=1}^d a_{ij}(x)\zeta_i\zeta_j \geq M|\zeta|^2$, $x \in U$, $\zeta \in \mathbb{R}_d$ [29,48]. To confirm condition (ii), it is sufficient to establish the existence of a non-negative C^2-function V and a neighborhood U such that for some $\mathcal{K} > 0$, $LV < -\mathcal{K}$, $x \in \mathbb{R}^d \setminus U$ [49].*

3. Theoretical Analysis

Stochastic Lyapunov functions play a crucial role in understanding the long-term behavior of stochastic systems and assessing the impact of randomness on system dynamics. However, the derivation and implementation of stochastic Lyapunov functions involve a rigorous mathematical process to analyze the stability of stochastic systems. In the following discussion, we shall construct suitable stochastic Lyapunov functions to obtain the extinction and stationary distribution and ergodicity results for the stochastic system.

3.1. Extinction of the Stochastic Epidemic Model (3)

In this subsection, we will explore the sufficient criteria for the extinction of the infected individuals. Set

$$\mathcal{R}_0^s \doteq \frac{2\beta\delta_1(\delta_0 + \delta_1)}{a[(\delta_0 + \delta_1)^2(\delta_0 + \delta_2 + \delta_3 + \frac{1}{2}\sigma_3^2) \wedge \frac{1}{2}\delta_1^2\sigma_2^2]}.$$

Theorem 1. *Let $(S(t), E(t), I(t), R(t), V(t))$ be the solution of model (3) with any initial value $(S(0), E(0), I(0), R(0), V(0)) \in \mathbb{R}_+^5$. If $\mathcal{R}_0^s < 1$ and $\delta_0 > \frac{\sigma_{max}^2}{2}$, then the solution of model (3) satisfies*

$$\lim_{t \to \infty} \frac{1}{t} \int_0^t S(u)du = \frac{A(\delta_0 + \eta)}{\delta_0^2 + \eta\delta_0 + \mu\delta_0}, \qquad \lim_{t \to \infty} \frac{1}{t} \int_0^t V(u)du = \frac{A\mu}{\delta_0^2 + \eta\delta_0 + \mu\delta_0},$$

$$\lim_{t \to \infty} \frac{1}{t} \int_0^t E(u)du = \lim_{t \to \infty} \frac{1}{t} \int_0^t I(u)du = \lim_{t \to \infty} \frac{1}{t} \int_0^t R(u)du = 0.$$

Proof. Let $Q(t) = \delta_1 E(t) + (\delta_0 + \delta_1)I(t)$. By applying Itô's formula, we obtain

$$
\begin{aligned}
d\ln Q(t) = & \left[\frac{\frac{\delta_1\beta SI}{1+aS+bI} - (\delta_0+\delta_1)(\delta_0+\delta_2+\delta_3)I}{\delta_1 E + (\delta_0+\delta_1)I} - \frac{\delta_1^2\sigma_2^2E^2 + (\delta_0+\delta_1)^2\sigma_3^2 I^2}{2[\delta_1 E + (\delta_0+\delta_1)^2 I]^2}\right]dt \\
& + \frac{\delta_1\sigma_2 E}{\delta_1 E + (\delta_0+\delta_1)I}dB_2(t) + \frac{(\delta_0+\delta_1)\sigma_3 I}{\delta_1 E + (\delta_0+\delta_1)I}dB_3(t) \\
\le & \frac{\delta_1\beta}{a(\delta_0+\delta_1)}dt - \frac{1}{[\delta_1 E + (\delta_0+\delta_1)I]^2}\left[((\delta_0+\delta_1)^2(\delta_0+\delta_2+\delta_3) + \frac{1}{2}(\delta_0+\delta_1)^2\sigma_3^2)I^2\right. \\
& \left. + \frac{1}{2}\delta_1^2\sigma_2^2E^2\right]dt + \frac{\delta_1\sigma_2 E}{\delta_1 E + (\delta_0+\delta_1)I}dB_2(t) + \frac{(\delta_0+\delta_1)\sigma_3 I}{\delta_1 E + (\delta_0+\delta_1)I}dB_3(t) \\
\le & \frac{\delta_1\beta}{a(\delta_0+\delta_1)}dt - \frac{1}{2(\delta_0+\delta_1)^2}\left[(\delta_0+\delta_1)^2(\delta_0+\delta_2+\delta_3+\frac{1}{2}\sigma_3^2) \wedge \frac{1}{2}\delta_1^2\sigma_2^2\right]dt \\
& + \frac{\delta_1\sigma_2 E}{\delta_1 E + (\delta_0+\delta_1)I}dB_2(t) + \frac{(\delta_0+\delta_1)\sigma_3 I}{\delta_1 E + (\delta_0+\delta_1)I}dB_3(t).
\end{aligned}
\tag{5}
$$

Integrating (5) from 0 to t, combining with Lemma 2, and noting $\mathcal{R}_0^s < 1$, we have

$$
\lim_{t\to\infty} sup\frac{lnQ(t)}{t} \le \frac{\delta_1\beta}{a(\delta_0+\delta_1)} - \frac{1}{2(\delta_0+\delta_1)^2}\left[(\delta_0+\delta_1)^2(\delta_0+\delta_2+\delta_3+\frac{1}{2}\sigma_3^2) \wedge \frac{1}{2}\delta_1^2\sigma_2^2\right] < 0 \quad a.s.,
$$

which implies that

$$
\lim_{t\to\infty} E(t) = 0, \quad \lim_{t\to\infty} I(t) = 0 \quad a.s..
$$

In other words, the susceptible individuals $E(t)$ and the infectious individuals $I(t)$ will both exponentially approach zero with probability one. From model (3), it is evident that $\lim_{t\to\infty} R(t) = 0$ a.s. This implies that

$$
\lim_{t\to\infty}\frac{1}{t}\int_0^t E(u)du = \lim_{t\to\infty}\frac{1}{t}\int_0^t I(u)du = \lim_{t\to\infty}\frac{1}{t}\int_0^t R(u)du = 0 \ a.s.
$$

On the other hand, according to model (3), we have

$$
dS(t) = \left(A - \frac{\beta SI}{1+aS+bI} - (\delta_0+\mu)S + \eta V\right)dt + \sigma_1 S(t)dB_1(t) \tag{6}
$$

Integrating (6) from 0 to t on both sides, we can derive

$$
S(t) - S(0) = At - \int_0^t \frac{\beta S(u)I(u)}{1+aS(u)+bI(u)}du - \int_0^t (\delta_0+\mu)S(u)du + \int_0^t \eta V(u)du + \int_0^t \sigma_1 S(u)dB_1(u).
$$

And then, we can obtain

$$
(\delta_0+\mu)\int_0^t S(u)du \le At - \int_0^t (\delta_0+\mu)S(u)du + \int_0^t \eta V(u)du + \int_0^t \sigma_1 S(u)dB_1(u). \tag{7}
$$

In the same way, we can obtain

$$
(\delta_0+\eta)\int_0^t V(u)du \le \int_0^t \mu S(u)du + \int_0^t \sigma_5 V(u)dB_5(u). \tag{8}
$$

According to (7) and (8), we can obtain

$$
(\delta_0+\mu-\frac{\eta\mu}{\delta_0+\eta})\int_0^t S(u)du \le At + \frac{\eta\sigma_5}{\delta_0+\eta}\int_0^t V(u)dB_5(u) + \int_0^t \sigma_1 S(u)dB_1(u). \tag{9}
$$

By dividing both sides of (9) by t, taking the limit superior, and combining this result with Lemma 2, one can deduce that

$$\lim_{t\to\infty}\frac{1}{t}\int_0^t S(u)du = \frac{A(\delta_0+\eta)}{\delta_0^2+\eta\delta_0+\mu\delta_0}\ a.s.$$

And similarly, we can obtain

$$\lim_{t\to\infty}\frac{1}{t}\int_0^t V(u)du = \frac{A\mu}{\delta_0^2+\eta\delta_0+\mu\delta_0}\ a.s.$$

This completes the proof. □

3.2. *Stationary Distribution and Ergodicity of the Stochastic Model (3)*

Theorem 2. *Assume $R_0 > 1$, where R_0 is defined in (2). If the following conditions are satisfied:*
(i)

$$\begin{aligned}
m_1 &= 2\delta_0 - \sigma_1^2 > 0,\\
m_2 &= 2\delta_0 - \sigma_2^2 > 0,\\
m_3 &= \frac{4\delta_1(\delta_0+\delta_3)+2(2\delta_0+\delta_3(\delta_0+\delta_2+\delta_3))-(2\delta_0+2\delta_1+\delta_3)\sigma_3^2}{2\delta_1} > 0,\\
m_4 &= \frac{4\delta_0\delta_2+2\delta_0(2\delta_0+\delta_3)-(2\delta_0+2\delta_2+\delta_3)\sigma_4^2}{2\delta_2} > 0,\\
m_5 &= \frac{2\delta_0\mu+2\delta_0(\delta_0+\eta)-(\mu+\delta_0)\sigma_5^2}{\mu} > 0;
\end{aligned}$$

(ii)

$$0 < F < \min\Big(m_1\theta_1^2 S^{*2}, m_2\theta_2^2 E^{*2}, m_3\theta_3^2 I^{*2}, m_4\theta_4^2 R^{*2}, m_5\theta_5^2 V^{*2}\Big),$$

where

$$\begin{aligned}
F =& \frac{2\delta_0\sigma_1^2 S^{*2}}{2\delta_0-\sigma_1^2}+\frac{2\delta_0\sigma_2^2 E^{*2}}{2\delta_0-\sigma_2^2}+\frac{[4\delta_1(\delta_0+\delta_3)+2(2\delta_0+\delta_3)(\delta_0+\delta_2+\delta_3)](2\delta_0+2\delta_1+\delta_3)\sigma_3^2 I^{*2}}{\delta_1[4\delta_1(\delta_0+\delta_3)+2(2\delta_0+\delta_3)(\delta_0+\delta_2+\delta_3)-(2\delta_0+2\delta_1+\delta_3)\sigma_3^2]}\\
&+\frac{[4\delta_0\delta_2+2\delta_0(2\delta_0+\delta_3)](2\delta_0+2\delta_2+\delta_3)\sigma_4^2 R^{*2}}{\delta_2(4\delta_0\delta_2+2\delta_0(2\delta_0+\delta_3)-(2\delta_0+2\delta_2+\delta_3)\sigma_4^2)}+\frac{2\delta_0(\mu+\eta+\delta_0)(\delta_0+\mu)\sigma_5^2 V^{*2}}{\mu[2\delta_0(\mu+\eta+\delta_0)-(\delta_0+\mu)\sigma_5^2]},
\end{aligned}$$

$$\begin{aligned}
\theta_1 &= \frac{2\delta_0}{2\delta_0-\sigma_1^2},\ \theta_2 = \frac{2\delta_0}{2\delta_0-\sigma_2^2},\\
\theta_3 &= \frac{4\delta_1(\delta_0+\delta_3)+2(2\delta_0+\delta_3)(\delta_0+\delta_2+\delta_3)}{4\delta_1(\delta_0+\delta_3)+2(2\delta_0+\delta_3)(\delta_0+\delta_2+\delta_3)-(2\delta_0+2\delta_1+\delta_3)\sigma_3^2},\\
\theta_4 &= \frac{4\delta_0\delta_2+2\delta_0(2\delta_0+\delta_3)}{4\delta_0\delta_2+2\delta_0(2\delta_0+\delta_3)-(2\delta_0+2\delta_2+\delta_3)\sigma_4^2},\ \theta_5 = \frac{2\delta_0(\mu+\eta+\delta_0)}{2\delta_0(\mu+\eta+\delta_0)-(\delta_0+\mu)\sigma_5^2}
\end{aligned}$$

and S^*, E^*, I^*, R^*, V^* are defined as the endemic equilibrium of the deterministic model (1), then there exists a unique stationary distribution $\pi(\cdot)$ for the stochastic model (3) with any initial value $X_0 \in \mathbb{R}_+^5$ and it has the ergodic property.

Proof. Since $R_0 > 1$, there is an endemic equilibrium $P* = (S^*, E^*, I^*, R^*, V^*)$ of the deterministic model (1). Then, we have

$$\begin{aligned} &A = \frac{\beta S^* I^*}{1 + aS^* + bI^*} + (\delta_0 + \mu)S^* - \eta V^*, \quad \frac{\beta S^* I^*}{1 + aS^* + bI^*} = (\delta_0 + \delta_1)E^*, \\ &\delta_1 E^* = (\delta_0 + \delta_2 + \delta_3)I^*, \quad \delta_2 I^* = \delta_0 R^*, \quad \mu S^* = (\delta_0 + \eta)V^*. \end{aligned} \tag{10}$$

Define

$$\mathcal{V}(X) = \mathcal{V}_1(X) + \frac{2\delta_0 + \delta_3}{2\delta_1}\mathcal{V}_2(X) + \frac{2\delta_0 + \delta_3}{2\delta_2}\mathcal{V}_3(X) + \frac{\delta_0}{\mu}\mathcal{V}_4(X), \tag{11}$$

where

$$\begin{aligned} &\mathcal{V}_1(X) = (S - S^* + E - E^* + I - I^* + R - R^* + V - V^*)^2, \\ &\mathcal{V}_2(X) = (I - I^*)^2, \quad \mathcal{V}_3(X) = (R - R^*)^2, \quad \mathcal{V}_4(X) = (V - V^*)^2. \end{aligned}$$

Then, $\mathcal{V}$ is positive definite and $\lim_{|X| \to \infty} \mathcal{V}(X) = \infty$. By virtue of (10), we can obtain

$$\begin{aligned} L\mathcal{V}_1 =& 2[(S - S^*) + (E - E^*) + (I - I^*) + (R - R^*) + (V - V^*)][A - \delta_0(S + E + I + R + V) \\ & - \delta_0 I] + \sigma_1^2 S^2 + \sigma_2^2 E^2 + \sigma_3^2 I^2 + \sigma_4^2 R^2 + \sigma_5^2 V^2 \\ =& 2[(S - S^*) + (E - E^*) + (I - I^*) + (R - R^*) + (V - V^*)][-\delta_0(S - S^*) - \delta_0(E - E^*) \\ & - (\delta_0 + \delta_3)(I - I^*) - \delta_0(R - R^*) - \delta_0(V - V^*)] + \sigma_1^2 S^2 + \sigma_2^2 E^2 + \sigma_3^2 I^2 + \sigma_4^2 R^2 + \sigma_5^2 V^2 \\ \leq& 2[-\delta_0(S - S^*)^2 - \delta_0(E - E^*)^2 - (\delta_0 + \delta_3)(I - I^*)^2 - \delta_0(R - R^*)^2 - \delta_0(V - V^*)^2 \\ & - (2\delta_0 + \delta_3)(E - E^*)(I - I^*) - (2\delta_0 + \delta_3)(I - I^*)(R - R^*) - 2\delta_0(S - S^*)(V - V^*)] \\ & + \sigma_1^2 S^2 + \sigma_2^2 E^2 + \sigma_3^2 I^2 + \sigma_4^2 R^2 + \sigma_5^2 V^2, \end{aligned}$$

$$\begin{aligned} L\mathcal{V}_2 &= 2(I - I^*)[\delta_1(E - E^*) - (\delta_0 + \delta_2 + \delta_3)(I - I^*)] + \sigma_3^2 I^2 \\ &= -2(\delta_0 + \delta_2 + \delta_3)(I - I^*)^2 + 2\delta_1(E - E^*)(I - I^*) + \sigma_3^2 I^2, \end{aligned}$$

$$\begin{aligned} L\mathcal{V}_3 &= 2(R - R^*)[\delta_2(I - I^*) - \delta_0(R - R^*)] + \sigma_4^2 R^2 \\ &= -2\delta_0(R - R^*)^2 + 2\delta_2(I - I^*)(R - R^*) + \sigma_4^2 R^2, \end{aligned}$$

$$\begin{aligned} L\mathcal{V}_4 &= 2(V - V^*)[\mu(S - S^*) - (\delta_0 + \eta)(V - V^*)] + \sigma_5^2 V^2 \\ &= -2(\delta_0 + \eta)(V - V^*)^2 + 2\mu(S - S^*)(V - V^*) + \sigma_5^2 V^2. \end{aligned}$$

This implies that

$$
\begin{aligned}
\mathcal{L}V =& \mathcal{L}V_1 + \frac{2\delta_0+\delta_3}{2\delta_1}\mathcal{L}V_2 + \frac{2\delta_0+\delta_3}{2\delta_2}\mathcal{L}V_3 + \frac{\delta_0}{\mu}\mathcal{L}V_4 \\
\leq & -2\delta_0(S-S^*)^2 - 2\delta_0(E-E^*)^2 - \left[2(\delta_0+\delta_3) + \frac{(2\delta_0+\delta_3)(\delta_0+\delta_2+\delta_3)}{\delta_1}\right](I-I^*)^2 \\
& -2\left[2\delta_0 + \frac{\delta_0(2\delta_0+\delta_3)}{\delta_2}\right](R-R^*)^2 - \left[2\delta_0 + \frac{2\delta_0(\delta_0+\eta)}{\mu}\right](V-V^*)^2 + \sigma_1^2 S^2 + \sigma_2^2 E^2 \\
& + \frac{(2\delta_0+2\delta_1+\delta_3)\sigma_3^2}{2\delta_1}I^2 + \frac{(2\delta_0+2\delta_2+\delta_3)\sigma_4^2}{2\delta_2}R^2 + \frac{(\delta_0+\mu)\sigma_5^2}{\mu}V^2 \\
= & -(2\delta_0-\sigma_1^2)\left(S - \frac{2\delta_0}{2\delta_0-\sigma_1^2}S^*\right)^2 - (2\delta_0-\sigma_2^2)\left(E - \frac{2\delta_0}{2\delta_0-\sigma_2^2}E^*\right)^2 \\
& - \left(\frac{2\delta_1(\delta_0+\delta_3)}{\delta_1} + \frac{(2\delta_0+\delta_3)(\delta_0+\delta_2+\delta_3)}{\delta_1} - \frac{2\delta_0+\delta_2+\delta_3}{2\delta_1}\sigma_3^2\right) \times \\
& \left(I - \frac{2\delta_1[2\delta_1(\delta_0+\delta_3)+(2\delta_0+\delta_3)(\delta_0+\delta_2+\delta_3)]}{4\delta_1(\delta_0+\delta_3)+2(2\delta_0+\delta_3)(\delta_0+\delta_2+\delta_3)-(2\delta_0+2\delta_1+\delta_3)\sigma_3^2}I^*\right)^2 \\
& - \left(\frac{2\delta_0\delta_2}{\delta_2} + \frac{2\delta_0(2\delta_0+\delta_3)-(2\delta_0+2\delta_2+\delta_3)}{2\delta_2}\right) \times \\
& \left(R - \frac{4\delta_0\delta_2+2\delta_0(2\delta_0+\delta_3)}{4\delta_0\delta_2+2\delta_0(2\delta_0+\delta_3)-(2\delta_0+2\delta_2+\delta_3)\sigma_4^2}R^*\right)^2 \\
& - \left(\frac{2\delta_0\mu+2\delta_0(\delta_0+\eta)-(\mu+\delta_0)\sigma_5^2}{\mu}\right)\left(V - \frac{2\delta_0(\mu+\eta+\delta_0)}{2\delta_0(\mu+\eta+\delta_0)-(\delta_0+\mu)\sigma_5^2}V^*\right)^2 + F \\
= & -m_1(S-\theta_1 S^*)^2 - m_2(E-\theta_2 E^*)^2 - m_3(I-\theta_3 I^*)^2 - m_4(R-\theta_4 R^*)^2 \\
& - m_5(V-\theta_5 V^*)^2 + F
\end{aligned}
$$

If F satisfies the following criteria

$$0 < F < \min\left(m_1\theta_1^2 S^{*2}, m_2\theta_2^2 E^{*2}, m_3\theta_3^2 I^{*2}, m_4\theta_4^2 R^{*2}, m_5\theta_5^2 V^{*2}\right),$$

then the ellipsoid

$$m_1(S-\theta_1 S^*)^2 + m_2(E-\theta_2 E^*)^2 + m_3(I-\theta_3 I^*)^2 + m_4(R-\theta_4 R^*)^2 + m_5(V-\theta_5 V^*)^2 = F$$

is completely contained within $\mathbb{R}_+^5$. One can choose U to be any neighborhood of the ellipsoid such that $\bar{U} \subset \mathbb{R}_+^(5)$, where $\bar{U}$ is the closure of U. Thus, we get $\mathcal{L}V(X) < -1$ for $X \in \mathbb{R}_+^5 \setminus U$, thus indicating the condition in Lemma 3 hold. Therefore, the stochastic model (3) possesses a stationary distribution and exhibits ergodicity. □

4. Numerical Simulations and Data Interpretation

Since the emergence of COVID-19 in late December 2019, the pandemic remains a substantial concern. However, the situation appears to have improved with the availability of vaccines. The purpose of this section is to provide a numerical example illustrating our main results, and offer recommendations for controlling pandemic based on data from COVID-19.

4.1. Model Validation

Based on official data and the research of various scholars, we have conducted a simple data analysis to obtain important parameters, presented in Table 2.

Table 2. Relevant variables and parameter values.

Parameter	Value	Reference
A	100,000	Estimate
a	0.5	[50]
b	0.5	[50]
δ_0	7.14×10^{-3}	[51]
μ	0.4	Estimate
η	0.3	[52]
δ_1	0.2	[53]
δ_2	0.02	[53]
δ_3	0.2	Estimate
σ_1	0.06	Estimate
σ_2	0.115	Estimate
σ_3	0.03	Estimate
σ_4	0.008	Estimate
σ_5	0.008	Estimate
$S(0)$	11,081,000	[53]
$E(0)$	600	[53]
$I(0)$	410	[53]
$R(0)$	30	[53]
$V(0)$	0	[53]

We set $\beta = 1.398 \times 10^{-3}$, and obtain $\mathcal{R}_0^s = 0.8759 < 1$ and $\delta_0 = 7.14 \times 10^{-3} > \frac{\sigma_{max}^2}{2} = 6.6125 \times 10^{-3}$ by using these parameter values. The dynamics of model (3) is presented in Figure 1. It shows that the disease will become extinct, which supports the results stated in Theorem 1.

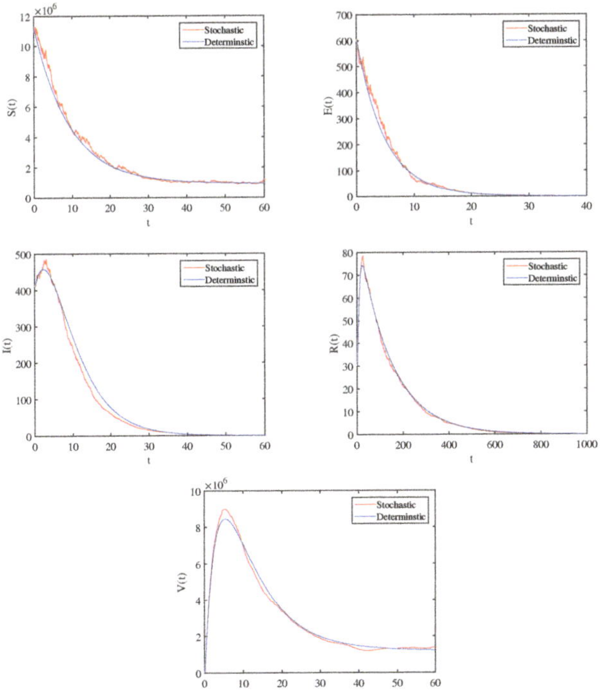

Figure 1. The spread of COVID-19 when $\mathcal{R}_0^s < 1$.

We set $\beta = 0.1898$ and $\sigma_2 = 0.07$, and the other parameter values used are those given in Table 2. Then, we obtain $R_0 = 2.1929 > 1$, and $m_1 = 0.0107$, $m_2 = 0.0094$, $m_3 = 0.5098$, $m_4 = 0.131$, $m_5 = 0.0252$, $0 < F = 1.9007 \times 10^9 < \min(m_1\theta_1^2 S^{*2}, m_2\theta_2^2 E^{*2}, m_3\theta_3^2 I^{*2}, m_4\theta_4^2 R^{*2}, m_5\theta_5^2 V^{*2}) = 1.9410 \times 10^9$. The dynamics of model (3) is presented in Figure 2. This indicates that the disease will prevail by our analytical results stated in Theorem 2.

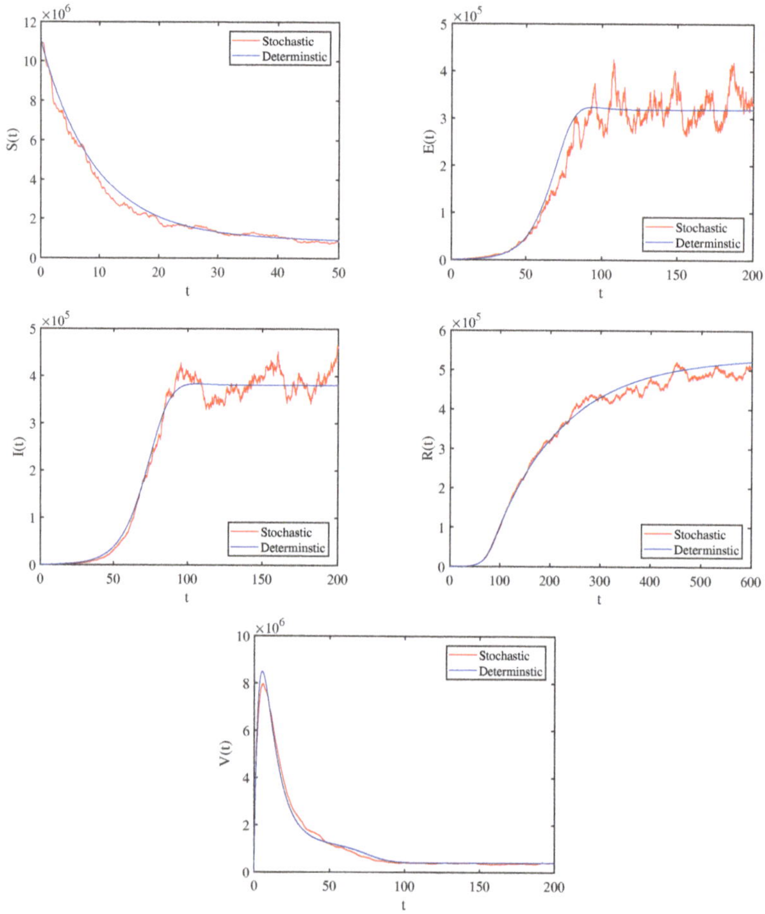

Figure 2. The spread of COVID-19 when $\mathcal{R}_0 > 1$.

4.2. Sensitivity Analysis of R_0 and $\mathcal{R}_0^s$

To effectively control infectious diseases, it is crucial to investigate the impact of various factors on disease transmission. Therefore, in this study, we examine the relationship between certain parameters and $\mathcal{R}_0^s$ and R_0, as well as potential measures to mitigate the spread of disease.

Firstly, we demonstrate the influence of the pertinent parameters on the threshold $\mathcal{R}_0^s$, as depicted in Figure 3a,b.

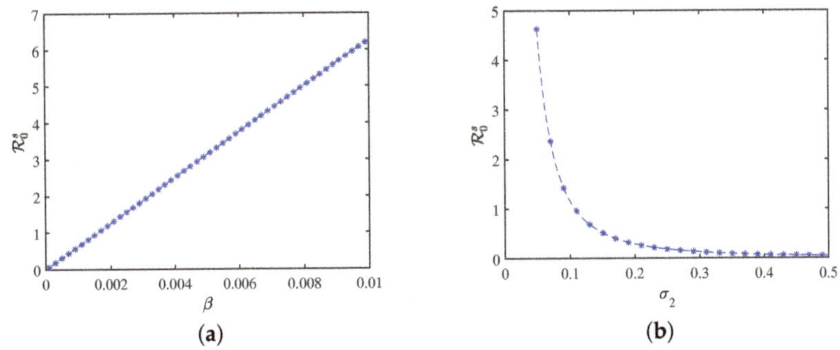

Figure 3. The relationship between $\mathcal{R}_0^s$ and related parameters. (**a**) Relationship between $\mathcal{R}_0^s$ and β. (**b**) Relationship between $\mathcal{R}_0^s$ and σ_2.

Upon setting $\beta \in [10^{-4}, 10^{-2}]$ while keeping the remaining parameter values unchanged from those presented in Table 2, we observe that $\mathcal{R}_0^s$ exhibits a decreasing trend as β decreases (refer to Figure 3a). Similarly, under the constant parameter values specified in Table 2, when σ_2 varies within the range [0, 0.5] and $\beta = 1.398 \times 10^{-3}$, we note that $\mathcal{R}_0^s$ displays a decreasing pattern as σ_2 increases (see Figure 3b). This observation indicates that the introduction of random fluctuations in our stochastic model can effectively suppress disease outbreaks.

We further investigate the relationship between several parameters and the value of R_0, as depicted in Figure 4. According to the definition of R_0 in Equation (2), it is evident that R_0 decreases as β decreases or μ increases. To clearly illustrate the impact of β and μ on R_0, we fix $A = 10$, $\delta_0 = 0.01$, $\delta_1 = 0.1$, $\delta_2 = 0.01$, $\delta_3 = 0.15$, $a = 0.01$, and vary β within the range [0.01, 0.1] and μ within the range [0, 0.8]. Through the analysis of Figure 4, it is evident that by reducing interpersonal contact and promoting vaccination efforts, the spread of the disease can be effectively controlled, aligning with the current strategies implemented in response to the ongoing pandemic.

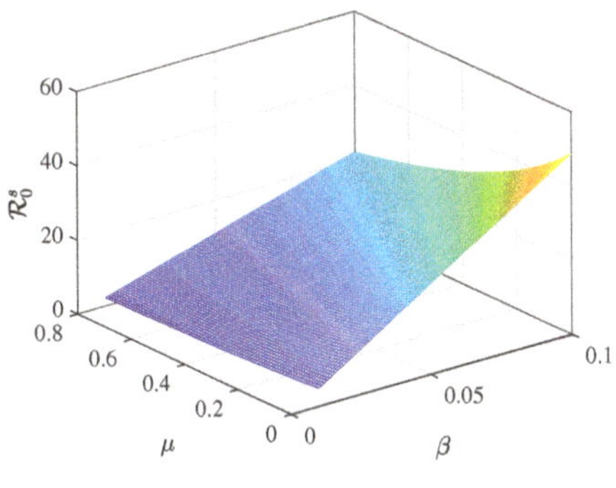

Figure 4. Relationship between $\mathcal{R}_0$ and β, μ.

5. Concluding Remarks

In this paper, we considered a stochastic SVEIR epidemic model with a nonlinear incidence rate. We utilized two key values to determine the system dynamics: one is defined as $\mathcal{R}_0^s$, and the other is the reproduction number R_0 of the corresponding deterministic model. We demonstrated that when $\mathcal{R}_0^s < 1$, the disease will become extinct. On the other hand, if $R_0 > 1$ and the other parameter values satisfy the conditions in Theorem 2, the disease will persist.

We extracted feasible coefficients from published studies on COVID-19 transmission to exemplify our findings. Through our sensitivity analysis, we revealed that the stochastic model, with the introduction of random fluctuations, can effectively mitigate disease outbreaks. Specifically, the contact transmission rate β and the vaccination rate coefficient μ exert substantial influence on the value of $\mathcal{R}_0^s$. These results indicate that reducing interpersonal contact and increasing vaccine usage are effective strategies for controlling epidemic spread.

The utilization of stochastic Lyapunov functions and numerical simulations with COVID-19 data accentuates the symmetrical interplay between random fluctuations, vaccination efficacy, and disease containment. This symmetrical perspective enhances our understanding of epidemic dynamics and underscores the importance of balanced strategies in mitigating disease outbreaks. As such, this study aligns with the principles of symmetry, emphasizing the harmonious interactions and equilibrium present in epidemic modeling and control efforts.

Finally, it should be noted that there are several areas that warrant further investigation in the field of stochastic epidemic modeling. For instance, (1) in the model we assumed Brownian noise, but in reality, some cases involve Lévy noise; (2) in the numerical simulation part, we assumed certain parameter values, but the actual parameter values are still uncertain; (3) the conditions outlined in Theorem 2 are intricate; (4) the nonlinear incidence rate may vary when modeling different diseases; (5) since most vaccines have a time limit, it is essential to incorporate this limitation into the model. In our future work, we will focus on addressing these questions.

Author Contributions: X.W.: conceptualization, investigation, writing—original draft. L.Z.: conceptualization, discussing, writing—review and editing. X.-B.Z.: discussing, writing—review and editing. All authors have read and agreed to the published version of the manuscript.

Funding: This work was partly supported by the Natural Science Foundation of Shaanxi Province (No. 2023-JC-YB-083), and the National Natural Science Foundation of China (Nos. 12361041, 12061033, 12201499).

Data Availability Statement: Data are contained within the article.

Conflicts of Interest: The authors declare that they have no known competing financial interests or personal relationships that could have appeared to influence the work reported in this paper.

References

1. Naheed, A.; Singh, M.; Lucy, D. Numerical study of SARS epidemic model with the inclusion of diffusion in the system. *Appl. Math. Comput.* **2014**, *229*, 480–498. [CrossRef] [PubMed]
2. Huo, H.F.; Feng, L.X. Global stability for an HIV/AIDS epidemic model with different latent stages and treatment. *Appl. Math. Model.* **2013**, *37*, 1480–1489. [CrossRef]
3. Pongsumpun, P.; Tang, I.M. Dynamics of a new strain of the H1N1 influenza a virus incorporating the effects of repetitive contacts. *Comput. Math. Methods Med.* **2014**, *2014*, 487974. [CrossRef] [PubMed]
4. Sen, M.; Ibeas, A. On an SE(Is)(Ih)AR epidemic model with combined vaccination and antiviral controls for COVID-19 pandemic. *Adv. Differ. Equ.* **2021**, *2021*, 92. [CrossRef]
5. Xing, Y.; Zhang, L.; Wang, X. Modelling and stability of epidemic model with free-living pathogens growing in the environment. *J. Appl. Anal. Comput.* **2020**, *10*, 55–70. [CrossRef]
6. Zhang, L.; Xing, Y.F. Stability Analysis of a Reaction-Diffusion Heroin Epidemic Model. *Complexity* **2020**, *2020*, 3781425. [CrossRef]
7. Wang, X. An SIRS Epidemic Model with Vital Dynamics and a Ratio-Dependent Saturation Incidence Rate. *Discret. Dyn. Nat. Soc.* **2015**, *2015*, 720682. [CrossRef]
8. Beretta, E.; Takeuchi, Y. Global stability of an SIR epidemic model with time delays. *J. Math. Biol.* **1995**, *33*, 250. [CrossRef] [PubMed]
9. Ruan, S.; Wang, W. Dynamical behavior of an epidemic model with a nonlinear incidence rate. *J. Differ. Equ.* **2003**, *188*, 135–163. [CrossRef]
10. Xiang, H.; Wang, Y.; Huo, H. Analysis of the binge drinking models with demographics and nonlinear infectivity on networks. *J. Appl. Anal. Comput.* **2018**, *8*, 1535–1554. [CrossRef]
11. Rui, X.; Ma, Z. Global stability of a delayed SEIRS epidemic model withsaturation incidence rate. *Nonlinear Dyn.* **2010**, *61*, 229–239. [CrossRef]

12. Alexander, M.; Moghadas, S. Bifurcation analysis of an SIRS epidemic model with generalized incidence. *SIAM J. Appl. Math.* **2005**, *65*, 1794–1816. [CrossRef]
13. Watmough, J.; Mccluskey, C.; Gumel, A. An SVEIR model for assessing potential impact of an imperfect anti-SARS vaccine. *Math. Biosci. Eng.* **2006**, *3*, 485–512. [CrossRef] [PubMed]
14. Khan, M.A.; Badshah, Q.; Islam, S.; Khan, I.; Khan, S.A. Global dynamics of SEIRS epidemic model with non-linear generalized incidences and preventive vaccination. *Adv. Differ. Equ.* **2015**, *2015*, 88. [CrossRef]
15. Khan, M.A.; Khan, Y.; Khan, S.; Islam, S. Global stability and vaccination of an SEIVR epidemic model with saturated incidence rate. *Int. J. Biomath.* **2016**, *9*, 59–83. [CrossRef]
16. Liu, X.; Yang, L. Stability analysis of an SEIQV epidemic model with saturated incidence rate. *Nonlinear Anal. Real World Appl.* **2012**, *13*, 2671–2679. [CrossRef]
17. Yang, Y.; Zhang, C.; Jiang, X. Global stability of an SEIQV epidemic model with general incidence rate. *Int. J. Biomath.* **2015**, *8*, 1550020. [CrossRef]
18. Xu, Z.; Liu, X. Backward bifurcation of an epidemic model with saturated treatment function. *J. Math. Anal. Appl.* **2008**, *348*, 433–443. [CrossRef]
19. Kyrychko, Y.N.; Blyuss, K.B. Global properties of a delayed SIR model with temporary immunity and nonlinear incidence rate. *Nonlinear Anal. Real World Appl.* **2005**, *6*, 495–507. [CrossRef]
20. Farrington, C.P. On vaccine efficacy and reproduction numbers. *Math. Biosci.* **2003**, *185*, 89–109. [CrossRef]
21. Agaba, G.O.; Kyrychko, Y.N.; Blyuss, K.B. Dynamics of vaccination in a time-delayed epidemic model with awareness. *Math. Biosci.* **2017**, *294*, 92. [CrossRef] [PubMed]
22. Gao, D.P.; Huang, N.J.; Kang, S.M.; Zhang, C. Global stability analysis of an SVEIR epidemic model with general incidence rate. *Bound. Value Probl.* **2018**, *2018*, 42. [CrossRef] [PubMed]
23. Rao, F.; Mandal, P.; Kang, Y. Complicated endemics of an SIRS model with a generalized incidence under preventive vaccination and treatment controls. *Appl. Math. Model.* **2019**, *67*, 38–61. [CrossRef]
24. Liu, X.; Takeuchi, Y.; Iwami, S. SVIR epidemic models with vaccination strategies. *J. Theor. Biol.* **2008**, *253*, 1–11. [CrossRef] [PubMed]
25. He, Z.L.; Nie, L.F. The Effect of Pulse Vaccination and Treatment on SIR Epidemic Model with Media Impact. *Discret Dyn. Nat. Soc.* **2015**, *2015*, 3129–3132. [CrossRef]
26. Zhang, T. Permanence and extinction in a nonautonomous discrete SIRVS epidemic model with vaccination. *Appl. Math. Comput.* **2015**, *271*, 716–729. [CrossRef]
27. Spencer, S. Stochastic Epidemic Models for Emerging Diseases. Ph.D. Thesis, University of Nottingham, Nottingham, UK, 2008.
28. Beddington, J.R.; May, R.M. Harvesting Natural Populations in a Randomly Fluctuating Environment. *Science* **1977**, *197*, 463–465. [CrossRef] [PubMed]
29. Gard, T.C. *Introduction to Stochastic Differential Equations*; Marcel Dekker Inc.: New York, NY, USA, 1988; Volume 84, p. 19.
30. Mao, X. *Stochastic Differential Equations and Applications*, 2nd ed.; Academic Press: Cambridge, MA, USA, 2006.
31. Jiang, D.; Shi, N.; Li, X. Global stability and stochastic permanence of a non-autonomous logistic equation with random perturbation. *J. Math. Anal. Appl.* **2008**, *340*, 588–597. [CrossRef]
32. Lahrouz, A.; Omari, L. Extinction and stationary distribution of a stochastic SIRS epidemic model with non-linear incidence. *Stat. Probab. Lett.* **2013**, *83*, 960–968. [CrossRef]
33. Chen, C.; Kang, Y. The asymptotic behavior of a stochastic vaccination model with backward bifurcation. *Appl. Math. Model.* **2016**, *40*, 6051–6068. [CrossRef]
34. Liu, Q.; Jiang, D.; Shi, N.; Hayat, T.; Alsaedi, A. Stationary distribution and extinction of a stochastic SIRS epidemic model with standard incidence. *Physica A Stat. Mech. Its Appl.* **2017**, *469*, 510–517. [CrossRef]
35. Zhang, X.; Huo, H.; Xiang, H.; Meng, X. Dynamics of the deterministic and stochastic SIQS epidemic model with non-linear incidence. *Appl. Math. Comput.* **2014**, *243*, 546–558. [CrossRef]
36. Liu, S.; Zhang, L.; Xing, Y. Dynamics of a stochastic heroin epidemic model. *J. Comput. Appl. Math.* **2019**, *351*, 260–269. [CrossRef]
37. Zhang, L.; Liu, S.; Zhang, X. Asymptotic behavior of a stochastic virus dynamics model with intracellular delay and humoral immunity. *J. Appl. Anal. Comput.* **2019**, *9*, 1425–1442. [CrossRef]
38. Cai, Y.L.; Kang, Y.; Wang, W.M. A stochastic SIRS epidemic model with nonlinear incidence rate. *Appl. Math. Comput.* **2017**, *305*, 221–240. [CrossRef]
39. Allen, L. *An Introduction to Stochastic Processes with Applications to Biology*; CRC Press: Boca Raton, FL, USA, 2010.
40. Mao, X.; Marion, G.; Renshaw, E. Environmental Brownian noise suppresses explosions in population dynamics. *Stoch. Process. Their Appl.* **2002**, *97*, 95–110. [CrossRef]
41. Zhang, X.B.; Liu, R.J. The stationary distribution of a stochastic SIQS epidemic model with varying total population size. *Appl. Math. Lett.* **2020**, *116*, 106974. [CrossRef]
42. Zhang, X.B.; Zhang, X.H. The threshold of a deterministic and a stochastic SIQS epidemic model with varying total population size. *Appl. Math. Model.* **2021**, *91*, 749–767. [CrossRef]
43. Britton, T. Stochastic epidemic models: A survey. *Math. Biosci.* **2010**, *225*, 24–35. [CrossRef]
44. Ball, F.; Neal, P. A general model for stochastic SIR epidemics with two levels of mixing. *Math. Biosci.* **2002**, *180*, 73–102. [CrossRef] [PubMed]

45. Yang, Q.; Jiang, D.; Shi, N.; Ji, C. The ergodicity and extinction of stochastically perturbed SIR and SEIR epidemic models with saturated incidence. *J. Math. Anal. Appl.* **2017**, *388*, 248–271. [CrossRef]
46. Khasminiskii, R.Z. *Stochastic Stability of Differential Equations*; Springer: Berlin/Heidelberg, Germany, 2012.
47. Zhang, X.; Huo, H.; Xiang, H.; Shi, Q.; Li, D. The threshold of a stochastic SIQS epidemic model. *Physica A Stat. Mech. Its Appl.* **2017**, *482*, 362–374. [CrossRef]
48. Strang, G. *Linear Algebra and Its Applications*; Harcourt Brace Jovanovich: Orlando, FL, USA, 1988.
49. Zhu, C.; Yin, G. Asymptotic properties of hybrid diffusion systems. *SIAM J. Control Optim.* **2007**, *46*, 1155–1179. [CrossRef]
50. Sinan, M.; Ali, A.; Shah, K.; Assiri, T.A.; Nofal, T.A. Stability Analysis and Optimal Control of COVID-19 Pandemic SEIQR Fractional Mathematical Model with Harmonic Mean Type Incidence Rate and Treatment. *Results Phys.* **2021**, *22*, 103873. [CrossRef] [PubMed]
51. Chen, M.; Li, M.; Hao, Y.; Liu, Z.; Hu, L.; Wang, L. The introduction of population migration to SEIAR for COVID-19 epidemic modeling with an efficient intervention strategy-ScienceDirect. *Inf. Fusion* **2020**, *64*, 252–258. [CrossRef] [PubMed]
52. Al Kaabi, N.; Zhang, Y.; Xia, S.; Yang, Y.; Al Qahtani, M.M.; Abdulrazzaq, N.; Nusair, M.A.; Hassany, M.; Jawad, J.S.; Abdalla, J.; et al. Effect of 2 Inactivated SARS-CoV-2 Vaccines on Symptomatic COVID-19 Infection in Adults: A Randomized Clinical Trial. *JAMA* **2021**, *326*, 35–45. [CrossRef] [PubMed]
53. Wang, X.; Tang, S.; Chen, Y.; Feng, X.; Xiao, Y.; Xu, Z. When will be the resumption of work in Wuhan and its surrounding areas during COVID-19 epidemic? A data-driven network modeling analysis. *Sci. Sin. Math.* **2020**, *50*, 969–978. (In Chinese)

MDPI AG
Grosspeteranlage 5
4052 Basel
Switzerland
Tel.: +41 61 683 77 34

Symmetry Editorial Office
E-mail: symmetry@mdpi.com
www.mdpi.com/journal/symmetry

www.ingramcontent.com/pod-product-compliance
Lightning Source LLC
Chambersburg PA
CBHW062101220926
51850CB00010B/2843
* 9 7 8 3 7 2 5 8 6 5 6 8 0 *